HUMAN REASONING

HUMAN REASONING

RUSSEL REVLIN and **RICHARD E. MAYER**
University of California, Santa Barbara

1978

V. H. WINSTON & SONS
Washington, D.C.

A HALSTED PRESS BOOK

JOHN WILEY & SONS
New York   Toronto   London   Sydney

Copyright © 1978, by V. H. Winston & Sons, a Division of
Scripta Technica, Inc.

V. H. Winston & Sons, a Division of Scripta Technica, Inc.,
Publishers
1511 K Street, N.W., Washington, D.C. 20005

Distributed solely by Halsted Press, a Division of John Wiley
& Sons, Inc.

Library of Congress Cataloging in Publication Data
Main entry under title:

Human reasoning.

   Includes indexes.
   1. Reasoning.   I. Revlin, Russell.   II. Mayer,
Richard E., 1947–
BC177.H85   160   77-16599
ISBN 0-470-99357-X

Composition by Marie A. Maddalena, Scripta Technica, Inc.

DEDICATION

For Nancy and Scott and in memory of Allen Revlis (RR)
To Beverly, Kenny, David and to my parents and brothers (RM)

CONTENTS

LIST OF CONTRIBUTORS

Lyle E. Bourne, Jr., University of Colorado

James R. Erickson, University of Texas at Arlington

Lawrence T. Frase, National Institute of Education

Richard A. Griggs, University of Florida

John R. Hayes, Carnegie-Mellon University

Mary Henle, Graduate Faculty, New School for Social Research

Von Otto Leirer, University of California, Santa Barbara

Richard E. Mayer, University of California, Santa Barbara

Denise M. Podeschi, Washington University

George R. Potts, University of Denver

Russell Revlin, University of California, Santa Barbara

C. Susan Robinson, Carnegie-Mellon University

Herman Staudenmayer, National Jewish Hospital and Research Center

Robert S. Wyer, Jr., University of Illinois at Urbana-Champaign

PREFACE

This volume is intended to provide a comprehensive, current, and integrative summary of research on the cognitive processes involved in human reasoning. In order to assure both a thorough and timely treatment of the subject, we invited contributions from researchers who represent a diversity of theories and methods, but who are actively working at the forefront of the field. We asked them to summarize their recent work and their on-going projects. In order to provide an integrated treatment, we encouraged interaction among the contributors. We met formally as a group to present and discuss preliminary papers at the "Symposium on Deductive Reasoning" held at the Meeting of the American Psychological Association in 1976. After all contributors had an opportunity to hear and read the other papers, they wrote more complete versions and circulated them with an expressed commitment to try to relate their work to that of the others. Finally, comments were solicited for each paper to be included in the final versions presented here. Further, an introductory chapter is included which explicitly points out the commonalities and major disagreements contained in these papers as well as provides a general, historical background for them.

Both the quality and diversity represented by these papers attest to human reasoning as an exciting area of cognitive psychology in which real progress is being made. There appears to be a unanimity among these papers in emphasizing the encoding of the problem's information and the construction of a representational formalism for answering questions. As a result of this treatment, it is possible to demonstrate that in some cases, incorrect answers to logical problems are due to the nature of the reasoner's encoding of the problem and not to faulty reasoning per se. The emphasis on encoding encourages us that advances in other areas of cognitive psychology are being brought to bear on the general problem of human inference.

We would like to thank each of the contributors to this volume. Their efforts to produce an integrated and current volume on human reasoning are much appreciated. We also would like to thank the staff of V. H. Winston & Sons for their cooperation on this project.

In addition, the first author wishes to acknowledge his indebtedness to George E. Mount, John R. Hayes, and Herbert H. Clark who in their own fashion left me alone to be free to understand human inference in my own way and in my own time. Most especially, my thanks are owed to my wife, Nancy Revlin, for her encouragement and criticism and for her efforts to provide me with the free time so that I might complete this project.

R.R.

The second author wishes to express thanks to those who have been my teachers, colleagues, and students for teaching me and stimulating me to think about human cognition. A special debt is due James Greeno in this regard. Finally, I am thankful for the encouragement of my parents, James and Bernis Mayer, my brothers, Bob and Bernie Mayer, and of course, Beverly, Kenny and David.

R.M.

Russell Revlin
Richard Mayer

FOREWORD

The present volume makes us aware of significant changes in the investigation of human reasoning—most specifically of syllogistic reasoning—in the last 10 or 15 years. The frequent errors made in solving syllogisms are no longer simply accepted at face value as indications of faulty reasoning; rather, attention has turned to the processes responsible for errors. Such a shift leads, perhaps inevitably, to an interest in the subject's interpretation of the premises; given the individual's understanding of the premise, the conclusion most often follows logically. The context in which inferences are made has been manipulated with consequent changes in the understanding of premises. The investigation of syllogistic reasoning has been extended from the study of (I think inappropriately maligned) categorical syllogisms to that of hypothetical syllogisms. Reasoning is now being studied in relation to such processes as memory, reading, persuasion, and the like. This volume contains studies of problem solving as well as the solving of syllogisms, with the implicit invitation to relate the two kinds of tasks and the approaches to them. All these changes seem to me to represent important advances.

Perhaps most important of all, a majority of the contributors to this volume consider syllogistic reasoning a rational process. This has not always been the case. No longer is the reasoner seen as using the problem as a vehicle for the expression of his wishes and prejudices in total disregard of the laws of logic. Nor are illogical logics invented to account for his errors. The human being, homo sapiens, it appears, is capable of rational thinking.

Of course, processes other than (or in addition to) reasoning may be at work when a subject is given a logical task. He may guess, he may follow learned rules for solving syllogisms, he may judge the empirical truth of a conclusion rather than its logical necessity. A number of the present authors have suggested the operation of processes in addition to deductive inference. For example, Potts sees errors based on a tendency to treat set inclusion relations in terms of the similarity of terms; this is more an evasion of the logical task than a violation of logic. Again, Frase suggests a process formally similar to the atmosphere effect: Particular premises may produce a feeling of uncertainty which is reflected in the avoidance of a universal conclusion. In this case, the extralogical process may produce correct solutions. Almost the only discussion of errors of ratiocination in this collection is Grigg's assertion that most subjects do not assume transitivity. Since the relation of class inclusion is transitive, the failure to assume transitivity is an abandonment of logic; it means thinking illogically. I will return to this problem.

But if errors of ratiocination seems to be largely absent from the studies here assembled, is a new kind of irrationality being introduced? No investigator in the field of syllogistic reasoning can deny that errors are very frequent. "For *most* syllogisms the modal response is incorrect," says Erickson. If the errors are in the interpretation of premises, are not such errors just as irrational as errors of ratiocination? If we are to hold to a conception of rational human thinking, as most of the present authors do, we need to try to understand these errors, not just incorporate them into our models. I would suggest that we look closely at the material we present to our subjects and the terms in which it is cloaked.

A few remarks may be in order about the language of syllogisms. It is, after all, not surprising that difficulties arise in the understanding of premises. Logic has developed a special language suited to its own purposes. *Is* in the categorical syllogism is not the *is* of common discourse, but means *is included in*. The logical meaning of *some* has long been recognized as a source of difficulty for untrained subjects. Even the meaning of *all* should be given attention. De Morgan suggests that most people use the term not as a universal, but to signify *more than most*. Nevertheless, we present problems to subjects in this special language because it resembles the English language. That resemblance makes matters confusing indeed, since we are using homonyms of words in ordinary English usage without telling our subjects that they are homonyms. Correspondingly, efforts to clarify various logical meanings have resulted in improved performance in solving syllogisms.

Let us look more specifically at a few common errors and the attempts to understand them. The most frequent error here reported is the illicit conversion. "All A are B" is converted into "All B are A"; "Some A are not B" becomes "Some B are not A." May such conversions "be viewed as an irrationality in an otherwise logical system?" ask Revlin and Leirer. They reject the suggestion, viewing conversion as a part of the very process of solving syllogisms, operating unless blocked.

Why does conversion occur? Revlin and Leirer suggest three bases for conversions, licit or illicit. Now widely recognized is the ambiguity of the copula, much earlier described by Chapman and Chapman; the copula is understood to refer not to set inclusion, as intended by logicians, but to identity, so that if A = B, B = A. In addition, Revlin and Leirer suggest that certain communicative presuppositions, as well as the assumption of symmetry of relations, account for the conversion. Other contributors to this volume make some or all of the same assumptions. Griggs, e.g., posits the assumption of symmetry of relations to account for conversion errors; many of Erickson's subjects interpret *A* propositions in terms of set identity rather than set inclusion.

But why, we must still ask, do we make the assumption of symmetry of relations? Why do linguistic conventions favor conversions? It is not enough to locate errors in the premises rather than in the reasoning process. They must still be understood if thinking is to be regarded as rational. Perhaps a new look at the *material* we present to subjects will be helpful. We note at once that premises of a given kind do not permit just any errors. What are the errors that given premises permit and encourage?

I would suggest first that it is too simple to regard the copula as signifying equality, although it may do so in some cases, particularly cases in which the premises are stated in the abstract form, "All A are B." But when we say that "John is a boy," we are well aware that he is also a member of the Doe family, and an 11-year-old, and a resident of Bucks County. We are likewise aware that there are other boys. Thus, we do not equate *John* and *boy*. In this example, as perhaps in most ordinary discourse, we are able to use the copula correctly.

If the copula misleads, it may do so by seeming to put the two terms of an *A* proposition on an equal footing, whereas the logical meaning is precisely that they are *not* on an equal footing, but one is subordinate to the other.

The same kind of analysis would seem to apply to the illicit conversion of *O* propositions: the conversion of "Some A are not B" to "Some B are not A." "Some plants are not green things" becomes "Some green things are not plants." This conversion would be correct if the meanings of our proposition were exhausted by the following two Venn diagrams:

It is only the case:

which shows that the conversion is illicit. Why do we tend not to think of this case?

Chapman and Chapman suggest that—so far as experience in the real world goes—we can afford to ignore this third representation of the proposition. But an interpretation in terms of experience cannot handle the conversion when the terms are symbolic. Nor does experience always support the conversion. There is no temptation to convert the proposition "Some coins are not dimes."

Once again, it seems to me, the copula puts the terms of the proposition on an equal footing, thus hiding the relation of class inclusion, which is a relation of subordination-superordination.

In the present case a further difficulty exists. "Some plants are not green things" suggests—if we get that far in our thinking—that *green things* is the superordinate term; but, as the diagram shows, *plants* is the class in which *green things* are to be included.

If this analysis is correct, *A* and *O* propositions remind us of leading questions. Since their demands are misleading, subjects interpret these propositions incorrectly, just as leading questions or "trick" problems almost force us to wrong assumptions.

Again if the analysis is correct, it should be possible to reword premises to make them easier to understand correctly. As one strategy, if the copula is the culprit, it may be eliminated, as in the following sets of premises due to Lewis Carroll:

> Nothing inteliigible ever puzzles me.
> Logic puzzles me.

or

> All my sisters have colds.
> No one can sing who has a cold.

Other strategies might be devised to test the more important possibility that the statement of the premises is misleading with respect to the relations involved. (I have tried a few. They didn't work, but it is altogether possible that they were not radical enough to dispel such sturdy assumptions.)

A somewhat different problem arises in connection with another common error. No valid conclusion follows from two particular premises; subjects, nevertheless, often draw conclusions from such premises. Here is a problem I once used; subjects were asked to evaluate the conclusion.

'Some of the warriors at Troy carried daggers, said Schliemann, and this king was a warrior at Troy. So of course he carried a dagger.'[1]

The first premise is commonly interpreted to mean that only some (not all) of the warriors at Troy carried daggers. It must then be assumed—if one is to accept the conclusion—that the king is one of this group. Why should one make such an assumption? A possibility worth investigating is that the mere presentation of the premises together leads to the assumption of their mutual relevance. "Why do you tell me these two things?" a subject might wonder. "They must have something to do with each other."

(Another possible interpretation of the error in this case belongs to the problem area discussed by Wyer and Podeschi. The quantifier *some* may drop out and the term *warriors* may then be understood to mean *all warriors*. This appears to have happened with some of my subjects, as shown by their choice of Venn diagrams.)

Other examples might be analyzed, pointing to new directions for research. But one large problem for the present interpretation of syllogistic reasoning remains: the seeming failure of Griggs's subjects to assume transitivity, thus to reason logically within the syllogistic framework. It may be remarked that his results were obtained with sorites, not with simple syllogisms. Sorites permit new errors, not found with syllogisms. They were, furthermore, obtained with passages (with one exception) employing extraneous material in addition to the premises of interest to the investigator. This procedure serves the important purpose of making the paragraph seem more natural to subjects, but it also offers additional opportunities for confusion. Other properties of the paragraph illustrated seem to me to invite confusion. Griggs attributes his results in large part to erroneous logical processing. Before accepting such an important conclusion, I would like to see what results are obtained with less confusing and with simpler material (syllogisms rather than sorites). When empirical results are puzzling, it is a good idea to reserve judgment until they have been replicated under simplified, thus more understandable, conditions. I

---

[1] I am aware that the subject of the minor premise is a singular term, not a particular. It was introduced for the sake of the story in which the syllogisms were presented. The king (Agamemnon) may be treated as a member of the class *kings*, thus as a particular.

would like assurance that Griggs's subjects understood and accepted their task and understood the language in which the problems were phrased. Indeed, I would like to know specifically how they interpreted the premises. I have never found errors which could unambiguously be attributed to faulty reasoning. If they are found under clear conditions, I will be forced to a drastic revision of my view of the relation of logic to thinking.

This kind of uncertainty about where we stand is one of the things that makes the present volume so fascinating. Another is, of course, that the research bears directly on one of the central problems of the nature of human nature: the rationality of human thinking. All the contributors to this volume are engaged in active research programs on human reasoning, and their work will help to clarify this issue. These papers have a good deal in common as well as significant diversity. I hope that the diversity will remain, for a time at least, not only for the adventure and suspense it provides, but in order that we do not come to a premature closure of this important and undoubtedly most complex issue.

Mary Henle
Graduate Faculty
New School for Social Research

INTRODUCTION

AN INFORMATION PROCESSING FRAMEWORK FOR RESEARCH ON HUMAN REASONING

Richard E. Mayer and
Russell Revlin
University of California, Santa Barbara

> Nothing intelligible ever puzzles me.
> Logic puzzles me.
> —Lewis Carroll, 1887

There can be no doubt that making inferences is a fundamental human process. It has intrigued investigators for a millenium not only because we are able to do it so well (who could doubt the correct conclusion to the foregoing problem?), but also because on some occasions, we seem to fail so miserably at it. For example, in the following argument, a commonly drawn conclusion (starred) does not follow unambiguously from the information given:

> All hammers are tools.
> Some tools are sale items.
> *Some sale items are hammers.

What cognitive processes and structures must the reasoner employ in such circumstances to permit him to reach the decision illustrated here, and how

1

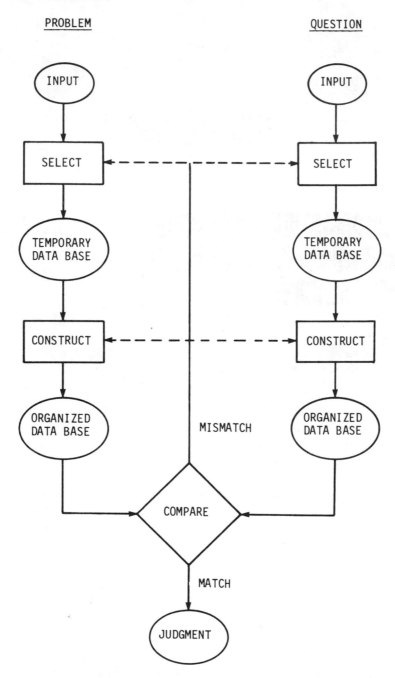

Fig. 1. A general model of reasoning.

can knowledge of such processes account for the decisions that people reach in everyday life?

The presence of these questions is visible in much of the recent research on human reasoning. The approach taken is to try to infer the logical processes and representation mechanisms that people possess and to describe the way the reasoner assembles those components to answer questions across a variety of situations, which may range from the child's representation of the physical world to the abstraction of meaning and the comprehension of connected discourse. This approach permits a description of the rational competence of people and in doing so provides an account of both the valid and invalid decisions that people reach in the course of everyday inference.

GENERAL FRAMEWORK

In understanding current research on reasoning, we find it useful to formulate a general model of inference to serve not only as a tentative model of human processing but also as a kind of organizing scheme for evaluating the locus of the many research projects in this area. This framework divides the process of making an inference into two major stages, Encoding and Question-answering, and subdivides each stage into three operations: Selection, Construction, and Comparison. The general functioning of these components is illustrated in Figure 1 and will be briefly described below.

Encoding

When a reasoner encodes the material from which he must make an inference, he first attends to the presented data and chooses the relevant features to be understood. This operation on the input is termed SELECT and may be guided by an external statement of a problem, subtleties in the form of the information presented, or specific past experience with such materials. We acknowledge, of course, that each of these potential sources of input *into* the SELECT operation are also elements that must be *acted upon* by the SELECT operation. Once the critical elements are stored in the reasoner's data base, he is said to operate on those elements to CONSTRUCT a formalism for representing the information in a manner amenable to later question-answering. This act of CONSTRUCT might also be termed a process of translation because it is said to transform the initial data base into a new one that may include both new elements and a new organization.

Question-answering

In a sense, we never observe the inference process, we only conjecture about its presence from the answers that reasoners give to our questions. In order to respond to questions in a manner that will satisfy an observer that the reasoner is indeed making an inference, the student must give the proper interpretation to the question. To do this, he must repeat the Encoding operations of SELECT and CONSTRUCT. Only this time, these operations take the Question as their input. When the reasoner has constructed an appropriate format for understanding the question, he must then COMPARE this formalism with that given for the input materials (e.g., evidence, premises, facts, etc.) to determine whether the formalism for the question is congruent with that of the initial data base. The result of the COMPARE operation might be either a simple Yes/No response or, as a function of the task requirements, may entail a second CONSTRUCT operation either on the evidence data base (guided by a SELECT operation that results from a failure of COMPARE) or a CONSTRUCT operation on the Question data base. That is, when the reasoner is unable to answer the question posed, he may transform his current knowledge of the evidence, or he may try to reinterpret the question so that it is congruent with his initial data base.

The reader will notice that there is no single operation in this framework that can be pointed to as an inference. Rather, what we would call 'inference' (in everyday speech) inheres in every operation: Inference is part and parcel of selecting relevant information from the evidence that is presented; inference guides the construction of a formalism; inference aids in determining which data base is to be transformed when the question is not readily answerable. Consequently, there is no single operation that can be labeled 'inference'; there are only elementary information processes that combine to produce the observed judgment that is called an inference.

This framework serves to organize the current research on human inference by determining on which operation each study is focused. It is not an oversimplification to say that all of the contributions in this volume present research concerned with the Encoding Process. That is, each of the projects examines either the reasoner's selection of information to be included in his data base or his understanding of those materials in terms of the organization of the data base. While Question-encoding is part and parcel of each of the models presented, many of the studies conclude that the decisions reached—whether valid or invalid—reflect rational operations acting on the incorrect representation of the reasoner's data base. Hence, even invalid conclusions may ultimately be shown to be rational ones. This is possible even if the reasoner's representation of the presented information is not veridical.

OUTLINE OF THE BOOK

The present volume contains a series of manuscripts concerning current research methods, results, and theories on human reasoning. While this collection does not represent an exhaustive survey of research on human inference, it is representative of the focal points around which both current research and theory have concentrated during the past few years. That is, it embodies the paradigms and issues of current concern in the work on human inference. The reader need only compare two chapters (selected at random) to notice that while the studies cover historically distinct paradigms, there are commonalities between them—not only in the general approach to the various problems but also in the details of the mechanisms that are employed. It is a tribute to the strength of the *Zeitgeist* that workers dealing with disparate tasks seem to conceptualize them in the same way.

These commonalities in both the approaches and mechanisms across inference tasks augur well for a unified view of human reasoning. This will be accomplished either by virtue of a single model that can account for the inferences across all tasks, or, more likely, we will be able to describe a sufficient set of processing and representational mechanisms that can be assembled in different ways for different tasks.

This volume has been divided into three major categories based on the type of task investigated.

Part 1 deals with traditional syllogistic reasoning tasks as well as applications of these tasks to "social" settings. The chapter by Erickson investigates performance on abstract syllogisms such as:

All A are C.
All A are B.
What can be concluded?

Revlin and Leirer report on factors influencing syllogistic reasoning with concrete rather than abstract terms. In particular, the role of personal bias is investigated by using syllogisms such as:

All blacks in Neuberg are welfare recipients.
Some welfare recipients in Neuberg are residents of Pennton.
What can be concluded?

The chapter by Staudenmayer and Bourne deals with conditional reasoning tasks of the form:

If there is an A on the front, then there is a 1 on the back.
There is an A on the front.
Is there a 1 on the back?

The final contribution in this section, by Wyer and Podeschi, concerns the factors that influence solutions to concrete problems—specifically, how students evaluate statements in terms of the evidence presented. For example:

> Tribes are primitive, communal, agricultural societies.
> Primitive societies buy bees.
> Communal societies buy bees.
> Agricultural societies do not buy bees.
> Do tribes buy bees?

Part 2 deals with drawing inferences from prose that contains set inclusion or linear ordering information. This work can be seen as extending the work on syllogistic reasoning to a new, broader area. For example, all three chapters deal with drawing inferences from set inclusions such as (Frase, 1969, 1970):

> All the Fundalas are outcasts from other tribes in Central Ugala. These people are isolated from other tribes because it is the custom in this country to get rid of certain types of people. All the outcasts of Central Ugala are hill people. The hills provide a most accommodating place to live. All the hill people of Central Ugala are farmers. The upper highlands provide excellent soil for cultivation. All the farmers of this country are peace loving people which is reflected in their artwork. All together, there are about fifteen different tribes in this area.

Questions involving inference could be: "Fundalas are hill people?" (1 inference) or "Fundalas are peace loving?" (4 inferences), etc.

In addition, all three chapters deal with linear orderings which have historical roots in the linear syllogisms (e.g., Clark, 1969). For example:

> In a small forest just south of nowhere, a deer, a bear, a wolf, and a hawk were battling for dominion over the land. It boiled down to a battle of wits, so intelligence was the crucial factor. The bear was smarter than the hawk, the hawk was smarter than the wolf, the wolf was smarter than the deer . . . Each of the battles was decided in its own way and tranquility returned to the area. (Potts, 1972, p. 730)

In this case inferences of one step are required to answer "Is the bear smarter than the wolf?"; two steps are required for "Is the bear smarter than the deer?".

Potts' deals with a theory of the memory structures supporting inference from text and compares it with work on "real" information such as reaction time studies on verification of information presumed to be in semantic memory. New data are presented that support a "similarity" theory of memory representation.

Griggs attempts to reconcile differences between inference performance on linear orderings and on set inclusions embedded in text. New data are presented that support the idea that all differences may be accounted for by assuming that subjects have difficulty with transitivity and conversion when they are confronted with set inclusions.

Frase attempts to provide a general overview of work on drawing inference from text. After summarizing the major results of his own series of experiments, he outlines a general framework for discussing the role of inference in reading.

Part 3 is concerned with the SELECT (Robinson & Hayes) and CONSTRUCT operations (Mayer) in mathematical inference, specifically focusing on solving algebra problems. For example, Robinson and Hayes present subjects with an algebra story problem and examines how students decide on what aspects of the problem are relevant to its solution. The problem concerns a crop-dusting plane that carries "2000 pounds of dusting compound, 250 pounds of fuel" and must cover a rectangular field of specified dimensions during a 3-hour period.

Mayer explores four types of mathematical inference tasks, including quantitative linear orderings such as:

In a certain forest the animals are voting for their leader. The frog gets 10 times as many votes as the rabbit. The hawk gets 20 times as many votes as the bear. The frog gets 40 times as many votes as the bear.

Another mathematical reasoning task involves algebraic substitution in which the reasoner learns:

$$H = E - B$$
$$M = O \times H$$
$$O = Y \times C$$

and then is asked questions such as "Given Y, C, and H, could you find M?"

FORMAL REASONING TASKS

Interest in formal syllogisms has always been two-fold: as formal expressions of rules of inference and as didactic devices for illustrating such rules. No doubt, Aristotle, the person credited with their development, had both functions in mind in his capacity as scientist and instructor. Through the 20 centuries of their existence, such problems have stood as the paradigm for logical thought (especially in the Latin church) and as a tool for instructing students in the proper rules of inferences. In this latter role, categorical syllogisms invariably find their way into texts on rhetoric and on improving thinking ability; they have even been incorporated into games to casually inculcate formal principles of reasoning (see, e.g., the books of Lewis Carroll and recent logic games such as *Propaganda, Wff & Proof*, etc.).

The presence of this prolific literature on formal reasoning attests to the mystery of the process. Surely, if we all reasoned according to the logician's formalisms, such great interest in logical arguments would hardly be warranted, and the systems of Boole, Venn, and Euler would not have been needed. The fact is that we are frequently presented with an anomaly: People who appear to be otherwise quite rational often fail to solve categorical and conditional syllogisms according to the rules of logic; i.e., some logical people appear to be illogical. The history of psychological research on categorical reasoning in this century reflects a perplexity with this problem. If reasoners are not reasoning according to the logician's rules, what rules are being used, and how can students be trained to relinquish these rules, and what impact on everyday reasoning do such rules have? A dichotomy discernable in the present literature is whether the researcher asks what processes students use when they are said to reason (e.g., Erickson, Revlin & Leirer), or whether he tries to posit a set of rules that reasoners might be following in dealing with a specific task (e.g., Staudenmayer & Bourne). The former approach is not tied to an *a priori* view of the reasoner and, consequently, is freer to explore process and mechanisms and to give generality to those components which may have independent motivation from other tasks.

Categorical Reasoning

Research on syllogistic reasoning during this past century can be divided into three overlapping lines: (a) fundamental research designed to ascertain the nature of the inference process; (b) studies which use the syllogism as a diagnostic standard against which to compare the performance of various groups; and (c) studies which use the syllogism in its most traditional sense (e.g., Boole, 1854) as a model of human thought.

Fundamental research. The fundamental research on human inference reflects an emphasis on either the reasoner's encoding of the materials (CONSTRUCT) or on the inference rules which operate on that encoding (e.g., COMPARE, CONSTRUCT). The earliest work on categorical syllogisms in the United States fortuitously combined an emphasis on both aspects of the inference process. Wilkins (1928) examined the effect on rational choice of the ease of encoding (concrete vs. abstract problems) and believability of the logical conclusions. A major finding of that study was that the variability in performance resulted from the complexity of the materials and that beliefs only marginally contributed to the reasoners decisions—certainly, the rationality of the judgments did not reflect the overwhelming presence of alogical or illogical inference rules.

This emphasis on the encoding process as a critical component for rational judgments pervades the more recent literature as well. Richter (1957), in analyzing decision errors, points to the reasoner's difficulty in deciding what task he is being asked to perform (SELECT). The research of Ceraso and Provitera (1971), Chapman and Chapman (1959), Dickstein (1976), Erickson (1974), Henle (1962), Revlis (1975a, 1975b), and Whimbey and Ryan (1969) all attest to the importance of the reasoner's understanding of the materials and his ability to store that representation in memory. That is, when we are able to state the reasoner's representation for the premises in a syllogism, we only need to posit a simple COMPARE mechanism to account for the range of decisions that reasoners make—both the logically correct and incorrect ones.

Concurrent with the work on specifying the fundamental encoding processes is an opposing tradition which seeks to posit alogical inference rules and to develop a kind of "psycho-logic" to explain the decisions (primarily focusing on the errors) that reasoners reach in categorical reasoning problems. This view was presented in the seminal work of Woodworth and Sells (1935) and Sells (1936), who showed that many decisions reflect both an insufficient processing of the reasoning materials on abstract syllogisms and a nonrational decision rule. Woodworth and Sells developed the "atmosphere" hypothesis to account for reasoning errors. It claims that when reasoners fail to appreciate the relation expressed in the premises of a syllogism, their decision reflects a superficial match (COMPARE) between the "global impression" of the premises with the atmosphere of the conclusion. For example, when solving the following syllogism, the reasoner is said to gain a particular-affirmative impression (atmosphere) from each of the premises and will, therefore, on some occasions accept a conclusion that also has a particular-affirmative atmosphere:

Some B are C.
Some A are B.
*Some A are C.

That is, reasoners both ignore the normative (even rational) encoding and apply an alogical rule in accepting conclusions. The hypothesis about the source of reasoner's decisions was applied only to an explanation of reasoning errors—no statement was made concerning the processes entailed in making a correct inference nor did Woodworth and Sells specify the occasions on which a reasoner would fail to appreciate the relation expressed in the premises. This analysis of reasoning has been examined in several studies (e.g., Begg &

Denny, 1969; Chapman & Chapman, 1959; Dickstein, 1975; Morgan & Morton, 1944; Revlis, 1975b; Simpson & Johnson, 1966) with equivocal results (e.g., Morgan & Morton, 1944, Revlis, 1975b), in part a consequence of the insufficient specification of the original hypothesis.

While the atmosphere hypothesis is readily construed as focusing on an alogical inference mechanism, it can as easily be categorized as a model which emphasizes the encoding process. To wit: Reasoners are claimed to employ an impoverished representation of the premises. In this case, there is no reason to believe that the COMPARE mechanism is any different than when the reasoner encodes the materials with a full (logical) reading. In fact, the Conversion Model offered by Revlin and Leirer (see chapter 3) claims that the atmosphere components are actually part of the initial stage in the comprehension of quantified relations and result in an encoding to which the reasoner (under specified circumstances) may retreat as a function of the problem's configuration.

Other alogical and illogical mechanisms have also been posited for both concrete and abstract syllogisms by Chapman and Chapman (1959), Dickstein (1976), Frase (1966a, 1966b, 1968), and Pezzoli and Frase (1968) as well as by researchers in the social-psychological tradition. All of this work promotes a view of the reasoner as a quasi-rational being who uses illogical processes when he reasons about events in the world; i.e., the reasoner is said to make deductions that do not follow rationally from the premises, but rather reflect "interrupts" in rational processing. These cause students to accept conclusions in which they have a particular emotional stake rather than conclusions that follow logically from the premises. This is somewhat akin to a juror who disregards the evidence of a case and reaches a verdict based on the emotional background of the testimony. This research tends to disregard the earlier findings of Wilkins (1928)—without justification (see Feather, 1965; Janis & Frick, 1943; Janis & Terwilliger, 1962; Kaufman & Goldstein, 1967; Lefford, 1946; Morgan & Morton, 1944; Thistlethwaite, 1950; Thouless, 1959; Wilson, 1965; Winthrop, 1946). While most of the traditional studies support the view of humans as irrational information processors, there are findings to the contrary—namely, Henle (1962), Henle and Michael (1956), Revlin and Leirer (see chapter 3 in this volume). Revlin and Leirer point out that many of the aforementioned findings largely reflect systematic confoundings in the preparation of the stimulus materials.

The syllogism as a diagnostic standard. The second research approach consists of studies which seek to use syllogisms as a diagnostic metric for assessing attitudes and beliefs (see the social-psychological literature cited above) and for distinguishing among people in terms of their putative thought processes. Hence, syllogisms have found their way onto intelligence tests (e.g., Guilford, 1959; Thurstone, 1938) as well as onto tests to diagnose and distinguish among clinical groups (e.g., Feather, 1965; Gottesman & Chapman, 1960; Von Domarus, 1944).

The syllogism as a model of human thought. Throughout the centuries, there have been advocates of the categorical syllogism as a model of human thought (e.g., Boole, 1854). Most recently, McGuire (1966a, 1966b, 1966c) has used the syllogism and a mathematical model for information integration to predict attitude change under various conditions of information presentation. This approach argues that beliefs are consistent and that information presented concerning one belief in a network can influence the other beliefs in that network roughly in a way that would follow if reasoners' decisions from their beliefs followed the categorical reasoning paradigm.

Current research. In a sense, the very recent work on categorical reasoning brings the literature full circle—it is now possible to think of humans as rational information processors whose decisions follow logically from their encoding of the materials reasoned about (Erickson, 1974; Johnson-Laird, 1970, 1975; Revlis, 1975a, 1975b). The current research seeks to describe a set of sufficient processes to account for both "correct" and "incorrect" inferences on such tasks. Much of this work focuses on how the reasoner understands both the material he is asked to reason about and the nature of the task. In this light, the reader will note that all four chapters that deal with formal inference in this volume (Erickson, Revlin & Leirer, Staudenmayer & Bourne, and Wyer & Podeschi) examine the reasoner's understanding of the premises of the problems and how such an understanding may account for *all* of the judgments made by the reasoner. Thus, the authors are providing general models of inference instead of detailing post hoc mechanisms that apply to narrowly defined classes of behavior—a frequent characteristic of the previous literature on formal inference.

Erickson emphasizes the importance of the reasoner's encoding processes. His research proceeds in two phases. First, he determines the probabilities associated with the reasoner's understanding of variously quantified propositions. Second, he uses these measures to predict the reasoners' decisions on abstract syllogisms—decisions which are said to rationally reflect the "diagrams" or representations that the reasoners have selected for the premises. The predictions of such an approach are evaluated in terms of a three-stage model of formal reasoning.

The research of Revlin and Leirer emphasizes the reasoner's encoding processes. Their chapter evaluates the Conversion Model of Formal Reasoning (Revlis, 1975b), which makes explicit predictions concerning the reasoners' decision when solving categorical syllogisms. After reviewing the evidence in support of the model's predictions on abstract and neutral-concrete syllogisms, the authors examine the model's accuracy in accounting for decisions on problems where (a) the logically required conclusion either agrees or conflicts with common beliefs (where the reasoner's representation of the premises was controlled), and (b) the logically required conclusion is neutral with respect to belief, but the representation of the "controversial" premises is free to vary (evaluated by means of a questionnaire). The results show that the traditional belief-bias effect in syllogistic reasoning can be viewed as a result of rational operations performed on a highly personalized data base. The data also affirm that a model which posits an underlying rationality to human decisions can account for apparently irrational choices.

Conditional Reasoning

The development of models and methodologies in categorical reasoning was paralleled by similar developments in conditional reasoning. In these tasks the reasoner would be told to assume that a rule was true (e.g., "If p, then q"), and then he would be asked about the truth of its components given evidence about other components (e.g., given that p was true, the reasoner would be asked whether q was also true). This task was seen as the embodiment of scientific thinking and as such, it was expected to serve as a useful metric for gauging cognitive development. Although such reasoning tasks were included on standardized tests (e.g., Burt, 1919), the work of Piaget appears to have given impetus to subsequent research—especially on conditional reasoning in children (e.g., Osherson, 1975; but see also Ennis, 1975). Such problems also find their way into the social-psychological and clinical literature, side-by-side with categorical syllogisms (e.g., Roberge & Paulus, 1971; Thistlethwaite, 1950). Indeed, recent work shows great commonalities in the processes employed to solve these problems in terms of the interpretation of the relational terms and in the importance of the concreteness of the categories reasoned about (compare Revlin & Leirer with Staudenmayer & Bourne, this volume). In a review of the literature, Evans (1973) shows that students employ similar levels of partial encoding and analysis (reading-off the formalism) in conditional and categorical syllogisms (see also Revlis, 1975a).

The research of Staudenmayer and Bourne emphasizes the importance of the reasoners' encoding processes for decisions on conditional syllogisms. They asked students to solve conditional reasoning problems in which the experimenter controlled the students' knowledge of the nature of the classes reasoned about. By dichotomizing groups of subjects in terms of their knowledge of the categories and their interpretation of the logical connective, Staudenmayer and Bourne are able both to account for the reasoners' decisions in the traditional conditional reasoning task and to illuminate the nature of the selection task in which reasoners evaluate conditional statements (see Appendix at the end of this chapter).

Belief Generalizations

The research on social inference (i.e., the chapter by Wyer & Podeschi) is of a piece with the formal reasoning tasks: Reasoners are asked to evaluate generalizations in accord with presented evidence. This task is different from other syllogisms in that the relational terms and the form are less restricted here than with standard syllogisms.

Social inference tasks of this sort were developed to assess the processes entailed when people reason about classes and events that are related to information already available in their long-term knowledge. Early work tested Abelson's Set Model of belief generalizations (Gilson & Abelson, 1965) which was embodied as a computer model of belief systems (Abelson & Carroll, 1965). As with other interesting paradigms, it has taken on a life of its own as researchers expand the materials and conditions in an effort to isolate fundamental processes and to evaluate alternate models (e.g., Abelson & Kanouse, 1966).

In current paradigms, students are given beliefs about subordinates and superordinates of a concept and are asked whether or not they would generalize the same belief to the concept itself. The results show that the willingness of reasoners to accept inductions or deductions is closely related to the relational terms (verbs). Some verbs generalize well from subordinate evidence, but poorly from superordinate evidence (these are called positive manifest verbs; they express concrete relations, e.g., *buy* or *produce*). Other verbs are most effective with superordinate evidence (these are called negative subjective verbs; they express negative orientation or mental states, e.g., *hate* or *fear*).

The presence of these relational terms affects the amount of evidence that reasoners require before they are willing to accept a generalization. This is as if the implicit quantifier associated with the generalization varies with the relational term (e.g., Abelson & Kanouse, 1966). That context affects the implicit and explicit quantifiers is demonstrated in psycholinguistic studies by Johnson-Laird (1969a, 1969b) and is shown to be a result of more general linguistic processes by Lawler (1972). This suggests that the inferences that reasoners are willing to make are reliant on the encoding of the test generalization (Question-answering) and the outcome of the COMPARE operator which must make use of quantificational elements. The Wyer and Podeschi research expands the paradigm to cover explicit aspects of the reasoner's encoding of the evidence and the question and shows that the relational terms are not the sole influence on how the reasoner constructs his representational formalism for answering such questions.

LINEAR ORDERING TASKS

Two contributions in this volume (by Potts and Griggs) are concerned with the reasoner's memory for ordered information. For example, Potts presents students with information of the form $A > B$, $B > C$, $C > D$, $D > E$ and then asks students whether specific relations are true or false of the ordering they were presented (e.g., $A > C$ or $A > E$). Some of these relations are verbatim matches with the original input, and some are inferentially true (or false) of the encoded material. The paradigms currently employed permit an evaluation of whether information is stored in a static, quasi-veridical form or whether it undergoes some transformation. Once again we find a relation between memory coding and inference.

These tasks have their genesis in the work on comparative judgments made by children (e.g., Burt, 1919; Donaldson, 1963; Piaget, 1921) where children were given two- or three-term series problems (e.g., "Tom is taller than John;" "John is taller than Bill") and asked to evaluate the truth or falsity of a question regarding who was the greatest (or least) on the relevant dimension (e.g., "who's tallest?").

These are symbolic comparative judgment tasks in the sense that the reasoner is asked to compare symbolic terms which vary along some dimension just as one might compare the physical stimuli to which the symbols correspond. Historically, formal models were inferred to account for the inferences in both adults and children. These models varied in terms of the formalism upon which inference processes operate and included a string manipulation model (Hunter, 1956), an imagery model (Huttenlocher, 1968), a propositional encoding (Clark, 1969), and a constructivist model (Barclay, 1973). Details may be found in a review by Johnson-Laird (1972).

Much of the research has concentrated on the two strongest models, that of Huttenlocher (1968; Huttenlocher & Higgins, 1972) and Clark (1969, 1971). Huttenlocher's model has its genesis in the social-psychological literature by Desoto (Desoto, 1961; Desoto, London, & Handel, 1965; Handel, Desoto, & London, 1968), where the claim was made that people have a predilection for linear orderings; i.e., they construct spatial analogs of the ordering, a representational formalism that permits reasoners to answer a question by reading off the material "top-down" or "left-right." The materials could include evaluative terms (e.g., *good/bad*) or perceptual ones (e.g., *light/dark, high/low*). Huttenlocher's work provided a formal framework for these conjectures, and she made the strong claim that the way reasoners mentally manipulate the comparative terms is isomorphic to the way they manipulate concrete objects.

The contrasting model by Clark claimed that reasoner's encode the material in an abstract, semantic representation and that the comparative judgments were made by manipulating and comparing these abstract codes. The evidence for the representation posited was gathered from both independent linguistic considerations and from experiments on memory for comparative sentences.

Potts' work can be seen as an extension of this reasoning/memory paradigm in two ways. First, he expanded the memory task to include many more relational terms than three. Second, Potts guised the problem within the context of a paragraph memory task rather than either a sentence memory task or a straightforward inference task. His objective, of course, was the same as Huttenlocher and Clark—namely, to use a memory paradigm to assess the reasoner's representation of ordered material and to determine whether reasoners made inferences about that ordering in the act of encoding the material.

Potts' findings were originally interpreted along the lines of a constructivist approach (Barclay, 1973) by showing that the reasoner appears to know more than the veridical statements that he committed to memory. And, in fact, the hallmark of Potts' effect is that inferences from the presented information are often better recalled than the originally presented information.

However, Potts has suggested that the representation for this information, necessary to account for the effect, is a linear ordering similar to that posited earlier by Desoto et al. (1965), where reasoners' data base is so constructed that the elements in the input are ordered along a continuum (see Moyer, 1973). Ease of answering questions is seen as a function of comparing two objects on this continuum (several models for such a comparison have been described by Moyer and Bayer (1976).

History seems to repeat itself, however: Banks (1977) argues for a more abstract, semantic code being employed in both the representation in the data base and in the comparison of the data base and the question, much in the form of Clark's (1969) model of linear reasoning. Interestingly, Potts acknowledges the presence of semantic factors when making analogies judgments with class inclusion relations (see Griggs, this volume).

Research on memory for inclusion relations by Griggs is similar to the work of Potts in two ways. First, it also has its genesis in the syllogistic reasoning literature. The series of class inclusion relations that comprise Griggs' task are formally defined as *sorites* and were briefly investigated by Sells (1936) in a categorical reasoning task.

All P are Q.
All Q are R.
All R are S.
*All S are P?
All P are S?

Students' recall for such relations was studied in the context of recall for connected discourse by Dawes (1964, 1966), working within the framework established by Bartlett (1932). Dawes ignored the encoding/question-answering processes and argued that the reasoners' ability to answer questions concerning the material was attributable to a distortion in the data base as a result of the decay of information over time (i.e., "simplification").

The reworking of the paradigm by Frase (1969), however, is more in keeping with the framework adopted here: He analyzed both the reasoner's encoding of quantified relations and separated the encoding from the question-answering component. Griggs' research represents an effort to assess both components and to compare the findings on memory for inclusion relations (sorites) with memory for linear orderings (linear syllogisms).

MATHEMATICAL INFERENCE

Inferential reasoning is not confined to the boundaries of the syllogism, nor even only to the domain of logical prose. Another rich source of information concerning inference may be found in the study of mathematical problem solving. In particular, inference is required to solve what Hinsley, Hayes, and Simon (1977) refer to as "those popular 20th century fables called algebra word problems." Although there are, of course, many other areas in mathematics that may be relevant, this section will focus mainly on studies of inference in algebra substitution problems.

The study of algebraic problem solving is useful for several reasons. Work in this area allows a complement and extension of theories developed from work on syllogistic and prose inference. In particular, one might be interested in whether reasoning with numbers (what could be called "quantitative reasoning") is the same as deductions performed on information that is non-numeric. In addition, algebra problems have some advantage over other prose "stories" because there is a precise mathematical notation available for representing the information. Finally, there are immediate practical benefits associated with an understanding of mathematical reasoning, including improved instruction and a higher level of mathematical "literacy" in the general public.

Subjects' Representation of Problems

One of the primary research issues has been what could be called the "representational problem"—how do subjects translate the presented problem into an internal representation, and how does that representation influence problem solving? Paige and Simon (1966) investigated this question by presenting a series of algebra story problems to tenth graders and asking them to draw a picture representing each problem before solving the problem. Several of the problems included contradictions and ambiguities such as:

> A board was sawed into two pieces. One piece was two-thirds as long as the whole board and was exceeded in length by the second piece by four feet. How long was the board before it was cut? (p. 119)

The students who correctly solved the problem (or who recognized the contradictions) were more likely to produce an integrated picture, e.g., one board showing part to be 2/3 X and the other part to be 2/3 X + 4. However, subjects who failed to find the correct answer tended to draw unintegrated pictures, such as making one separate drawing for each sentence or major clause in the story.

Bobrow (1968) developed a program called STUDENT that attempts to solve algebra story problems. A typical problem is as follows:

> The gas consumption of my car is 15 miles per gallon. The distance between Boston and New York is 250 miles. What is the number of gallons of gas used on a trip between New York and Boston? (p. 174–175)

The first step is to translate the external representation of the problem into an internal representation. The program derived the following equations from the story:

> (Distance between Boston and New York) = (250 miles)
> (X1) = (Number of gallons of gas used on trip between New York and Boston)
> (Gas consumption of my car) = (15 miles/1 gallon)

An additional piece of information from long-term memory is retrieved:

> (Distance) = (Gas consumption) X (Number of gallons of gas used)

Next, STUDENT must decide that some of the variables are identical, e.g., "distance" is the same as "distance between Boston and New York." Finally, the actual computations are carried out, yielding the answer:

> The number of gallons of gas used on a trip between New York and Boston is 16.66 gallons.

As with Paige and Simon's study, the crucial stage in STUDENT's solution is that of setting up the internal representation (i.e., building the equations).

Schwartz and his colleagues (Polich & Schwartz, 1974; Schwartz, 1971; Schwartz & Fattellah, 1972) have investigated the ways in which adults represent information required to solve "who-done-it"-type deductive reasoning problems. One consistent finding is that subjects are more likely to use a matrix format for representing the information if large amounts of information are presented, and subjects who choose to use a matrix representation tend to perform better on the task. Other less successful protocols given by Schwartz's subjects included rewriting the problem in sentence form, grouping the data, forming a network, or "miscellaneous" techniques. Schwartz's findings are consistent with the idea that how a problem is translated into an internal representation is a critical stage in determining reasoning performance.

In a more recent study, Hinsley, Hayes, and Simon (1977) found that subjects were quite proficient at categorizing algebra story problems into category types such as distance-rate-time, scale conversion, triangle, interest, river current, etc. Eighteen different types of problems were revealed, and the authors argue that when subjects decide on what type of problem they are given, their expectancy serves as a schema for organizing the information. Presumably, many errors in solving algebra problems occur because subjects misinterpret the type of problem and thus form an incorrect internal representation of the facts. This idea is consistent with the findings of Loftus and Suppes (1972) that sixth graders tend to make more errors when a given story problem is of a different type from the preceding one.

Presentation

A second basic research issue concerns what could be called the "presentation problem"–determining the effect of how the presented information is organized on a subject's ability to solve the problem. For instance, Posner (1973) provides an example of a common algebra story problem:

> Two trains stations are fifty miles apart. At 2 p.m. one Saturday afternoon two trains start toward each other, one from each station. Just as the trains pull out of the stations, a bird springs into the air in front of the first train and flies ahead to the front of the second train. When the bird reaches the second train, it turns back and flies toward the first train. The bird continues to do this until the trains met. If both trains travel at the rate of twenty-five miles per hour and the bird flies at a hundred miles per hour, how many miles will the bird have flown before the trains meet? (p. 150–151)

According to Posner, the above problem is much more difficult than asking "How much time will the bird have been flying?" By focusing on the bird's flight, the subject might attempt to calculate the bird's distance on each trip between the trains.

Similarly, Maier and Burke (1967) found that certain minor changes in how a problem is presented can greatly change the difficulty. For example, the horse problem states, "A man bought a horse for $60 and sold it for $70. Then he bought it back again for $80 and sold it for $90. How much did he make in the horse business?" (p. 305). This problem was very difficult for Maier and Burke's subjects, but the solution rate increased dramatically when the problem was presented as two separate transaction, one concerning a white horse and one concerning a black horse.

More recently, Hayes and Simon (1974) have developed problem isomorphs for the tower of Hanoi problem. For example, the problem could be represented in the form of three monsters holding three different-sized globes ("monster problem") or in terms of tea-pouring ritual involving three people ("tea ceremony problem"). One of the major findings of these studies is that very different patterns of solution behavior are obtained for different isomorphs of the same problem, even though all the problems share the same formal characteristics. Similarly, Mayer (1976) found that different ways of presenting a series of conditional branching statements (e.g., in English or as flow diagrams) resulted in different error patterns.

Apparently, the way that a story problem is organized and the things that are emphasized tend to influence the way in which the subject translates the problem into an internal representation. In a recent study Mayer and Greeno (1975) provided evidence that algebraic information that is presented as a meaningful story is stored in a more flexible way than identical information presented as a set of nonsense equations. Clearly what is needed to resolve both the "presentation problem" and the "representation problem" is a more precise language for characterizing the internal representation of problems. Hayes and Simon's UNDERSTAND is one promising movement in that direction.

Process

A third major research area is what could be called the "process problem"—determining how the subject carried out the required inference steps. Findings in this area are essentially the reserve of Potts' (1972, 1974) "distance effect" obtained with non-numeric information and suggest that different processing is required for these two types of situations. For example, Loftus and Suppes (1972) and Suppes, Loftus, and Jerman (1969) presented 100 story problems to sixth graders. A typical problem is: "At the tree nursery, Tom counted 28 rows of pine trees. The forester said that there were 575 trees in each row. How many trees were there at the nursery?" (Loftus & Suppes, 1972, p. 437). Among the factors increasing the subjects' difficulty in answering these problems was the number of different operations required.

There is also some evidence concerning the processes that subjects use to solve algebra substitution problems. For example, Malin (1973) isolated a "forward" and "backward" processing strategy for solving algebra problems consisting of three interlocking three-term equations. Hayes' (1965, 1966) classic work on "spy problems" also indicates that an important strategy used by subjects in solving substitution problems is breaking a problem down into subparts (or subgoals).

Finally, Groen and Parkman (1972) and Resnick (1976; Woods, Resnick, & Groen, 1975) have provided process models to account for reaction time performance in solving simple addition and subtraction problems, respectively. These models encourage the development of similar process models for more complex algebraic tasks.

Current Research

The Robinson and Hayes chapter in this volume concerns the important issue of how subjects decide what is "relevant" and what is not relevant from the information presented in an algebra story problem. It seems to focus on what we have called the SELECT stage of solving reasoning problems, i.e., the selection of to-be-represented information. In the studies reported, subjects were presented a problem in the form of cumulative segments; for each segment the subject was asked to indicate whether or not the information was necessary to solve the problem. The problem was presented twice in this manner, but some subjects were given the question to-be-answered *before* each reading, and others were given the question *after* each reading. Results indicated an increase in performance (both a drop in "false alarms" and an increase in "hits") from presentation 1 to presentation 2, especially for the question-after group; the question-before group performed quite well on both passes. One tentative conclusion is that providing the question before reading served as an advance organizer (Ausubel, 1968) which allowed subjects to establish the appropriate "schema" (Hinsley et al., 1977) for the problem. Robinson and Hayes argue that once the subject has developed a schema for the problem (i.e., once the subjects knows what the question is), selective attention "demons" can be adjusted appropriately.

The contribution by Mayer (chapter 10) deals with the role of meaningfulness (e.g., whether information is presented as nonsense equations or as a story) in how information is represented in memory. In other words, while Robinson and Hayes focus on the selection of information to be encoded, Mayer focuses on the quality of structuring of the resulting internal representation. In a series of experiments using four separate tasks (algebra substitution, spy problems, linear ordering, base 3 arithmetic), the general method was to present identical information in meaningful and in rote formats and then to measure problem-solving performance (either response time or error rate) for problems requiring varying amounts of inference. For algebra substitution and spy problems, results indicated that meaningful presentation resulted in faster inferences and were consistent with the idea that better integrated cognitive structures were acquired from meaningful as opposed to rote presentations. For linear orderings and arithmetic problems meaningful and rote subjects displayed entirely different patterns of performance, and several qualitatively different types of cognitive structures were suggested. The results indicate that the same information may be represented in memory in several different "correct" ways.

COMMON THEMES

The contributors to this volume were selected because their work appeared to be representative of the "hot" areas in human reasoning during the past five years. Our original goal was to juxtapose such research in the remote hope that some common strains could be found among the projects and thereby promote some integration of the areas. We were delightfully surprised when we studied the manuscripts: The commonalities were both obvious and important. In spite of the fact that many different types of inference tasks were explored, the researchers had developed similar analytical concepts and often described similar mechanisms as well.

Encoding

The most striking commonality among the studies is the emphasis on how reasoners encode the represent information. Since the tasks presented here are word problems in one form or another, linguistic encoding is critical. Each researcher seems to focus on a slightly different aspect of the encoding process.

For example, Erickson investigates how the premises are interpreted by the reasoner (the first stage in his three-stage model). His analysis is based on the idea that when an ambiguous proposition is given, subjects tend to select just one of the possible interpretations in a manner analogous to selecting a Venn diagram. Thus, a proposition like "Some A are B" could be interpreted as an overlap relationship or as a set-subset relationship, but not both at the same time. The reasoner's decisions are said to reflect this encoding.

Revlin and Leirer also rely heavily on the mechanism for interpreting propositions; however, these authors are able to account for many interesting effects by suggesting that subjects are required by linguistic conventions to convert each proposition. For example, "All A are B" would be interpreted as "All B are A".

Similarly, Staudenmayer and Bourne note that many errors found in conditional and biconditional reasoning tasks can be accounted for by the subject's interpretation of biconditional or conditional propositions and the size of the categories reasoned about.

Wyer and Podeschi point to the influence of linguistic context on how propositions are interpreted and the evidential context for inductive and deductive decisions.

Potts' contribution on inference from text attempts to develop a theory of how information is represented in memory. Potts' model is based on the idea that elements are encoded in terms of their similarity, i.e., the number of common features.

Griggs deals with two basic encoding assumptions that subjects tend to make when dealing with set inclusions from text: conversion and lack of transitivity.

Finally, Frase points out that two major problems in encoding are partial encoding (encoding only a part of the presented information, such as in a feature abstraction model) and optional encoding (encoding something different from what was presented, such as the converse of sentences).

There are three traditional forms of the syllogism: set inclusion, linear ordering, and conditional. The present studies indicate that for each type subjects have trouble interpreting asymmetrical relations. For example, Staudenmayer and Bourne find that subjects tend to impose symmetry by giving conditional premises (such as "If p, then q") a biconditional interpretation ("If q, then p"). Similarly, with set inclusion propositions Revlin and Leirer note conversions of asymmetric premises such as "All A are B" into "All B are A." Potts and Griggs also report that subjects have difficulty with asymmetrical linear ordering relations and tend to interpret "A is greater than B" as "A and B are different from one another." A second problem that permeates several types of reasoning is the problem of indeterminancy—where there is more than one conclusion following from the premises. In all types of syllogisms there is also evidence that subjects tend to interpret ambiguous situations as being more restricted than they are.

In the section on mathematical reasoning, Robinson and Hayes show that a subject's "schema" for an algebra story problem can influence what is attended to and selected for further thought. Mayer emphasizes the idea that the same formal information may be represented in the reasoner's memory in qualitatively different ways and that different patterns of inference performance can be accounted for in terms of differences in underlying memory representations. These studies point to the role of the reasoner's expectancies and past experiences in selecting and organizing to-be-reasoned-upon information.

Cognitive Structures

Most of the research presented here is also concerned with the cognitive structures (formalisms) that the reasoner constructs in order to answer questions. For example, both Revlin and Leirer and Erickson explicitly present the formalisms that may be assumed to underlie syllogistic reasoning performance. While Revlin and Leirer rely on an encoding of a lingusitic transformation of the proposition and Erickson relies on an imaginal representation of the set-subset relation, both models may be expressed in sufficient detail to invite empirical testing. Potts' similarity model for representing logical information acquired from text is an attempt to relate this work to the existing rich literature on semantic memory for categorical information. Indeed, the debate between Griggs and Potts is on the issue of whether this formalism is sufficient or needed. Mayer explicitly suggests some possible cognitive structures that subjects can acquire from the format in which mathematical problems are presented, and he relates patterns of performance to the representations. In this, several different formalisms are possible for the same presented information. Although Robinson and Hayes do not explicitly suggest the structure of the representation supposed to be acquired by their subjects, the authors look at how one's notion of the task affects the formalism constructed.

Past Experience

A related issue is how the reasoner's knowledge comes into play in solving problems. For example, Revlin and Leirer, Staudenmayer and Bourne, and Wyer and Podeschi manipulate the nature of the categories reasoned about and note the effect on reasoners' decisions. While Wyer and Podeschi and Staudenmayer and Bourne manipulate the nature and size of categories within the experiment, Revlin and Leirer make use of questionnaires and word norms to predict decisions from hypothesized knowledge of the subjects.

Potts' model of memory representation also relies on the subject's past experience with the features of presented categories. The tendency to convert, noted by Griggs and others, may be seen as a general strategy that has been successful in the past. As Chapman and Chapman (1959) pointed out almost 20 years ago, many conversions are correct.

Robinson and Hayes show that students possess various problem-analyzers that are evoked in the control of certain types of problems. These analyzers must certainly reflect experience with algebra word problems. Mayer reports that meaningfulness of presentation influences how information is structured in memory; this is consistent with the idea that past experience is used to encode meaningful information, but is not as effective with less meaningful material. This work has implications for possible differences in performance on concrete and abstract syllogisms.

Extensions of Paradigms

Another common theme reflected in this volume is the attempt to go beyond the formal structure of traditional abstract syllogisms. For example, Revlin and Leirer and Wyer and Podeschi extend the paradigm to concrete, English sentences that could be found in discourse. Further, the work of Frase, Potts, and Griggs investigates inferential reasoning based on reading from text. Finally, Robinson and Hayes and Mayer explore the world of algebra story problems in a further extension; these tasks require a form of inference that is based on numerical quantities. The extension of the inferential reasoning paradigm to diverse (but related) tasks is an important step in determining the general characteristics of human inferential reasoning in "natural" settings.

DISAGREEMENTS

The reader should be aware that while these studies demonstrate a convergence of thinking on many issues concerning human inference, much remains to be clarified. The research projects summarized here contain contrasting as well as congruent elements. Griggs and Potts, using similar paradigms for studying ordering relations (linear and class inclusions), come to different conclusions concerning the place of abstract and real-world material in inference tasks of this sort. This leads to quite different explanations for their respective findings (see Potts' reply to Griggs).

In categorical reasoning, Revlin and Leirer and Erickson view the inference process quite differently. Revlin and Leirer appear to argue for a propositional interpretation of premises and a logical (though unspecified) deduction operation on specified encoding. Erickson attests to the importance of the encoding process, but sees the inference tasks as a result of probabilistic manipulation of Venn diagrams from whence the conclusion is read off.

Staudenmayer's work contrasts sharply with the views of Wason and Johnson-Laird (1972) on the selection task and on conditional reasoning in general. Basically, Staudenmayer and Bourne demonstrate that knowledge of the categories affects the deductions independently of how the reasoner interprets the relational terms (i.e., either biconditional or conditional). This strongly argues against the generality of previous work with abstract situations (i.e., the selection task of Wason & Johnson-Laird, 1972) and permits a bridge between abstract and concrete problems.

The work of Wyer and Podeschi dramatically extends the seminal work of Abelson and Kanouse (1966) on evidence-reasoning and evaluates a series of models (Venn diagrams of Erickson, linear models of Anderson, etc.). These authors demonstrate that the traditional crop of models do not adequately account for the dynamics of such reasoning tasks and argue (in contrast to Revlin) that the reasoner evokes new inference rules as a function of the stimulus elements in the problem.

Another unresolved issue is whether the same information can be organized into qualitatively different representations. In the section on mathematical reasoning, Mayer suggests that qualitatively different structures can be acquired from the same material; however, Robinson and Hayes deal mainly with the question of how much information is encoded rather than how the pieces of information are organized by the subject. If the same information can be structured in different ways in memory, Mayer's theory would lead to different predictions than one that considers only how much is encoded.

THE FUTURE OF HUMAN REASONING

Having attempted to refrain (as much as possible) from outrageous speculations and comments up to this point, we would like to exercise the editors' privilege to close this chapter by summarizing, speculating, and giving our view of the future. After studying the research presented in this volume, we remain convinced that the study of human reasoning is an exciting and growing area and that it has potential importance for a great many theoretical and practical issues. What is most exciting about editing this volume is that we are given a sense that progress has been made. There appears to be a convergence across research paradigms to a similar view of human rationality. For example, the better our understanding of the reasoner's representation of the problem and its materials, the more rational his choices appear. We are able to say that recent research has isolated hitherto unexplored factors in the encoding process that require precise modeling: (a) subjects assume that asymmetrical relations are symmetrical; (b) the representational formalism appears to vary with the size of the categories reasoned about—in a way that suggests that Euler rather than Venn diagrams might be an appropriate analog in formal reasoning tasks; (c) Long-Term Memory particiaptes fully in the establishment of a representational formalism even when abstract or nonsensical materials are involved. We can say that a number of interesting models and theories of how information is represented have been developed and are now in the process of "fighting it out" in the laboratory. We can say that research on reasoning is vital enough to have expanded to new areas, including both text and mathematical reasoning.

We see future research continuing with a two-fold emphasis. First, there appears to be a resurgence of interest in the traditional, formal paradigms both because they are of historical interest and because they provide a well-defined domain in which to probe human rational competence. Second, there is a concomitant expansion of research beyond the confines of the formal problems to evaluate reasoning models in the context of discourse, reading, and mathematics. Research in both of these ways will show the promise of developing detailed processing models of reasoning—models which not only can account for reasoning errors but also tell us why reasoners are sometimes correct in their judgments.

We are encouraged by the development of explicit theories of the encoding process, the organization of the mental representation, and the question-answering process. We foresee a continued sharpening of existing theories and the development of new ones. In particular, it is encouraging to note the development of specifically testable theories such as Revlin's Conversion Model or Potts' Similarity Model or Erickson's Set Model or Mayer's Integrated and Rote Models. Clearly, all of these models will ultimately be shown to be incorrect, or at least, incomplete; however, by positing explicit models and mechanisms, these researchers have helped to define the issues that must be tested in the future.

One related issue concerns the types of theories which need to be constructed. Clearly, the studies presented herein point to the immediate need for a thorough-going model of inference which adequately specifies the selection and encoding processes and provides some detail concerning the cognitive structure of the representation that is acquired by the reasoner. The nature of the question-answering process has only been touched upon in this volume. The process model on the horizon must give adequate attention to structure as well as process: All of the present papers suggest that the ability to predict and explain reasoners' judgments rely on a detailed specification of their representation of the problem's materials.

Can one general model be developed to account for behavior in all reasoning tasks? We don't know; but even if general models are not forthcoming, it seems to us a reasonable strategy to continue to try to model as precisely as we can each particular situation individually—borrowing the mechanisms from other models wherever possible. Out of this work will emerge a set of basic components that are shared by all tasks.

It is our hope that researchers will make better use of the developments in the larger field of cognitive psychology. Potts' attempt to integrate reasoning research with that of semantic memory is an encouraging sign in this direction. Since the consensus of this volume is that memory representation is a critical factor in reasoning, a closer look at existing memory models is in order.

We also see the field as having more to say about real-world situations and practical applications of reasoning research. This, we hope, reflects an increment in the maturity of the field rather than a return to nonexperimental approaches to human reasoning. For example, research on inference from text might lead to implications for the organization of texts, especially in the sciences and mathematics. Further, a theory of mathematical reasoning could generate diagnostic procedures and guide instruction; e.g., the performance of problem solvers could be analyzed to determine what component process or structure is missing, and then that component could be taught.

In short, we look to the future with optimism. Although the present state of our understanding of human reasoning does not allow us to form closure on many issues, progress has been made. At this point, we are not yet ready to disagree with Carroll that "Logic is unintelligible," but it is not quite as unintelligible as it was when Carroll wrote.

REFERENCES

Abelson, R. P., & Carroll, J. D. Computer simulation of individual belief systems. *American Behavioral Scientist*, 1965, 8, 24–30.

Abelson, R. P., & Kanouse, D. E. Subjective acceptance of verbal generalizations. In S. Feldman (Ed.), *Cognitive consistency*. New York: Academic Press, 1966.

Ausubel, D. P. *Educational psychology: A cognitive view*. New York: Holt, Rinehart & Winston, 1968.

Banks, W. P. Encoding and processing of symbolic information in comparative judgments. In G. Bower (Ed.), *The psychology of learning and motivation*, 1977, in press.

Barclay, J. The role of comprehension in remembering sentences. *Cognitive Psychology*, 1973, 4, 229–254.

Bartlett, F. C. *Remembering: A study in experimental social psychology*. Cambridge: University Press, 1932.

Begg, I., & Denny, J. Empirical reconciliation of atmosphere and conversion interpretations of syllogistic reasoning. *Journal of Experimental Psychology*, 1969, 81, 351–354.

Bobrow, D. G. Natural language input for a computer problem solving system. In M. Minsky (Ed.), *Semantic information processing*. Cambridge, Mass.: MIT Press, 1968.

Boole, G. *An investigation of the laws of thought*. London: Macmillan, 1854.

Burt, C. The development of reasoning in school children. *Journal of Experimental Pedagogy*, 1919, 5, 68–77; 121–127.

Ceraso, J., & Provitera, A. Sources of error in syllogistic reasoning. *Cognitive Psychology*, 1971, 2, 400–414.

Chapman, L. J., & Chapman, J. P. Atmosphere effect re-examined. *Journal of Experimental Psychology*, 1959, 58, 220–226.

Clark, H. H. Linguistic processes in deductive reasoning. *Psychological Review*, 1969, 76, 387–404.

Clark, H. H. More about "adjectives, comparatives and syllogisms": A reply to Huttenlocher and Higgins. *Psychological Review*, 1971, **78**, 505–514.

Cohen, M. R., & Nagel, E. *An introduction to logic.* New York: Harcourt, 1934.

Dawes, R. Cognitive distortion. *Psychological Reports*, 1964, **14**, 443–459.

Dawes, R. Memory and distortion of meaningful written material. *British Journal of Psychology*, 1966, **57**, 77–86.

Desoto, C. B. The predilection for single orderings. *Journal of Abnormal and Social Psychology*, 1961, **62**, 16–23.

Desoto, C., London, M., & Handel, S. Social reasoning and spatial paralogic. *Journal of Personality and Social Psychology*, 1965, **2**, 513–521.

Dickstein, L. S. Effects of instructions and premise order on errors in syllogistic reasoning. *Journal of Experimental Psychology: Human Learning and Memory*, 1975, **1**, 376–384.

Dickstein, L. S. Differential difficulty of categorical syllogisms. *Bulletin of the Psychonomic Society*, 1976, **8**, 330–332.

Donaldson, M. *A study of children's thinking.* London: Tavistock, 1963.

Ennis, R. H. Children's ability to handle Piaget's propositional logic: A conceptual critique. *Review of Educational Research*, 1975, **45**, 1–41.

Erickson, J. R. A set analysis theory of behavior in formal syllogistic reasoning tasks. In R. L. Solso (Ed.), *Theories of cognitive psychology: The Loyola symposium.* Hillsdale, N.J.: Erlbaum, 1974.

Evans, J. On the problems of interpreting reasoning data: Logical and psychological approaches. *Cognition*, 1973, **1**, 373–384.

Feather, N. T. Acceptance and rejection of arguments in relation to attitude strength, critical ability, and intolerance of inconsistency. *Journal of Abnormal and Social Psychology*, 1965, **69**, 127–136.

Frase, L. T. Belief, incongruity, and syllogistic reasoning. *Psychological Reports*, 1966, **18**, 982. (a)

Frase, L. T. Validity judgments of syllogisms in relation to two sets of terms. *Journal of Educational Psychology*, 1966, **57**, 239–245. (b)

Frase, L. T. Associative factors in syllogistic reasoning. *Journal of Experimental Psychology*, 1968, **76**, 407–412.

Frase, L. T. Structural analysis of the knowledge that results from thinking about text. *Journal of Educational Psychology Monograph*, 1969, **60**(6, Part 2).

Frase, L. T. The influence of sentence order and amount of higher level text processing upon reproductive and productive memory. *American Educational Research Journal*, 1970, **7**, 307–319.

Gilson, C., & Abelson, R. P. The subjective use of inductive evidence. *Journal of Personality and Social Psychology*, 1965, **2**, 301–310.

Gottesman, L., & Chapman, L. J. Syllogistic reasoning errors in schizophrenia. *Journal of Consulting Psychology*, 1960, **24**, 250–255.

Groen, G. J., & Parkman, J. M. A chronometric analysis of simple addition. *Psychological Review*, 1972, **79**, 329–343.

Guilford, J. P. Three faces of intellect. *American Psychologist*, 1959, **14**, 469–479.

Handel, S., Desoto, C., & London, M. Reasoning and spatial representations. *Journal of Verbal Learning and Verbal Behavior*, 1968, **7**, 351–357.

Hayes, J. R. Problem topology and the solution process. *Journal of Verbal Learning and Verbal Behavior*, 1965, **4**, 371–379.

Hayes, J. R. Memory, goals, and problem solving. In B. Kleinmuntz (Ed.), *Problem solving: Research, method, and theory.* New York: Wiley, 1966.

Hayes, J. R., & Simon, H. A. Understanding written problem instructions. In L. W. Gregg (Ed.), *Knowledge and cognition.* Hillsdale, N.J.: Erlbaum, 1974.

Henle, M. On the relation between logic and thinking. *Psychological Review*, 1962, **69**, 366–378.

Henle, M., & Michael, M. The influence of attitudes on syllogistic reasoning. *Journal of Social Psychology*, 1956, **44**, 115–127.

Hinsley, D. A., Hayes, J. R., & Simon, H. A. From words to equations. In P. Carpenter & M. Just (Eds.), *Cognitive processes in comprehension.* Hillsdale, N.J.: Erlbaum, 1977.

Hunter, I. The solving of three-term series problems. *British Journal of Psychology*, 1956, **48**, 286–298.

Huttenlocher, J. Constructing spatial images: A strategy in reasoning. *Psychological Review*, 1968, **75**, 550–560.

Huttenlocher, J., & Higgins, E. T. On reasoning, congruence, and other matters. *Psychological Review*, 1972, **79**, 420–427.

Janis, I., & Frick, F. The relationship between attitudes toward conclusions and errors in judging logical validity of syllogisms. *Journal of Experimental Psychology*, 1943, **33**, 73–77.

Janis, I., & Terwilliger, R. An experimental study of psychological resistances to fear arousing communication. *Journal of Abnormal and Social Psychology*, 1962, **65**, 403–410.

Johnson-Laird, P. N. On understanding logically complex sentences. *Quarterly Journal of Experimental Psychology*, 1969, **21**, 1–13. (a)

Johnson-Laird, P. N. Reasoning with ambiguous sentences. *British Journal of Psychology*, 1969, **60**, 17–23. (b)

Johnson-Laird, P. N. The interpretation of quantified sentences. In G. B. Flores d'Arcais & W. J. M. Levelt (Eds.), *Advances in psycholinguistics.* Amsterdam: North-Holland, 1970.

Johnson-Laird, P. N. The three-term series problem. *Cognition*, 1972, **1**, 57–82.

Johnson-Laird, P. N. Models of deduction. In R. Falmagne (Ed.), *Reasoning: Representation and processes in children and adults.* Hillsdale, N.J.: Erlbaum, 1975.

Kaufman, H., & Goldstein, S. The effects of emotional value of conclusions upon distortions in syllogistic reasoning. *Psychonomic Science*, 1967, **7**, 367–368.

Lawler, J. Generic to a fault. *Papers from the Eighth Regional Meeting of the Chicago Linguistic Society.* Chicago: University of Chicago Press, 1972.

Lefford, A. The influence of emotional subject matter on logical reasoning. *Journal of General Psychology*, 1946, **34**, 127–151.

Loftus, E. F., & Suppes, P. Structural variables that determine problem-solving difficulty in computer assisted instruction. *Journal of Educational Psychology*, 1972, **63**, 531–542.

Maier, N. R. F., & Burke, R. J. Response availability as a factor in the problem-solving performance of males and females. *Journal of Personality and Social Psychology*, 1967, **5**, 304–310.

Malin, J. E. T. *An analysis of strategies for solving certain substitution problems.* Ann Arbor, Mich.: Human Performance Center Tech. Rep. No. 40, 1973.

Mayer, R. E. Comprehension as affected by structure of problem representation. *Memory & Cognition*, 1976, **4**, 249–255.

Mayer, R. E., & Greeno, J. G. Effects of meaningfulness and organization on problem solving and computability judgments. *Memory & Cognition*, 1975, **4**, 356–362.

McGuire, W. J. Cognitive consistency and attitude change. *Journal of Abnormal and Social Psychology*, 1960, **60**, 345–353. (a)

McGuire, W. J. Direct and indirect persuasive effects of dissonance producing messages. *Journal of Abnormal and Social Psychology*, 1960, **60**, 354–358. (b)

McGuire, W. J. A syllogistic analysis of cognitive relationships. In M. J. Rosenberg & C. I. Hovland (Eds.), *Attitude organization and change.* New Haven: Yale University Press, 1960. (c)

Morgan, J. J., & Morton, J. T. The distortion of syllogistic reasoning produced by personal convictions. *Journal of Social Psychology*, 1944, **20**, 39–59.

Moyer, R. F. Comparing objects in memory: Evidence suggesting an internal psychophysics. *Perception and Psychophysics*, 1973, **13**, 180–184.

Moyer, R. F., & Bayer, R. H. Mental comparison and the symbolic distance effect. *Cognitive Psychology*, 1976, **8**, 228–246.

Osherson, D. Logic and models of logical thinking. In R. Falmagne (Ed.), *Reasoning: Representation and processes in children and adults.* Hillsdale, N.J.: Erlbaum, 1975.

Paige, J. M., & Simon, H. A. Cognitive processes in solving algebra word problems. In B. Kleinmuntz (Ed.), *Problem solving: Research, method, and theory.* New York: Wiley, 1966.

Pezzoli, J. A., & Frase, L. T. Mediated facilitation of syllogistic reasoning. *Journal of Experimental Psychology*, 1968, **78**, 228–232.

Piaget, J. Une forme verbale de la comparison chez l'enfant. *Archives de Psychologie*, 1921, **18**, 141–172.

Polich, J. M., & Schwartz, S. H. The effect of problem size on representation in deductive problem solving. *Memory & Cognition*, 1974, **2**, 683–686.

Posner, M. I. *Cognition: An introduction.* Glenview, Ill.: Scott, Foresman, 1973.

Potts, G. R. Information processing strategies used in encoding of linear orderings. *Journal of Verbal Learning and Verbal Behavior*, 1972, **11**, 727–740.

Potts, G. R. Storing and retrieving information about ordered relationships. *Journal of Experimental Psychology*, 1974, **103**, 431–439.

Resnick, L. B. Task analysis in instructional design: Some cases from mathematics. In D. Klahr (Ed.), *Cognition and instruction*. Hillsdale, N.J.: Erlbaum, 1976.

Revlis, R. Syllogistic reasoning: Logical decisions from a complex data base. In R. Falmagne (Ed.), *Reasoning: Representation and processes in children and adults*. Hillsdale, N.J.: Erlbaum, 1975. (a)

Revlis, R. Two models of syllogistic reasoning: Feature selection and conversion. *Journal of Verbal Learning and Verbal Behavior*, 1975, **14**, 180–195. (b)

Richter, M. The theoretical interpretation of errors in syllogistic reasoning. *Journal of Psychology*, 1957, **43**, 341–344.

Roberge, J. J., & Paulus, D. H. Developmental patterns for children's class and conditional reasoning abilities. *Developmental Psychology*, 1971, **4**, 191–200.

Schwartz, S. H. Modes of representation and problem solving: Well evolved is half solved. *Journal of Experimental Psychology*, 1971, **91**, 347–350.

Schwartz, S. H., & Fattellah, D. Representation in deductive problem solving. *Journal of Experimental Psychology*, 1972, **95**, 343–348.

Sells, S. B. The atmosphere effect: An experimental study of reasoning. *Archives of Psychology*, 1936, **29**, 3–72.

Simpson, M. E., & Johnson, D. M. Atmosphere and conversion errors in syllogistic reasoning. *Journal of Experimental Psychology*, 1966, **72**, 197–200.

Suppes, P., Loftus, E. F., & Jerman, M. *Problem-solving on a computer-based teletype*. Stanford: Institute for Mathematical Studies in Social Sciences, Tech. Rep. No. 141, 1969.

Thistlethwaite, D. Attitude and structure as factors in the distortion of reasoning. *Journal of Abnormal and Social Psychology*, 1950, **45**, 442–458.

Thouless, R. Effect of prejudice on reasoning. *British Journal of Psychology*, 1959, **50**, 289–293.

Thurstone, L. L. Primary mental abilities. *Psychometric Monograph*, No. 1. Chicago: University of Chicago Press, 1938.

Von Domarus, E. The specific laws of logic in schizophrenia. In J. S. Kasanin (Ed.), *Language and thought in schizophrenia*. Berkeley: University of California Press, 1944.

Wason, P. C., & Johnson-Laird, P. N. *Psychology of reasoning: Structure and content*. London: Batsford, 1972.

Whimbey, A., & Ryan, S. Role of short-term memory and training in solving reasoning problems mentally. *Journal of Educational Psychology*, 1969, **60**, 361–364.

Wilkins, M. C. The effect of changed material on ability to do formal syllogistic reasoning. *Archives of Psychology*, 1928, **16**, 83 pp.

Wilson, W. R. The effect of competition on the speed and accuracy of syllogistic reasoning. *Journal of Social Psychology*, 1965, **65**, 27–32.

Winthrop, H. Semantic factors in the measurement of personality integration. *Journal of Social Psychology*, 1946, **24**, 149–175.

Woods, S. S., Resnick, L. B., & Groen, G. J. An experimental test of five process models for substraction. *Journal of Educational Psychology*, 1975, **67**, 17–21.

Woodworth, R. S., & Sells, S. B. An atmosphere effect in formal syllogistic reasoning. *Journal of Experimental Psychology*, 1935, **18**, 451–460.

APPENDIX TO CHAPTER 1

A singular advantage of using formal reasoning tasks to assess rational processes is that such tasks are well defined. While the "rules" and "procedures" may not always be clear to the student (e.g., Richter, 1957), the nature of the problems and their resolution are uniform and unambiguously specified in the body of logic. As such, formal reasoning tasks are excellent devices for probing rational processes because they provide a standardized format for eliciting students' decisions.

The long history of such tasks in psychological research has promoted the use of specialized terms for describing the problems and their outcomes. To facilitate reading of the contributions included in this collection, it would seem useful to clarify both the tasks and some of the terminology.

CATEGORICAL SYLLOGISMS

The formal, or categorical, syllogism consists of two propositions (called Premises) followed by one or more propositions (called Conclusions) which may or may not logically follow from the Premises:

(1) All M are P. (Major Premise)
Some S are M. (Minor Premise)
Therefore:
(a) All S are P;
(b) No S are P;
(c) Some S are P;
(d) Some S are not P;
(e) None of the above is proven.

Each proposition asserts a relation between two sets of terms. The major premise expresses the relation between the predicate of the conclusion (P) and another term (M). The minor premise expresses a relation between the subject of the conclusion (S) and the other term (M). The reasoner's task is to judge whether one of the conclusions can be validly inferred from the premises—i.e., whether one of the expressed relations between S and P can be unambiguously determined from the relations expressed in the premises (cf. Cohen & Nagel, 1934, for the formal rules for making this judgment). In the foregoing example, conclusion (c) is a deduction from the two premises. In part, this is a result of the special meaning of the term *some*. In traditional logic, the word *some* should be given a distributed interpretation: It means *at least one and possibly all*. In addition, although the reasoner knows that at least some of the S are P, it is also possible that all of the S are P. Since the reasoner cannot be certain that there are S which are not P, conclusion (d) is not a valid deduction—it does not necessarily follow from the information given in the premises.

The importance of the definition of *some* is also seen in syllogism (2):

All M are P.
All S are M.
Therefore:
(a) All S are P;
(b) No S are P;
(c) Some S are P;
(d) Some S are not P;
(e) None of the above is proven.

In this syllogism, the reasoner knows that since all of the S are M and all of the M in turn are P, therefore, all of the S are P (answer [a]). Because of the special meaning of *some* in these problems, it also follows that "Some S are P" (answer [c]). This is true because at least one member of the set S is a member of the set P (by virtue of the fact that "All S are P"). It goes without saying that clarification of the meaning of *some* is an important part of the instructions in syllogistic reasoning experiments.

Within each premise, the terms may appear in either of two orderings, with M as either the first or second term mentioned: orders (M–P or P–M; M–S or S–M). Consequently, there are four possible combinations of orderings for each syllogism (2 premises × 2 orders of terms). These are called Figures, and each one of the combinations has a special designation:

Figure I	Figure II	Figure III	Figure IV
M–P	P–M	M–P	P–M
S–M	S–M	M–S	M–S
S–P	S–P	S–P	S–P

The premises in the standard categorical syllogism are selected from only four types of propositions, determined by the orthogonal pairing of two features: Quantification [± Universal] and Polarity [± Affirmative]. An example of these premises is given in Table 1. Each one of the premises has a letter designation. Affirmative premises, universal and particular, are designated by A and I, respectively (the letters represent the first two vowels in *affirmo*); the designations for the negative premises, universal and particular, are E and O, respectively. These are the two vowels in *nego* (see Cohen & Nagel, 1934).

Notice that the premises assert a class inclusion relation between the subject and predicate categories. This relation is realized by the coupla *is a*. This restriction of the syllogism to cover only explicit class inclusion relations may be a recent innovation. There is some evidence that Aristotle's conception of the syllogism included modal relations (i.e., ones that expressed varying degrees of necessity) and psychological research during this past century is replete with variations on the traditional inclusion relation (e.g., Wilkins, 1928).

Since any of the four types of premises may be the major premise and any of the four may comprise the minor premise, there are 16 combinations of premise–types called *moods*. Each of these 16 moods can appear in any one of the four figures. Consequently, there are 64 possible syllogisms—only 19 of which are valid; i.e., they have an unambiguous conclusion.

Table 1. Categorical Premises

Designation	Features	Description	Example
A	[+Universal] , [+Affirmative]	Universal Affirmative	"All A are B"
E	[+Universal] , [–Affirmative]	Universal Negative	"No A are B"
I	[–Universal] , [+Affirmative]	Particular Affirmative	"Some A are B"
O	[–Universal] , [–Affirmative]	Particular Negative	"Some A are not B"

With this information in mind, we can characterize syllogism (1) as having an *A*-type major premise and an *I*-type minor premise. It has, therefore, an *AI* mood and is written in the first figure. It is designated as *AI*-1. The conclusion that validly follows from the premises is an *I* proposition.

CONDITIONAL SYLLOGISMS

The conditional or hypothetical syllogism consists of a statement of a relation (e.g., a rule) and one or more pieces of evidence concerning aspects of the rule. The reasoner's task is to decide whether a hypothetical condition could be true or false given the rule and the evidence presented. For example, a reasoner might be told that:

"If there is a solar eclipse, the streets are dark."
  [If p, then q]
"There is a solar eclipse." [p is true]
QUESTION: "Are the streets dark?" [Is q true?]

That is, the reasoner is told that if p is true, then condition q is true. The student would then be asked to assess the implications of knowing, e.g., that q is true. Or, perhaps that $\bar{q}$ ("not-q") is true, etc. The stated relation between p and q is said to be one of implication because the truth (or existence) of one of the states (p or q) can be determined in some cases as a result of knowing the truth (or existence) of the other event. The proposition p is said to be the *antecedent* of the rule, while the q condition is said to be the *consequent* of the rule.

In the traditional paradigms, reasoners are given the rule and the evidence (which either affirms or denies the antecedent or affirms or denies the consequent), and the reasoner is asked to evaluate the truth value of a potential conclusion. Sometimes the material is presented in an abstract form (with letters standing for events), while on other ocassions it is expressed as concrete categories. Concreteness of the propositions is an important variable in such studies and provides a means for separating representation from operations on such tasks. Sometimes the reasoner is restricted to saying *true* or *false* concerning the conclusion, while other paradigms permit the response *sometimes true/false*.

The logically defined acceptable conclusions for each of the evidence conditions are expressed in Table 2. Perhaps the best way to understand the relations expressed is to substitute the phrase "there is a vowel on the front" for p and the phrase "there is an even number on the back" for q. In this case. "If p, then q" is read: "If there is a vowel on the front, then there is an even number on the back." In the Staudenmayer and Bourne chapter in this volume, the convention is adopted to provide the reasoner with "given"

Table 2. Truth Table for the Rule, "If p, then q"

Evidence	Question	Formal decision	Informal decision
p	q	True	True
p	not-q	False	False
not-p	q	False	Sometimes true/false
not-p	not-q	False	Sometimes true/false
q	p	False	Sometimes true/false
q	not-p	False	Sometimes ture/false
not-q	p	False	False
not-q	not-p	True	True

information followed by a "question." The given information consists of a rule (e.g., "If there is a vowel on the front, then there is an even number on the back") and a piece of evidence (e.g., "there is a vowel on the front"). The question consists of a conclusion to be evaluated by the reasoner (e.g., "there is an even number on the back").

A special form of this kind of propositional reasoning has gained popularity in recent years. It is the selection task of Wason and Johnson-Laird (1972). In this task, students are asked to evaluate a rule (i.e., to test whether the rule is true or false given some evidence available to the reasoner). The student is told that he may select from among the available evidence those pieces he feels most germane to the evaluation of the rule. The student's selections are then evaluated in terms of the kind of inference rules that the reasoner may possess which could account for the selection made. For example, in the standard, four-card selection task, the student is shown four cards:

and is told a rule that must be tested: "If there is a vowel on one side of the card, there is an even number on the other." The reasoner is asked to select the minimal, sufficient pieces of evidence to test the rule. In this case, the rule could be expressed in the conditional form: If p (vowel), then q (even number), and the alternatives to be selected from are p(A), -p(B), q(2), -q(3). Clearly, to test the rule, one would want to examine to two conditions which must be true if the rule is true: p (vowel) and -q (odd number 3). In fact, inspection of the truth conditions in Table 2 shows that there are the two conditions for a rule of the form "If p, then q," which are true if the rule is true. A reasoner, making his decisions according to this formal system would then inspect p and not -q. If he turns the p card over and finds that there is an odd number on the other side, then he knows that p does not lead to q. If he turns over the odd number and finds that there is a vowel on the other side, then he knows that $-q$ does not imply $-p$ as would be predicted if the rule were true. This task has been studied in detail by Wason, Johnson-Laird and other collaborators, and a process model has been developed (Johnson-Laird, 1972). It is an imaginative paradigm in that it permits an examination of reasoning with a variety of materials and feedback conditions.

MODELS OF FORMAL REASONING

RESEARCH ON SYLLOGISTIC REASONING

James R. Erickson
University of Texas at Arlington

The central problem of logic is the classification of arguments so that all those that are good are thrown into one pile, and all those that are bad are thrown into another. Over several hundred years, logicians have worked on this problem—and are still at it. The logician, quite properly, is not particularly interested in the reasoning process, just in its outcome. As psychologists, however, we can be interested in both aspects of reasoning, the process and the outcome, but our main business is with the process. What I would like to do is discuss briefly some research which has been aimed at trying to understand processes which underlie reasoning behavior when we ask our subjects to deal with simple arguments.

The arguments we use are formal Aristotelian syllogisms. A syllogism is an argument in three sentences: two premises, and a conclusion. The major premise links the predicate (P) of the conclusion with a middle term (M), and the minor premise links the subject (S) of the conclusion with the middle

Preparation of this chapter was supported by Grant No. OR-76-32 from the Organized Research funds of the University of Texas at Arlington.

Table 1. Examples of Standard Terms Used to Describe Syllogisms

Examples of a syllogism

Major Premise	All churchgoers are honest	All M are P
Minor Premise	All politicians are churchgoers	All S are M
Conclusion	All politicians are honest	All S are P

Possible sentence types that can be used in a syllogism

A	All S are P	All psychologist are wise
E	No S are P	No poor research is published
I	Some S are P	Some elected officials are truthful
O	Some S are not P	Some professors are not rich

Possible syllogistic figures

Figure I (Forward chain)	Figure II (Stimulus equivalence)	Figure III (Response equivalence)	Figure IV (Backward chain)
M – P	P – M	M – P	P – M
S – M	S – M	M – S	M – S
S – P	S – P	S – P	S – P

term. Table 1 illustrates the main features. A valid syllogistic argument is one in which the conclusion necessarily follows from the premises. Another way of saying this is: If the premises are true, then the conclusion must be true in a valid argument. However, one should not confuse truth with validity. Validity has to do with the form of the argument, not the truth value of the statements in the argument. Only four kinds of sentences are allowed in a syllogism; these are illustrated in Table 1.

Finally, there are four syllogistic figures, formed by ordering the terms in the two premises as shown. As Frase pointed out several years ago (1968), these correspond to four well-known mediation paradigms, and I find them easier to remember by those labels than by Figures I to IV. A compact notation for a syllogism lists the mood and the figure. For example, an *EIO*–IV syllogism would have a universal negative major premise, a particular affirmative minor premise, and a particular negative conclusion, with the premises arranged as in Figure IV. Symbolically: "No P are M; Some M are S; therefore, Some S are not P." I might note that in our research, we use the letters A, B, and C rather than S, M, and P, and I will use them from now on.

In logic classes a fair amount of time is often spent teaching students how to tell valid syllogisms from invalid ones. The fact that the logic of these simple arguments has to be taught to college students—often laboriously—ought to give us a clue that the psychology of reasoning is certainly different from the logic of reasoning. One of our subjects can sit and stare for a minute or two at a syllogism stripped down to its bare essentials—with no verbal context to distract him—and come up with the wrong answer. In fact, for *most* syllogisms the modal response is incorrect. Why is this?

Over the last 30 or 40 years several answers to this question have been given. Some have essentially stated that people do not reason, instead respond to the surface form of the argument (e.g., Woodworth & Sells, 1935), or on the basis of personal prejudices, beliefs, etc. about the contents of the argument (e.g., Janis & Frick, 1943; Morgan & Morton, 1944; Thistlethwaite, 1950; see also Revlin & Leirer, chapter 3 of this volume). Others have suggested that people are indeed fairly good reasoners, but that they are prone to misunderstand or change the nature of the content of the argument in the course of dealing with it (e.g., Chapman & Chapman, 1959). Henle (1962) has presented a very lucid statement of this point of view, and Revlin and Leirer present some of their research testing this point of view in the next chapter. My viewpoint has been that our subjects, typical college students with no particular background in formal logic, are good reasoners as far as they go, but that they tend not to be very thorough.

Several investigators (e.g., Ceraso & Provitera, 1971; Henle, 1962; Neimark & Chapman, 1975) have taken note of the inherent ambiguity of typical syllogistic statements. I have found it useful to focus on this ambiguity and to try to model ways in which a subject might respond to it (Erickson, 1974). I like to think of syllogistic reasoning as a three-stage process. During the first stage the premises are interpreted, a process I think of as forming a set interpretation. The problem is the fact that abstract premises often have several set interpretations. For example, the statement "All A are B" could mean that A and B are identical or that A is a subset of B. Similarly, the statement "Some A are B" has four possible set interpretations because of the way the word *some* is used in logic. I assume that only one interpretation is used by each (naive) subject. Across a group of subjects, various set interpretations are chosen with some relative frequency, and these relative frequencies are parameters of the model. Stage II is a combination stage—during this stage the two interpreted premises (linking A with B and B with C) are combined in order to determine the set relationship between A and C. Again, as a starting point I have assumed that most subjects will choose only one of the possible ways of combining two set relations; the relative frequencies across a group of subjects of these combinations are also parameters of the model.

Stage III is a response stage. During this stage the subject reports on the set relationship between A and C, according to the demands of the experimenter.

If he is asked for a conclusion to a pair of premises, he must use an $A, E, I,$ or O sentence with A as the subject and C as the predicate. If the task is to judge the validity of a complete argument, we have explored—with some success—the notion that the subject will judge the argument to be valid if the verbal conclusion presented can be used to describe the derived set relation conclusion.

This kind of analysis has its share of problems, and the model used is far from perfect, but let me give you an idea of how far we can go with it. Briefly, what the model tries to do is to account for the probability with which each possible response is chosen to any possible syllogistic argument. The level of analysis is the individual syllogism. If it can do this, it can (automatically) account for other findings, e.g., the "atmosphere" effect, or "conversion" data, or the fact that particular groupings of syllogisms may be easier or harder than other groupings (e.g., Dickstein, 1975; Revlis, 1975a, 1975b).

I will concentrate on four syllogisms here—the four with AA premises. I choose them not because the model does particularly well or poorly with them, but because they are natural appearing arguments for most people, are likely to be fairly common, and because they illustrate many of the points I would like to make. In Figure I, the chaining paradigm, the premises are "All B are C and All A are B." This is *the* classic syllogism which everybody knows in the form: All men are mortal and Aristotle is a man; therefore, Aristotle is mortal. To these premises an A response is valid, but so is an I response because of the definition of the word *some* in logis. In Figure II, the stimulus equivalence paradigm, the premises are "All A are B and All C are B." This is an invalid argument, and the correct response is that no conclusion necessarily follows. Figure III, the response equivalence paradigm, is "All B are C and All B are A." From this it follows that "Some A are C." Figure IV, the backward chaining paradigm, is "All C are B and All B are A." From this it also follows that "Some A are C." Thus, one of the AA premise pairs has two valid conclusions, A and I; two have only a valid I conclusion; and one has no valid conclusion. Let us see how these arguments are analyzed and a conclusion chosen according to the model.

An A statement has two possible set interpretations, *set identity* and *set inclusion*. We have collected data from subjects asked to draw Venn diagram interpretations of all possible premises and premise pairs (Erickson, Wells, & Traub, 1974). In that study about 40% of our subjects systematically interpreted A-type statements in terms of set identity, and about 60% interpreted them in terms of set inclusion. Almost no subjects mixed the two kinds of interpretation. For example, if a subject interprets an A premise as an identity, he will almost always interpret another A premise the same way. This means that we need to examine only identity-identity interpretations and

Table 2. Illustrations of Possible Conclusions to Venn Diagram Premises

Premise pair		Possible conclusions				
		(AB)	(A) C	(C) A	(A)(C)	(A) (C)
(AB) (BC)	(All figures)	X				
(A) B (B) C	Figure I		X			
(A) B (C) B	Figure II	X	X	X	X	X
(B) A (B) C	Figure III	X	X	X	X	
(B) A (C) B	Figure IV		X			

inclusion-inclusion interpretations of AA syllogisms. Table 2 shows identity-identity premises and notes that an identity relation between A and C must result. When we asked subjects to draw a Venn conclusion to these two Venn premises, about 95% of them drew a set-identity conclusion, while about 5% of them illogically drew an overlap conclusion (Erickson et al., 1974).

Since all four of the AA syllogisms share identity-identity interpretations, presumably with the same probability, we expect a substantial proportion of A responses (All A are C) for all of them, since this is the most natural way to describe the fact that sets A and C are identical (subjects are forced to write an A, E, I, or O conclusion, with A as the subject and C as the predicate, or to respond that no response follows logically).

The four AA syllogisms differ with respect to subset-superset interpretations. Table 2 shows that for syllogism Figure I, the Venn conclusion that follows if A is a subset of B and B is a subset of C is that A is a subset of C. Again, subjects asked to draw a Venn conclusion to this pair of Venn premises draw the proper conclusion with probability about .85; but 5% of them draw an identity conclusion, and 10% of them draw an overlap conclusion. Thus, for Figure I both premise set-interpretations logically yield an A verbal conclusion, and we expect that a very high proportion of subjects will conclude that "All A are C," but that a few will respond "Some A are C."

Next, look at syllogism Figure II in Table 2 and note that if A and C are both subsets of B, *any* set relation between A and C is possible. We assume that some subjects will note this and decide that no conclusion follows necessarily. However, when we ask subjects to draw a Venn conclusion to this premise pair, most of them draw either a set-identity or a set-overlap conclusion (about 40% each), with the other three possible conclusions drawn occasionally, E most often. For this syllogism, then, we expect that almost all

Table 3. Conclusion Production Data from Several Studies Compared to Predictions from the Model

Premises	Conclusions	Erickson (1974)	Chapman and Chapman (1959)	Erickson (1975)	Traub (1977)	Ceraso and Provitera (1971)	Unweighted Mean	Predicted
Figure I	A[a]	.92		.93	.90	.87	.90	.96
All B are C	E	.02		.03	.01	.00	.02	0
All A are B	I[a]	.04		.02	.06	.03	.04	.04
	O	.02		0	.01	–	.01	0
	None	–[b]		.02	.01	.10	.04	0
Figure II	A	.62	.81	.80	.59	.42	.66	.68
All C are B	E	.03	.04	.03	.02	.01	.02	.04
All A are B	I	.33	.04	.05	.15	.22	.12	.08
	O	.02	.01	0	.02	–	.01	0
	None[a]	–	.09	.13	.22	.34	.20	.20
Figure III	A			.72	.59	.60	.63	.70
All B are C	E			.02	0	0	.01	0
All B are A	I[a]			.20	.30	.02	.21 (.30)	.30
	O			0	.01	–	.01	0
	None			.06	.09	.38	.18 (.06)	0
Figure IV	A	.66		.87	.56	–	.70	.62
All C are B	E	.02		.03	.02	–	.02	0
All B are A	I[a]	.30		.05	.34	–	.23	.38
	O	.03		.02	.02	–	.02	0
	None	–		.03	.05	–	.03	0

[a]Valid conclusion.
[b]This response alternative was not available to the subject.

subjects who use the identity interpretation and many of the subjects who use subset interpretations will choose the A response "All A are C." We expect some subjects to respond correctly, that no conclusion necessarily follows, and we also expect some E and I responses.

Next, look at syllogism Figure III in Table 2. If B is a subset of both A and C, any set relation between A and C is possible except the disjunctive one. When subjects were given this Venn premise, 55% of them drew an overlap relation, 30% an identity relation, and the other three conclusions were each chosen by about 5%. For Figure III, then, we expect that subjects using the identity relations will tend to respond that "All A are C," but that most subjects choosing subset interpretations will respond "Some A are C" (the valid conclusion) or "All A are C."

Finally, look at Figure IV in Table 2. If C is a subset of B and B is a subset of A, then C must be subset of A, and 85% of the subjects drew this relationship in the Venn premise study. Since we require a verbal conclusion with A as the subject, subjects who use subset-premise interpretations will tend to conclude "Some A are C," the valid conclusion, while those using premise-identity interpretations will tend to respond "All A are C."

Let us look briefly at some data. First, I will present data from what we call the production task in which the premise pair is given, and the subject is asked to produce a valid conclusion (or respond that no valid conclusion exists). I assume (with no real justification) that this task is equivalent to the multiple choice task where the five potential responses are given, and the subject chooses the one he likes best. In our laboratory we have run three fairly large-scale production task studies in which subjects responded to all potentially valid syllogisms and to at least some invalid ones (Erickson, 1974, 1975; Traub, 1977). Several other studies in the literature report responses to individual syllogisms, but mainly from invalid syllogisms; valid syllogisms have been rather neglected (e.g., Ceraso & Provitera, 1971; Chapman & Chapman, 1959). Predictions from the model are based on two sets of parameters—the probabilities of choosing particular set interpretations for each premise and the probabilities of choosing particular combinations for the two interpreted premises. Because of the large number of parameters potentially involved, we have tended to use the data from Erickson et al. (1974) as a guide in choosing parameter estimates. Recall that in that study we asked subjects to draw Venn interpretations to premise pairs and to draw Venn conclusions from Venn premises.

Table 3 shows the probability with which the various responses (A, E, I, or O or none [no valid conclusion]) were chosen in several studies where data from individual syllogisms are available (correct responses are indicated). I suspect that there may be an error in the data for Ceraso and Provitera's (1971) Table 1, since their data are so discrepant for Figure III, and that the

.38 and .02 should be reversed. As can be seen, the data tend to be rather stable for subjects from at least four universities. Unweighted mean choice proportions are also shown. For Figure III, the numbers in parentheses represent unweighted means if the .38 and .02 from Ceraso and Provitera (1971) were, indeed, inadvertently reversed.

Predictions from the model are shown in the last column, and they are obviously fairly close to the obtained data. These predictions were made using the parameters shown in Table 4. The data of Erickson et al. (1974) were used as a rough guideline in choosing these parameters. It might also be noted that these same parameter values are used in making predictions for any other syllogisms where they might be applicable. Across the entire set of syllogisms, correlations between model predictions and obtained data tend to be about .85 to .95 for valid syllogisms and a bit lower for invalid ones, on the order of .80 to .85.

We have run several studies to test the generality of the model. For example, instead of asking subjects to produce a conclusion, we have asked them to judge the validity of a complete syllogistic argument—what we call the judgment task (Traub & Erickson, 1975). As a starting point, we consider the possibility that the difference between the production and judgment tasks is in Stage III alone—that the first two stages are identical. Assume that a subject will call an argument valid if the verbal (presented) conclusion *can* be used to describe the symbolic (derived) conclusion from Stage II. The only

Table 4. Parameter Values Used in Predicting Performance on *AA* Syllogisms

---

Stage I   Premise interpretation
   All X are Y
         p(Identity interpretation) = .60
         p(Subset interpretations) = .40

Stage II   Premise combination

Interpreted premises			p(Conclusions)						
			(AC)	(A) C	(C) A	(AC)	(A)	(C)	?
(BC)	and	(AB) (All figures)	1	0	0	0	0	0	0
(B) (C)	and	(A) (B) (Figure I)	0	.9	0	.1	0	0	0
(C) (B)	and	(A) (B) (Figure II)	.20	0	0	.20	.10		.50
(B) (C)	and	(B) (A) (Figure III)	.20	.05	.05	.70	0	0	0
(C) (B)	and	(B) (A) (Figure IV)	.05	0	.85	.10	0	0	0

Table 5. Judgment Task Data Compared to Predictions From the Model

		Traub and Erickson (1975)	Sells (1936)	Prediction
Figure I	AAA[a]	.91	.92	.96
	AAI[a]	.75	.88	.71
	AAE	—	.17	0
Figure II	AAA	.47	.62	.68
	AAI	.46	.63	.56
	AAO	—	.17	.11
Figure III	AAA	.51	—	.70
	AAI[a]	.74	.88	.79
	AAE	—	.11	0
	AAO	—	.17	.30
Figure IV	AAA	.52	.55	.62
	AAI[a]	.71	.92	.81

[a] Valid syllogism.

new parameters which must be estimated are the probability that A, E, I, or O statements will be accepted as descriptions of the various set relations. We assume that an A conclusion will be acceptable for an identity or a subset-superset relation, an I or an O statement will be acceptable for a superset-subset or overlap relation, and an E statement for a disjoint relation. We estimate (purely on subjective grounds) that an I statement will be acceptable for an identity or a subset-superset relation with probability .7, and an O statement will be acceptable for a disjoint relation with the same probability. No other statements are acceptable. Obviously, the largest effects will be for particular (I or O) conclusions. While a subject will not produce a particular conclusion to describe a set relation where a universal statement (A or E) could be used, he will often judge that particular statements could be used.

Table 5 shows the probabilities with which various AA syllogistic arguments were judged to be valid. The data are from Traub and Erickson (1975) and from Sells (1936). It might be noted that one has to be careful in using Sells' data, since several of the syllogisms he used are incorrectly labeled

(Figures I and IV are often reversed). Predictions from the model are also shown. For these syllogisms, the model does fairly well, and across the set of syllogisms used by Traub and Erickson, the data-model correlation was about .90. Several qualitative features of the data are also accounted for within the framework of the model. For example, subjects are more accurate at judging that a valid syllogism is valid than at judging that an invalid syllogism is invalid, and as can be noted in Table 4, the probabilities of judging that the valid *I* conclusions are, indeed, valid are considerably higher than the probabilities of producing these *I* conclusions (Table 3).

Dickstein (1975) has recently shown that when subjects are cautioned about making conversion errors or probabilistic inferences, their performance improves. Whether our three-stage model can account for this improvement is an open question, since Dickstein did not provide data for individual syllogisms. However, it would be of some interest to see if these instructions change the probabilities with which premises are interpreted or combined, or if they increase the probability of more complete analysis (leading subjects to examine more than one interpretation or more than one combination). This would, of course, be the more desirable, since that is the road to good reasoning. However, this would require a more complex model, perhaps the complete combination model of Erickson (1974).

Ceraso and Provitera (1971) have shown that disambiguating premises improves performance. They gave subjects modified premises which were intended to specify set interpretations. The three-stage model accounts for this improvement in performance quite nicely, with no modifications required, by assuming that Stage I interpretations are determined by the modified premises (Erickson, 1974).

We have explored the possibility that this kind of modification can also be used to account for performance on syllogisms in which the premises specify real-world set relations. For example, a premise like "All cows are mammals" requires a subset interpretation, while one like "All people are humans" requires an identity relation. Our research in this area is just beginning. In a recent doctoral dissertation, Bruce Traub—who has been involved in much of the research mentioned here—examined performance on syllogisms where the material was chosen to reflect real-world set relations (Traub, 1977). His results are promising, but somewhat ambiguous, and suggest that both the real-world truth value (i.e., set relation) of the conclusion and the real-world set relations specified by the premises need to be taken into account. This was anticipated several years ago by Henle (1962) and stated more precisely in an unpublished dissertation by Pezzoli (1970), so it is hardly a startling new conclusion, but it bears repetition. The content of an argument has a definite influence on reasoning behavior, and a model developed for abstract reasoning may or may not apply to real-world problems. However, our research—and the research presented by Revlin and Leirer (see chapter 3)—indicates that this will be a fruitful area of research in the near future. I have not attempted the task, but I would be interested in whether or not our model could account for data from Revlin and Leirer's Experiment 2 by changing only Stage I parameters to reflect their manipulations.

I have tried to indicate some of the directions of our thinking and to demonstrate some areas where the three-stage model seems to apply and others where it needs further development. I do feel that our approach has some promise, but we need to see other kinds of processes developed to handle data at the level of the individual syllogism, for that is the way to rapid growth of our knowledge about reasoning processes.

REFERENCES

Ceraso, J., & Provitera, A. Sources of error in syllogistic reasoning. *Cognitive Psychology*, 1971, **2**, 400–410.

Chapman, L. J., & Chapman, J. P. Atmosphere effect re-examined. *Journal of Experimental Psychology*, 1959, **58**, 220–226.

Dickstein, L. S. Effects of instructions and premise order on errors in syllogistic reasoning. *Journal of Experimental Psychology: Human Learning and Memory*, 1975, **104**, 376–384.

Erickson, J. R. A set analysis theory of behavior in formal syllogistic reasoning tasks. In R. L. Solso (Ed.), *Theories of cognitive psychology: The Loyola symposium*. N.J.: 1974.

Erickson, J. R. *Responses to all possible syllogistic arguments*. Unpublished manuscript, University of Texas, 1975.

Erickson, J. R., Wells, G. L., & Traub, B. H. *Tests of a model of formal syllogistic reasoning*. Paper presented at the meeting of the Psychonomic Society, Boston, November, 1974.

Frase, L. T. Associative factors in syllogistic reasoning. *Journal of Experimental Psychology*, 1968, **76**, 407–412.

Henle, M. On the relation between logic and thinking. *Psychological Review*, 1962, **69**, 366–378.

Janis, I., & Frick, F. The relationship between attitudes toward conclusions and errors in judging logical validity of syllogisms. *Journal of Experimental Psychology*, 1943, **33**, 73–77.

Morgan, J. J., & Morton, J. T. The distortion of syllogistic reasoning produced by personal convictions. *Journal of Social Psychology*, 1944, **20**, 39–59.

Neimark, E. D., & Chapman, R. H. Development of the comprehension of logical quantifiers. In R. J. Falmagne (Ed.), *Reasoning: Representation and process*. Hillsdale, N.J.: Erlbaum, 1975.

Pezzoli, J. A. *Syllogistic inference: A problem-solving task*. Unpublished doctoral dissertation, University of Massachusetts, 1970.

Revlis, R. Syllogistic reasoning: Logical decisions from a complex data base. In R. Falmagne (Ed.), *Reasoning: Representation and process*. Hillsdale, N.J.: Erlbaum, 1975. (a)

Revlis, R. Two models of syllogistic reasoning: Feature selection and conversion. *Journal of Verbal Learning and Verbal Behavior*, 1975, **14**, 180–195. (b)

Sells, S. B. The atmosphere effect: An experimental study of reasoning. *Archives of Psychology*, 1936, **No. 200**, 1–72.

Thistlethwaite, D. Attitude and structure as factors in the distortion of reasoning. *Journal of Abnormal and Social Psychology*, 1950, **45**, 442–458.

Traub, B. H. *A set theory approach to deduction with meaningful syllogisms*. Unpublished doctoral dissertation, Ohio State University, 1977.

Traub, B. H., & Erickson, J. R. *Determinants of difficulty in judging the validity of syllogistic arguments*. Paper presented at the meeting of the Midwestern Psychological Association, Chicago, May 1975.

Woodworth, R. S., & Sells, S. B. An atmosphere effect in formal syllogistic reasoning. *Journal of Experimental Psychology*, 1935, **18**, 451–460.

THE EFFECTS OF PERSONAL BIASES ON SYLLOGISTIC REASONING: RATIONAL DECISION FROM PERSONALIZED REPRESENTATIONS

Russell Revlin and Von Otto Leirer
University of California, Santa Barbara

Although Aristotle offered the categorical syllogism as a paradigm for rationality more than twenty centuries ago, only recently has there been serious work on psychological models of such reasoning (see models by Erickson, 1974, and in Chap. 2 of this volume; Johnson-Laird, 1975; Revlis, 1975a, 1975b). While some of these models show an acceptable accuracy in predicting the decisions reached by students when solving a particular type of syllogism (abstract problems), so far only the Conversion Model of Revlis has successfully accounted for the variables that have been shown to be important for solving categorical syllogism—namely: (a) the validity of the problems (whether the syllogism has an ambiguous conclusion), and (b) the concreteness of the propositions (whether they are expressed as abstract relations with letters or as concrete ones with real-world categories). Unfortunately, none of

This work was funded in part by a grant to the first author from the Academic Senate of the University of California, Santa Barbara.

The authors wish to express their appreciation to Nancy Revlin for her comments on earlier drafts of this chapter.

51

these models has been extended to account for human inference in those special situations where human rationality is often called into question—occasions where people reason about controversial relations and appear to make capricious and irrational decisions. This chapter offers such an extension and aims to show that the Conversion Model can account for what has been traditionally viewed as irrational thought processes.

This notion of an irrational reasoner has been given renewed interest as a result of the acceptance of categorical syllogisms into the social psychological literature as a diagnostic metric for assessing attitudes and beliefs (e.g., McGuire, 1960; Morgan & Morton, 1944; Thistlethwaite, 1950; Winthrop, 1946). It is a frequent conclusion of such research with categorical syllogisms that the untrained reasoners are not strictly logical in their inferences and that they base their decisions primarily on personal knowledge and biases. For example, when solving syllogisms such as the following, the content of the propositions is said to have an effect on the reasoner's assessment of the validity of the overall argument:

(1) All Russians are Bolsheviks.
    Some Bolsheviks are undemocratic people.
    Therefore:
    (a) All undemocratic people are Russian;
    (b) No undemocratic people are Russian;
    (c) Some undemoractic people are Russian;
    (d) Some undemocratic people are not Russian;
    (e) None of the above is proven.

That is, when solving such syllogism, students do not appear to base their judgments on the logical form of the arguments but rather on the believability of the conclusions (e.g., Feather, 1965; Gordon, 1953; Janis & Frick, 1943; Janis & Terwilliger, 1962; Kaufman & Goldstein, 1967; Lefford, 1946; Morgan & Morton, 1944; Parrott, 1967, 1969; Wilkins, 1928; Wilson, 1965; Winthrop, 1946). In the syllogism presented above, students are claimed to accept conclusion (c) rather than (e)—the logically required answer—because they are supposed to believe that Russians are undemocratic people.

The Conversion Model of syllogistic reasoning provides an alternative interpretation of these data which will be examined here—namely, that deductive errors on categorical syllogisms are only indirectly affected by the problem's content because they are attributable to the reasoner's representation of the problem's propositions. The decisions neither reflect insufficiencies in the reasoner's logical skills nor any putative suspension of rationality. For example, one possible explanation of errors in (1) is that the proposition "All Russians are Bolsheviks" is converted in the process of comprehension so that the reasoner understands it to mean that not only are "All Russians

Bolsheviks," but it is also the case that "All Bolsheviks are Russians" (in fact, this is historically correct). If this converted interpretation is the first one employed by the reasoner when considering the composite meaning of the two premises of the syllogism (this would be an identity relation in Erickson's terms), then the conclusion that *Bolsheviks* and *Russians* share all properties in common is a rational one and in fact the reasoner is quite correct in asserting that "Some undemocratic people are Russian" (c) is a valid conclusion from the two premises of the syllogism.

The Conversion Model was purposefully developed as an alternative to the notion that reasoners' decisions are capricious and reflect idiosyncratic biases and that reasoners are susceptible to "interrupts" from the content of the material reasoned about. The view taken here is an old one and dates back at least to Wilkins (1928), but perhaps more appropriately to Henle (1962) who succinctly illustrated how reasoners might interpret the propositions of a syllogism in ways that the experimenter or logician did not intend. Henle's work is notable in this regard since her paper with Michael (Henle & Michael, 1956) stands as one of the few studies to challenge the view of human reasoners as illogical.

An advantage of the present formulation is that it extends Henle's criticisms of the existent literature by pointing out a critical confounding in the research on beliefs in formal reasoning—namely, such research invariably manipulated (however subtly) not only the belief status of the conclusions but also the kind of relations expressed in the premises. Syllogism (1) is a typical example in that one cannot tell whether the reasoner's decisions are a result of faulty inference or whether the decisions logically follow from an idiosyncratic (i.e., personalized) representation, as claimed by the Conversion Model. This difficulty in assessing the source of reasoning decisions is compounded because in most studies the "neutral" materials drive different representations of the propositions than the "controversial" materials with which they are contrasted. That is, the syllogisms' premises not only differed in emotional content and real-world believability, they also differed in the kinds of relations they expressed (e.g., class inclusion vs. identity relations). It is not surprising, therefore, that such ambiguous conditions have lead some researchers to conclude that the reasoner's beliefs about the truth of a syllogism's content affect the kinds of decisions that are reached—often at the expense of rationality.

Another difficulty with this literature is that its view of the reasoner is not motivated by a *general* model of formal inference. It claims only that when beliefs conflict with logic, the reasoner tends to make his decisions based on personal biases rather than on systematic rules of inference. Such an approach neither tells us how people reason with neutral materials nor where in the reasoning process personal beliefs come into play. This view asks us to accept that there are two reasoning systems: one evoked by abstract or neutral materials (a quasi-rational system producing dispassionate judgments); the second evoked by materials with real-world truth values (an irrational system producing emotional judgments). This poses difficulties for any model of inference which seeks to develop a minimal set of mechanisms that can account for all decisions in formal inference tasks.

The Conversion Model, which seeks to be such a general model, would at first seem an unlikely candidate to explain the effect of personal beliefs on rational judgments: How can a model with an underlying assumption of rationality account for data that appear to support irrational decision "rules"? Since the Conversion Model assumes that reasoners' decisions follow rationally from the nature of the representation of the syllogism's premises, it cannot entertain illogical inference rules. We must show, therefore, that the previous findings are artifacts of the confounding of Representation and Inference and that by independently varying these two factors, the influence of personal bias will be limited to the reasoner's understanding of the premises and not to a suspension of rationality when judging the conclusions.

These predictions from the Conversion Model were examined in two experiments that avoid the type of confounding mentioned above. In Experiment 1 the stimulus materials included syllogisms whose conclusions have different real-world truth values (i.e., some were believed true; others were believed false). These problems were selected so that the reasoner's interpretation of the premises would not bias the conclusion drawn. On such syllogisms, illogical decisions are properly ascribed to the inference rules (or response biases) that students employ rather than to the representation of the premises.

In Experiment 2 the students' knowledge of certain real-world categories was assessed by means of a questionnaire (e.g., the percentage of blacks on welfare; the percentage of welfare recipients who are black). Some of this information was incorporated into syllogisms with highly controversial subject matter in the premises but neutral conclusions. We then attempted to predict the conclusions reached by the reasoners based on their personal knowledge about the categories reasoned about. On such problems, illogical decisions are properly ascribed to the representation of the "controversial" premises and not to faulty inference rules.

Our purpose in this enterprise is two-fold. First, we wish to extend the Conversion Model—a model designed to account for decisions on problems with neutral content—so that it may predict decisions on problems which contain sentences that vary in believability and emotionality. Second, we wish to show that the component processes of this model are congruent with processes entailed in quite different reasoning tasks. In this way we hope to place in perspective the endeavors of many research projects and thereby to promote common modes of analysis so that ultimately we may have either a single model which can account for the decisions people reach on a variety of inference tasks or a handful of inference rules and processes which are combined in special ways for different reasoning tasks.

What follows in the next section of the chapter is a general description of the model's structure, the accuracy of its predictions for abstract and neutral syllogisms, and the generality of its mechanisms. The section is intended not only to explain the nature of the Conversion Model but also to describe the programmatic nature of our project on human inference. The reader already familiar with the model may wish to proceed directly to the section which presents the two experiments examining personal bias in reasoning. The last section of this chapter considers the general implications of the Conversion Model for human inference.

THE CONVERSION MODEL

The underlying assumption of the Conversion Model is that people are rational problem solvers: They are capable of reaching logically valid conclusions with little or no special training on the rules of logic. Further, when errors in reasoning occur, they are primarily attributable to the encoding of the problem materials and not to the rationality of the operations performed on that encoding. The following is an example of the kind of problems to which this approach is applied, and it includes a description of how this approach is realized as a process model of categorical decisions.

The Task

The formal, or categorical, syllogism consists of two propositions (called Premises) followed by one or more propositions (called Conclusions) which may or may not logically follow from the Premises:

(2) All M are P. (Major Premise)
Some S are M. (Minor Premise)
Therefore:
(a) All S are P;
(b) No S are P;
(c) Some S are P;
(d) Some S are not P;
(e) None of the above is proven.

Each proposition asserts a relation between two sets of terms. The major premise expresses a relation between the predicate of the conclusion (P) and another term (M). The minor premise expresses a relation between the subject of the conclusion (S) and the other term (M). The reasoner's task is to judge whether one of the conclusions can be validly inferred from the premises—i.e., whether one of the expressed relations between S and P can be unambiguously determined from the relations expressed in the premises (cf. Cohen & Nagel, 1934, for the formal rules for making this judgment). The accuracy of the reasoner's decisions varies across problems: The logically required conclusion is nearly always drawn for some syllogisms while an invalid conclusion is frequently accepted for other syllogisms (Morgan & Morgan, 1953; Revlis, 1975b).

Conversion Operation

The Conversion Model accounts for reasoning errors by focusing on the problem solver's representation of the syllogism's premises. The model claims that a primary source of erroneous decisions is that a conversion operation participates in the encoding of quantified propositions: When the reasoner is told, e.g., that "All A are B," he interprets this proposition to mean that the converse is also true—that "All B are A." Conversion as a source of errors in deductive reasoning was noted earlier by Wilkins (1928) as a form of interpretation that occurs on single-premise problems and on formal syllogisms.

Conversion in the encoding of quantified propositions may be based on one or more of the following three factors: first, on the ambiguity of the relational copula, *is a*, that appears in all standard syllogisms; second, on social-linguistic conventions for communicating; third, on elementary comprehension mechanisms for analyzing quasi-symmetrical relations. With respect to the first factor, Chapman & Chapman (1959) report that reasoners tend to encode *is a* as *is equal to* (an identity relation) rather than the logical *is included in* (where *A* is a subset of *B*, though possibly the only subset of *B*). As a consequence, Universal Affirmatives ("All A are B") have their meanings altered by conversion (conversion leaves unchanged the meaning of "No A are B" and "Some A are B"). A test of the importance of this factor for formal reasoning was described by Revlis (1975a), who showed that disambiguation of the relational term improved performance on syllogisms that contain Universal Affirmative relations, thereby supporting the contention that reasoning errors are attributable to the misinterpretation of the copula on Universal Affirmatives. However, Revlis (1975a) also observed a substantial, and unpredicted, improvement on all syllogisms. Consequently, while this specific interpretation of the relational term may contribute to conversion, it is clearly not the only relevant factor.

Communicative presuppositions contribute to the conversion interpretation primarily with respect to the encoding of Particular Negatives. The principle involved is that in the act of communicating a relation, the most informative form is used. For example, when a speaker asserts a Particular Negative (e.g., "Some plants are not green things"), the listener knows that the converse of the statement is also true ("Some green things are not plants"); this is so because if any universal relation between *plants* and *green things* were appropriate, (e.g., "All green things are plants" or "No green things are plants"), normal conventions of communication would require its use (cf. Grice, 1967; Haviland & Clark, 1974). Consequently, the assertion of a Particular Negative readily leads to the acceptance of its converse. Recent linguistic discussions of "conversational implications" provide further support for these two bases of conversion in normal speech (Gordon & Lakoff, 1971; Horn, 1972; Lakoff, 1970; see also the category-interchange hypothesis of Meyer, 1970.)

The third factor contributing to conversion is not as well supported as the previous two, but possesses excellent heuristic value. It is claimed that when comprehending quantified relations between distinct categories, there is an automatic operation that treats inputs as *symmetric*, so that on hearing, e.g., "All A are B," the listener automatically entertains the notion that "All B are A." This operator is said to apply to both abstract inputs (where letters stand for categories) and concrete ones as well (see below). As a result of this operator, the encoding for $A \rightarrow B$ relation (independent of quantifier) includes $B \rightarrow A$. While we do not have independent psycholinguistic evidence for this operator, it has become an integral part of explanations for categorical syllogisms as well as linear orderings (see chapter 6 by Potts and chapter 7 by Griggs). The basis for this operator is the notion that quantified relations are at least quasi-symmetric in the sense that for every quantified expression of the form "A relation$_1$ B," there is a true expression of the form "B relation$_2$ A." Such reversals of subject and predicate terms are the hallmark of symmetric relations; where true symmetry holds in just those cases where $relation_1 = relation_2$. In the case of the four categorical propositions ("All A are B;" "No A are B;" "Some A are B;" "Some A are not B"), two cases of true symmetry occur (conversion or reversal of subject and predicate classes): No A are B $\rightarrow$ No B are A; Some A are B $\rightarrow$ Some B are A. In addition, one case of limited symmetry occurs; All A are B $\rightarrow$ Some B are A. In all cases there appears to be at least an intuitive basis for asserting a quasi-symmetric relation between the subject and predicate classes in a syllogism. This immediate inference may be readily made by reasoners who do not adhere to formally constrained interpretations of these relations. Consequently, their decisions appear to be illogical while, in fact, they may be the result of the rigorous application of logical operators to a casually derived understanding of the relations.

The conversion operation—whatever factors contribute to its functioning—has important consequences for deductive reasoning. If a conversion operator participates in the encoding of quantified propositions, then the reasoner makes his validity judgments based on a representation of a syllogism that may be quite different from the one objectively presented. The following illustrates how conversion alters the presented syllogism:

(3) All C are B.   (4) All B are C.
    Some B are A.   Some A are B.
    Therefore: Therefore:
    No conclusion follows. Some A are C.

In syllogism (3) we cannot unambiguously determine the relation between A and C from the information provided in the premises. If the reasoner correctly encodes the propositions and reasons logically on this problem, he must decide that no valid conclusion is possible. However, the Conversion Model claims that while encoding the premises, the reasoner converts each one in turn so that the problem (after conversion) would appear to the reasoner as syllogism (4). This converted syllogism does have a solution, "Some A are C." Therefore, when the reasoner converts the propositions and applies correct logical operations, a new problem is produced with a conclusion that is inappropriate for the original syllogism.

Meaning Stack

We argue here that the encoding of syllogistic statements proceeds as a progressive extraction of elementary features. The historical sequence involved is analogous to the construction of a stack of meanings for each syllogistic statement. Figure 1 shows that this entails the isolation of orthographic/acoustic features: subject, object, relations, quantifiers. Most important for the present discussion is that the reasoner stores both the original (A-B) and the converted (B-A) propositions in his Data Base (with the converted proposition given priority in the "Stack" of meanings for the premises (i.e., its meaning is generated later than the unconverted one.)

While it is claimed that the conversion operator is evoked automatically, not every proposition will have its converted form stored in the meaning stack. For example, when the reasoner encodes information from concrete propositions, the converted meaning will not appear in his Data Base in just those cases where the meaning of the converted propositions does not make sense to the reasoner. Just as we generate only semantically meaningful readings of sentences, so too we may block the generation of pragmatically deviant sentences which result from the presence of a conversion operation. Thus, if the reasoner were told that "All horses are animals," he would balk at the idea that the statement might be interpreted to mean "All animals are horses." Yet, reasoners are quite willing to permit the conversion of other

MEANING STACK OF QUANTIFIED RELATIONS

⋮

CONVERSION: Quantifier(Predicate(Predicate <u>is</u> <u>a</u> Subject))

GLOSS: Quantifier(Subject(Subject <u>is</u> <u>a</u> Predicate))

⋮

RELATION: [<u>+</u>Universal], [<u>+</u>Affirmative]

TOPIC: Subject Term, Predicate Term

⋮

FORM: Phonological Features

⋮

Orthographic Features

FIG. 1. Meaning stack of quantified relations.

abstract or concrete propositions, e.g., when they are told that "All A are B" ("All B are A") or that "All Communists are protestors" ("All protestors are Communists") (Revlis, 1975a).

The Conversion Model claims that the explicit details of the nature of conversion coupled with a small set of processing assumptions can account for reasoning decisions. What is important to recognize here is that the encoding processes present in the comprehension of normal English expressions are also present at the encoding of syllogistic statements and that such processes affect the conclusions reached by the reasoner. Notice that by focusing on the representation of the premises, it becomes unnecessary to posit separate inference mechanisms to account for reasoning with different materials. The Conversion Model claims that the mechanisms remain constant across conditions; only the representation on which the mechanisms operate changes with the materials.

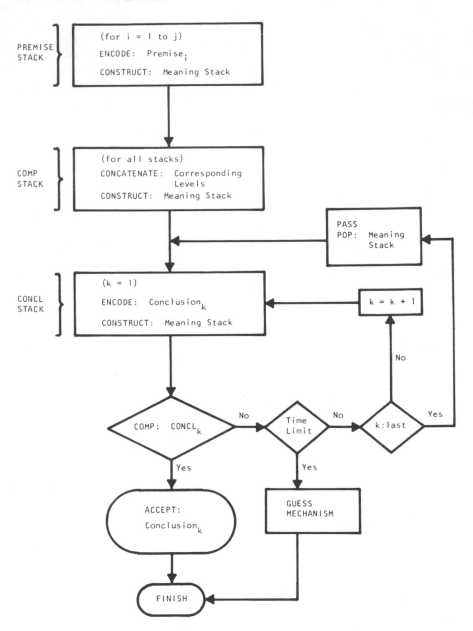

FIG. 2. Conversion Model of Formal Reasoning.

Processing Stages

The Conversion Model is shown in Figure 2; it consists of four processing stages: (a) an encoding stage, in which the individual premises are given a first reading and the meaning of each premise is stored as a stack of propositions; (b) a composite stage, in which logical operations work to produce a single predicate representing the information in the premises; (c) a conclusion-encoding stage, similar to the premise-encoding stage; (d) a comparison stage, where the composite information is compared with the encoded conclusion. This last stage also includes a decision substage in which the reasoner selects his response.

In addition to these four stages, the model makes several strong assumptions about the nature of the encoding of quantified propositions. First, it assumes that the reasoner applies a conversion operation in the encoding of each sentence. Second, both the converted and original forms of the propositions are stored in the reasoner's data base with the converted meaning at the "top" of a meaning stack. However, when such a meaning is "blocked," the unconverted (nonsymmetric form) is stored at the top of the meaning stack. Finally, both the composite representation and the conclusions provided are also subject to the conversion operation since they too are quantified propositions. The operation of each stage and the importance of the encoding assumptions are described below:

Stage 1: Encoding and conversion. In the first stage, the reasoner reads-in the premises and stores a representation of the individual propositions. The encoding process entails a conversion operator which acts upon the representation of propositional components, as shown in Figure 1. The notational form for this encoding may be a bracketed proposition (e.g., Clark, 1969) or a pictorial scheme such as Venn diagrams (see Chap. 2 by Erickson). While no notational form has been completely successful in predicting categorical reasoning decisions, any form selected must permit the encoding and decision processes described here.

The levels of the meaning stack (shown in Figure 1) embody the history of the encoding process, which proceeds through many steps including (a) a phonological representation of each premise, (b) isolation of subject, predicate, quantificational, and relational terms, (c) superficial reading based on the isolated elements, (d) deep structural reading of the propositions based on the isolated elements, and (e) operations on this reading including the conversion operation. This stack or "list" framework is in contrast to the model proposed by Erickson (1974) which embodies a briefly enduring array of possible representations (Venn diagrams); from these diagrams, the reasoner is said to idiosyncratically (or probabilistically) make a selection for each premise. The Conversion Model differs from Erickson's on several dimensions (see Chap. 2).

Stage 2: Composite representation. The composite representation of the pair of premises is constructed concurrently with the development of the individual meaning stacks. In this way, the composite stack (COMP) proceeds in a bottom-to-top manner just as the individual meaning stacks do. The levels of the COMP stack consist of concatenations of the successive "interpretations" given for the individual premises. Consequently, at the top of the stack is the composite representation given for converted interpretations of the two premises; the second level consists of the composite representation for the unconverted interpretations of the two premises; the third level consists of the composite representation of the "atmosphere" features; etc. The rules for constructing such composites can only be incompletely specified at present. Perhaps Johnson-Laird's (1975) link structure will account for the combination of the propositional representation (i.e., the top two encodings) while Revlis' (1975b) Feature Selection Model can account for the combination of the representation of the abstract features (i.e., the lower encodings).

Stage 3: Conclusion encoding. In this stage, the conclusion is encoded with conversion and represented in a form amenable to a comparison with the output of Stage 2.

Stage 4: Comparison. The reasoner compares the output of Stage 2 with the conclusion encoded in Stage 3. If the two propositions are congruent, the reasoner accepts the conclusion as "valid." In the experiments reported here, the reasoner is presented with five alternative conclusions. If the first conclusion and the COMP are incongruent, the reasoner considers the next conclusion offered. For those problems on which none of the propositional conclusion match the reasoner's composite predicate (i.e., a "none of the above" conclusion is the only one remaining to him), the reasoner makes a second PASS through the problem by selecting the next composite representation available to him in the COMP meaning stack. The PASS mechanism consists of a recovery of less derived composite representations by a back-up operation in memory which is accomplished by "popping" the top of the COMP meaning stack.

If the additional PASS does not result in a match with a propositional conclusion, and time remains, the reasoner will continue to pop the COMP stack until either a match is eventually found or time and/or motivation runs out. At this point (which obviously varies with people and conditions) the reasoner makes a fair GUESS from among the available conclusions. Both the PASS and GUESS mechanisms presuppose a response bias against accepting a nonpropositional conclusion ("none of the above") on such tasks. The plausibility of this assumption is well recognized (e.g., Chapman & Chapman, 1959; Dickstein, 1975; Revlis, 1975b; but see also Dickstein, 1976). The operation of these mechanisms will be described more fully when we consider the predictions of the model.

Predictions

The Conversion Model predicts the decisions reasoners will reach on each syllogism. These predictions will be described separately for invalid and valid syllogisms.

Invalid syllogisms. Invalid syllogisms are ones where no conclusion unambiguously follows from the premises, i.e., two or more contradictory conclusions may be entailed by the premises. On these problems, the logically required decision is that "no conclusion is proven." The model distinguishes between two types of invalid syllogisms: (a) those where conversion transforms the syllogism into one with a different conclusion (i.e., other than "no conclusion is proven") than would be prescribed by a logician; these are labeled DIFFERENT syllogisms; and (b) those where conversion produces a syllogism with the same conclusion as would be prescribed by a logician (i.e., "no conclusion" is the correct decision to be reached); these are labeled SAME-N syllogisms (same conclusion "none").

On the first PASS through all syllogisms, the representation of the premises entails a conversion operator which is reflected in the top encoding of the COMP stack. For DIFFERENT syllogisms, the top encoding will match a propositional conclusion, the reasoner will accept it as his decision, and the response will be scored as *incorrect* by the experimenter (0% correct is predicted).

For SAME-N problems, the converted syllogism requires a nonpropositional, "none" conclusion. Because he eschews such conclusions, the reasoner makes a second PASS through the problem and pops the proposition in the COMP stack. On the second PASS, the reasoner retrieves the encoding akin to the one that is logically prescribed. However, this interpretation will again result in a nonpropositional, "none" conclusion. If sufficient time is not available, the reasoner will make a fair GUESS from among the conclusions provided. As a result of the GUESS, a correct "none" response will occur on approximately 20% of the problems (when there are five alternatives to choose from, as in the present experiments).

These and other predictions from the model were examined by Revlis (1975b). The results are summarized in Table 1, which shows that when solving abstract syllogisms under modest time constraints (15 to 30 seconds), the subjects' performance on invalid DIFFERENT syllogisms approached 0% correct (observed = 6.5%), and performance on invalid SAME-N syllogisms did not differ statistically from the 20% correct predicted to occur by chance (observed = 15.3%).

Time is an important factor in these predictions because it determines the range of encodings from the COMP stack that will be tested for congruence with the available conclusions. The number of passes a reasoner can make will have a critical impact on the decisions he will reach on SAME-N syllogisms.

Table 1. Reasoning Accuracy Across Abstract Syllogisms[a]

Validity	Problem-type		
	SAME	NONE	DIFFERENT
Valid	72.8%	71.6%	12.6%
Invalid	15.3%	—[b]	6.5%

[a] Adapted from Revlis (1975b).
[b] Undefined.

For example, in those cases where there is sufficient time to make a third PASS, the reasoner retrieves that level of the meaning stack which contains the abstract features corresponding to [Subject], [Predicate], [Quantifier], and [Relation]. As with the other levels in the COMP stack, the reasoner compares the composite representation with that of the conclusion based on the relevant features.[1] The nature of this COMP representation and the comparison stage are described in the Feature Selection Model of Revlis (1975b). The methodologies employed in our research program guarantee that the reasoner will always find a match with the COMP representation if he has sufficient time to complete a third PASS. It should be noted that such third-PASS matches for SAME-N problems will invariably result in an illogical decision since the logically prescribed conclusion ("none of the above") never corresponds to the third-PASS features.

Support for this description of the decision process is provided by Revlis (1975b) who showed that the preponderant error on SAME-N syllogisms was the selection of conclusions that are congruent with the Extension-Polarity features of the premises: [±Universal] and [±Affirmative].

Valid syllogisms. Valid syllogisms are ones where a single conclusion unambiguously follows from the two premises. It is also the case with such problems that if a universally quantified conclusion is valid, then its particularly quantified form is also valid (though the reverse is not acceptable). For example, if "All A are B" is a valid conclusion to a syllogism, then "Some A are B" is also valid because of the special definition of *some* in such problems. That is, *some* is treated as meaning *a part, possibly all*—this is in contrast to the more restricted normal definition where *some* is treated as

[1] How such decisions are actually made and the kind of variability in response to such problems is given in Revlis, 1975a.

just *a part*. Clarification of this interpretation of *some* is an important part of the instructions on syllogistic reasoning tasks (cf. Frase, 1966).

The Conversion Model distinguishes among three types of valid syllogisms: (a) those where conversion results in the same conclusion as the presented problem, SAMES; (b) those where conversion produces a syllogism with a different propositional conclusion than the presented one, DIFFERENTS; (c) those where conversion results in a nonpropositional conclusion, NONES. For SAMES and DIFFERENTS, the reasoner finds a match between the converted encoding from the COMP stack and one of the propositional conclusions, and he accepts the conclusion logically required by his representation: SAME decisions will be scored as *correct* (100% correct is predicted) while DIFFERENT decisions will be scored as *incorrect* (0% correct is predicted).

For NONES, the reasoner finds no propositional conclusion congruent with his COMP representation and makes a second PASS, pops his top encoding, and compares the unconverted encoding with the conclusions. Since these are valid syllogisms, the reasoner will encounter a match with the correct conclusions and accept this conclusion as his decision. Consequently, on his second PASS, the reasoner's decisions will always be scored as *correct* (100% correct is predicted).

This characterization of valid syllogisms was examined by Revlis (1975b). As shown in Table 1, the predictions of the Conversion Model were confirmed. For example, reasoners' accuracy in their decisions is good when conversion does not alter the logically required conclusions (SAMES and NONES); when conversion alters the conclusion (DIFFERENTS), reasoners' accuracy is poor. These data show that given our hypothesis concerning the type of encoding employed by the reasoner and the assumption of rational decision processes, we are able to state with acceptable accuracy (approximately 70%) the decisions that reasoners actually reach when solving abstract categorical syllogisms.

The Conversion Model also accounts for the traditional finding that valid syllogisms are easier to solve than invalid ones. It does this in two ways. First, the conversion operator causes erroneous decisions to be made on 9 invalid syllogisms; in contrast, conversion leads to errors on only 3 valid syllogisms. Second, while the PASS mechanism leads to errors on many of the remaining invalid syllogisms, it actually leads to improved performance on 9 valid syllogisms (i.e., NONES) where on the first PASS the reasoner encounters a "none" conclusion, but where on the second PASS he reaches the logically prescribed conclusion. Notice that in explaining the validity effect, the Conversion Model need not entertain the notion that there are any intrinsic differences between valid and invalid syllogisms; it shows, e.g., that performance on DIFFERENTS will be the same for both valid and invalid syllogisms (see Table 1). The validity effect can, therefore, be most appropriately viewed as a consequence of the roughly automatic decision mechanisms that operate in categorical reasoning.

Concrete Syllogisms

While the Conversion Model has been developed to account for the decision processes of students when solving abstract syllogisms, the model is readily extended to the solution of concrete syllogisms (i.e., those with concrete class terms). A consistent finding on such problems is that students reason more accurately on concrete syllogisms than on abstract ones (e.g., Wilkins, 1928). This effect of concreteness may be a result of the differential availability of long-term memory (LTM) representations for the concrete categories and knowledge of their typical (or pragmatically permissible) relations. The Conversion Model claims that such knowledge is used in the encoding of the individual premises and that an interpretation of a premise will be automatically "blocked" in those instances when conversion results in a semantically deviant relation. Since we possess such knowledge for sentences of the form "All horses are animals" (where "All animals are horses" is not normally permitted), the Conversion Model claims that reasoning with conrete syllogisms should be more accurate than reasoning with abstract syllogisms where blocking the converted interpretation alters the reasoner's decision and requires him to select a more accurate conclusion. That is, concreteness should be an important factor in solving categorical syllogisms on just those problems where conversion alters the conclusion drawn: valid and invalid DIFFERENT syllogisms. In all other problems, reasoners should show the same performance on conrete and abstract syllogisms.

To test this hypothesis, Revlis (1975a) asked two groups of students to solve reasoning problems that contained premises either designed to permit conversion (5) or designed to block conversion (6).

(5) All history books are among the books on this corner of the shelf.
Some books on this corner of the shelf are rare volumes.
(6) All history books are among the books on this floor of the library.
Some books on this floor of the library are rare volumes.

Notice that for syllogisms like (5), most (if not all) elements of the predicate class (books on this corner of the shelf) are likely elements of the subject class (history books), thereby facilitating conversion. In contrast, for syllogisms like (6), there are many possible elements of the predicate class (books on this floor of the library) that are not likely elements of the subject

Table 2. Reasoning Accuracy Across Concrete Syllogism[a]

Category size	Convertibility	Problem-type	
		SAME	DIFFERENT
Explicit	Unblocked	76.5%	26.5%
	Blocked	76.5%	53.5%
Implicit	Unblocked	83.5%	40.0%
	Blocked	80.0%	60.0%

[a]Valid syllogisms; data from Revlis (1975a).

class (history books), thereby blocking conversion. To insure that students understood the implicit relations just described, two additional groups were given the same syllogisms with numbers added to indicate the sizes of the classes, thereby making the relative convertibility of the premises explicit.

The model makes two predictions with respect to the present experiment. First, it claims that students will show the same performance effect of conversion on concrete syllogisms as they do on abstract ones. For example, SAME syllogisms will be easier to solve than DIFFERENT syllogisms on problems like (5). Second, the model predicts that the relative convertibility of the premises will affect reasoning performance on DIFFERENT syllogisms, but will have no effect on SAMES (where the reasoner is said to reach the same conclusion as prescribed by logic even when he converts the premises). Thus, for DIFFERENT problems, the reasoner's decisions will be more accurate on syllogisms where conversion is blocked (6) than where it is not blocked (5); no such effect should appear for SAME problems.

The results of this experiment are presented in Table 2 which shows that for both the Implicit and Explicit groups, concrete syllogisms exhibit the same kind of conversion effect as abstract syllogisms. For unblocked problems, SAMES are solved more accurately than DIFFERENTS (Implicit: $F[1,29]$ = 23.8, $p < .001$; Explicit: $F[1,29]$ = 72.5, $p < .001$). This is also shown for blocked problems (Implicit: $F[1,29]$ = 9.2, $p < .01$; Explicit: $F[1,29]$ = 8.1, $p < .01$). More critically, there is an interaction between the type of materials—blocked or unblocked—and the type of problems—SAMES or DIFFERENTS—(Implicit: $F[1,58]$ = 4.4, $p < .05$; Explicit: $F[1,58]$ = 6.9, $p < .01$). What this shows is that over all conditions, blocked problems are solved more accurately than unblocked problems on just those syllogisms where the Conversion Model claims that the conversion operator has its effect, i.e., DIFFERENT syllogisms.

The Conversion Model makes the strong claim that performance on concrete syllogisms is usually superior to that found on abstract syllogisms because only the former permit conversion to be blocked in the encoding of the premises. If this analysis is correct, then reasoners should be as accurate (or, more appropriate, as inaccurate) on unblocked concrete syllogisms as they are on abstract ones but more accurate on blocked concrete syllogisms than on abstract ones. A comparison of the data in Table 1 and 2 confirms this hypothesis and strongly supports the argument that the concreteness effect in categorical reasoning is attributable to the encoding of the materials—specifically, to the activity of the conversion operator in the encoding of the categorical premises.

REASONING FROM PERSONAL KNOWLEDGE

After demonstrating that the Conversion Model can account for rational decisions with both abstract and concrete materials, we now turn to the most serious challenge for such a model: Can the Conversion Model account for ostensibly irrational decisions made by reasoners who are asked to make decisions concerning "emotional" or prejudicial materials? Since the Conversion Model cannot posit illogical inference rules, it must demonstrate that the "irrational" decisions can be accounted for in terms of how such materials are encoded by the reasoner. In other words, the influence of personal bias on categorical reasoning must be shown to be a result of how the reasoners understand the premises and not due to a suspension of rationality.

To extend the Conversion Model to categorical reasoning with controversial (or prejudicial) materials, we must first show that when encoding is held constant (either conversion always occurs or is always blocked) or rendered irrelevant (e.g., SAME syllogisms), there is no difference in the erroneous acceptance of conclusions that vary in real-world truth value. That is, reasoners will accept the logically prescribed conclusion independent of its empirical truth value. Second, we must show that when students reason with controversial materials, the decisions they reach can be predicted from their encoding of the premises (independently assessed by means of a questionnaire). These goals are part of the rationale for Experiments 1 and 2, respectively.

Experiment 1

The Conversion Model claims that when the premises of a syllogism are unambiguous, the conclusions reached will be rational—however controversial the alternatives may be. To examine this hypothesis, Revlin and Leirer (in preparation) asked 25 students to solve two types of valid syllogisms. In the first type, the logical conclusion is also one that the reasoner would select if his decisions were based on real-world truth values. For examples, in the following syllogism, answer (d) is both the logically valid as well as the empirically true conclusion:

(7) No members of the committee are women.
     Some U.S. Senators are members of the committee.
     Therefore:
     (a) All U.S. Senators are women;
     (b) No U.S. Senators are women;
     (c) Some U.S. Senators are women;
     (d) Some U.S. Senators are not women;
     (e) None of the above is proven.

Answer (c) is also empirically correct, but it does not pose a problem for analysis (see below). These problems are termed *LA* syllogisms because *L*ogic *A*grees with beliefs.

In the second type of syllogism, the logical conclusion would not be selected if the reasoner based his judgments on real-world truth values. For example, while the logical conclusion to the following syllogism is answer (d), the empirically true conclusion corresponds to answer (b):

(8) No U.S. Senators are members of the Harem Club.
     Some Arabian sheiks are members of the Harem Club.
     Therefore:
     (a) All Arabian sheiks are U.S. Senators;
     (b) No Arabian sheiks are U.S. Senators;
     (c) Some Arabian sheiks are U.S. Senators;
     (d) Some Arabian sheiks are not U.S. Senators;
     (e) None of the above is proven.

Notice that the premises of these syllogisms are "neutral"; they have no real-world truth value. In contrast, the conclusions do have empirical truth values. In addition, conversion of the premises does not alter the logically required conclusion. As stated earlier, irrational judgments are, therefore, a result of "faulty inference." These are termed *LC* syllogisms since *L*ogic *C*onflicts with beliefs. Of course, the Conversion Model is in the unenviable position of seeking an acceptance of the null hypothesis since it clearly predicts that reasoners will be as accurate on syllogisms where logic agrees with beliefs as on syllogisms where logic and beliefs conflict (LA = LC).

In the foregoing syllogisms, the conclusion can be said to be empirically based, general knowledge. (Other examples are "All brick layers are laborers" or "No ex-U.S. Vice Presidents are women" or "Some U.S. Senators are not women.") Since it is difficult to assess the strength of such beliefs, one half of the syllogisms in the experiment contained conclusions that are definitionally true, (e.g., "All popes in the Vatican are Catholics" or "No robots are people" or "Some animals are not mammals"). These problems were included to provide differential strength of belief. If students are selecting the conclusions on the basis of personal knowledge and beliefs, then such a tendency should be more pronounced for definitionally true conclusions than for empirically true ones.

The results of the experiment are presented in Table 3 and show that when solving valid categorical syllogisms, students are less accurate in their decisions when logic and knowledge conflict than when they agree, $F(1,24) = 13.5$, $p < .01$. While there is no difference overall in accuracy on problems with definitionally true or empirically true conclusions, strength of belief does interact with problem type, $F(1,24) = 9.1$, $p < .01$. Put another way, when logic and knowledge conflict, reasoners' accuracy deteriorates primarily in those cases where the conflict is between a logical conclusion and a definitionally true, strong conclusion (empirically true = 73.0% correct; definitionally true = 60.0% correct). While this trend reaches conventional levels of significance, it should be kept in mind that the effect of believability of the conclusions is quite limited; inspection of Table 3 shows that for all problems, reasoners overwhelmingly select the logically correct conclusion.

The importance of personal knowledge can also be assessed by asking whether the errors that do occur (despite the model's claims of perfect rationality) represent decisions to accept conclusions that are consistent with personal beliefs. That is, when students are not accepting the logical conclusion, are their decisions appreciably influenced by personal knowledge? Analysis of the percentage of errors presented in Table 4 shows that 47.8% of all errors for LC problems (Logic Conflicts with beliefs) occur when reasoners select the conclusion that agrees with their personal knowledge (e.g., answer

Table 3. Reasoning Accuracy with Believed Conclusions[a]

Type of problem	Type of belief		Total
	Definitionally true	Empirically true	
Logic Agrees with belief (LA)	88.0%	78.0%	83.0%
Logic Conflicts with belief (LC)	60.0%	73.0%	66.6%

[a]Chance performance is 20%.

Table 4. Percentage of All Errors Attributable to Accepting Conclusion[a]

Type of problem	Type of belief		Weighted total
	Definitionally true	Empirically true	
Logic Agrees with belief (LA)	9.1	50.0	35.3
Logic Conflicts with belief (LC)	32.5	70.4	47.8

[a]For LC problems, this is the believed conclusion; for LA problems this is the disbelieved conclusion.

[b] in syllogism [8]). This differs only slightly from the percentage of errors for LA syllogisms (Logic Agrees with beliefs) where 35.3% of the errors occur when students select answer (b). In addition, only 7.4% of the errors on LC-type problems are attributable to the selection of a "real-world" competitor to the logically required response (e.g., [c] vs. [d] in syllogism [7]).

While this traditional statistical analysis lends some credibility to the reality of the belief-bias effect, a more detailed inspection of the data (i.e., a subject-by-subject analysis) argues persuasively that personal bias has only a minimal influence on reasoning decisions. We will describe two aspects of the data in this regard. First, 67% of the belief errors (LC condition) were contributed by only 6 subjects who made the same error in the LA condition (they accepted conclusion [b]). Interestingly, this error in the LA condition is tantamount to accepting a conclusion that these subjects must clearly disbelieve (e.g., "No college students are seniors"). It is plausible, therefore, that much of the effect of personal bias is the result of a few students following an unpredicted reasoning process—but one that is clearly orthogonal to accepting conclusions based on their real-world truth value.

Second, it would seem that the most appropriate subjects to look at in evaluating the belief-bias effect are those who made no errors in the LA condition. If students are accepting conclusions based on their believability, then one would predict perfect performance in the LA condition and minimal performance in the LC condition. Therefore, we compared the performance of the 11 students who made no errors when belief and logic agree (LA) with their performance when belief and logic conflict (LC). We found that while their accuracy in the LC condition was lower than in the LA condition, it was not appreciably lower (88.7% compared with 100%, respectively). In addition, there was no clear difference between definitionally true conclusions and empirically true ones (86.4% compared with 90.9%). It is important to note that while subjects do select believed conclusions in the LC condition, such errors represent only 2% of all responses—an insignificant component of the total data.

There are at least two aspects of these findings that are critical for the Conversion Model. First, reasoners tend to make rational judgments even when such decisions conflict with their personal knowledge: There is only a small tendency to select believed conclusions when they conflict with logic. Second, when students fail to reach logical conclusions, it is not due to a total suspension of rationality in favor of personal biases: Only a small proportion of errors can be attributed to belief in the conclusions.

Experiment 2

If reasoners are not selecting the appropriate conclusion to syllogisms based on real-world truth values of the propositions, how do we account for the traditional finding of personal biases in formal judgments? The Conversion Model directs our attention not to the believability of the conclusions but to the personal encodings of the premises of the syllogism. When students are asked to reason about real-world, familiar categories, they may inadvertently fail to code the relations expressed in the problems with the appropriate contextual tags (cf. Anderson & Bower, 1973). That is, when the premises contain information about categories that are already available in the reasoners' long-term memories, they may provide the working memory with more information than was contained in the presented material. If one accepts the notion that the meaning of terms is, at least in part, determined by the immediate relations into which those terms enter in LTM (cf. Collins & Quillian, 1969), then even a simple semantic reading of the premises might entail "awareness" of relations among categories not specifically called for in the reasoning problem. Hence, the reasoner is making his judgments based on too much information and not on the specific content of the problem. And, of course, this is the hallmark of the effect of personal biases on syllogistic reasoning.

One way in which this may be manifested is in terms of the kinds of immediate inferences that the reasoners are willing to make when presented a proposition. For example, when shown the abstract relation, "All A are B," reasoners are quite willing to infer that it is also the case that "All B are A." But, as stated earlier, they may block conversion in some concrete relations as a function of their pragmatic implication. It is this kind of use of LTM or personal knowledge that the Conversion Model claims will affect the validity judgments on categorical syllogisms.

As discussed in an earlier section, Revlis (1975a) has already shown that reasoners' decisions change predictably as a function of whether the premises of the syllogism are converted or blocked when students encode neutral premises that describe relatively arbitrary relations. Of interest, however, is whether such an effect can be shown when the reasoners encode premises with controversial materials of the sort that has long been associated with belief-bias in syllogistic reasoning.

To test the hypothesis that the belief-bias effect is related to the personalized representation of the premises of a syllogism (and not to faulty inference rules), 34 students were asked to solve 16 syllogisms of the type shown below; the premises of these syllogisms had real-world truth values (of a sort) and were of a controversial nature. However, the conclusions were quite neutral. In this way, we felt we could isolate the effects of premise encoding from response biases in the selection of conclusions (see Experiment 1):

> (9) All blacks in Neuberg are welfare recipients.
> Some welfare recipients in Neuberg are residents of Pennton.
> Therefore:
> (a) All residents of Pennton are black;
> (b) No residents of Pennton are black;
> (c) Some residents of Pennton are black;
> (d) Some residents of Pennton are not black;
> (e) None of the above is proven.

Clearly, with such problems as (9), only the premises have a pre-experimental meaning to the reasoners—the relation between *blacks* and *welfare recipients*. Certainly, the reasoners have no knowledge about a mythical community of Neuberg and its residents, but they very well may have knowledge about the categories of *blacks* and *welfare recipients*. Indeed, it was expected that some of the reasoners would actually believe the converse of the major premise in syllogism (9)—i.e., that "All welfare recipients are black." If so, they should readily accept conclusion (d) since it logically follows from an identity encoding: *Blacks* and *welfare recipients* are coextensive groups.

In contrast, those reasoners who do not accept the converse of the major premise should not accept conclusion (d) and should respond by noting that conclusion (e) is the only logical conclusion.

To assess the kind of knowledge that such reasoners bring to bear in their encoding of these propositions, the students were asked to complete a 50-item questionnaire that was ostensibly designed to determine the breadth of knowledge of civics among Introductory Psychology students. Half of the students completed the questionnaire before seeing the reasoning task while the remaining half of the students completed the questionnaire following the task. The items on the questionnaire permitted us to determine separately the knowledge of the students on such topics as "What percentage of American

Table 5. Conditional Probabilities of Accepting Conversion Conclusions

Encoding	Questionnaire		Total
	First	Second	
Converted	.769	.819	.794
Blocked	.181	.333	.257

blacks are welfare recipients?" and in another question (25 items away), "What percentage of American welfare recipients are black?" By putting together the answers to these and other questions, we were able to characterize the reasoner as either a converter or nonconverter for each syllogism and to make predictions concerning the answers that would be logically dictated by the hypothesized encoding of the reasoner.

The results of this experiment are presented in Table 5, which shows that the conditional probability of selecting the "converted" response is considerably greater if the reasoner is a "converter" than if the reasoner did not convert the major premise of the syllogism.

The findings of these two experiments lend support to the contentions of the Conversion Model that the effect of personal biases on syllogistic reasoning judgments—shown so often in the literature—is, at least to a considerable degree, related to the reasoners' encodings of the premises of the syllogism and not to a suspension of rationality when making logical judgments. When faced with a conclusion that they must logically select but personally disbelieve, students overwhelmingly accept the logical nature of the task and make a rational choice. When asked to reason about controversial—if not emotional—material, students do not suspend rational choice, but rather their decisions are judicious ones flowing logically from their idiosyncratic understanding of the materials reasoned about.

IMPLICATIONS OF THE CONVERSION MODEL

The previous sections describe the Conversion Model of Formal Inference and detail how it accounts for the accuracy of students when they are asked to solve categorical syllogisms. This model has three noteworthy advantages over previous hypotheses or models of formal inference. First, it is able to account for the decisions of students on concrete as well as abstract syllogisms. Second, it is internally consistent in that it carried through its underlying assumption of human rationality to decisions which appear to be irrational. Third, its most salient feature is that it makes explicit, testable predictions concerning the decisions that students will reach on every syllogism. On this last point it should be noted that alternative hypotheses (e.g., the "atmosphere" hypothesis of Sells [1936], the "probabilistic inference" hypothesis of Chapman and Chapman [1959], the Structural Model of Johnson-Laird [1975]) all express their predictions in terms of response tendencies and describe a multitude of interpretations and decisions. Only the Conversion Model presents a completely determined approach: Each response is predicted. Consequently, the model can be evaluated in terms of its predictive accuracy. For example, the Conversion Model accurately predicts 70% of the decisions on abstract syllogisms (Revlis, 1975a), 74% of the decisions on neutral concrete problems (where conversion is permitted), and 70.3% on neutral concrete problems where conversion is blocked (Revlin, Ammerman, Petersen, & Leirer, in preparation).

Perhaps the most singularly important advantage of the present model over previous ones is that the Conversion Model offers a common framework for understanding decision-making with a variety of materials: abstract, concrete, blocked, converted, emotional, and neutral. This offers the possibility of a theoretical unification of apparently disparate paradigms and findings during the past half century of research on categorical reasoning. The model does this by focusing on the reasoner's encoding of variously quantified sentences and by assuming rational decision processes.

In the experiments presented here, we have undertaken to show that the Conversion Model can account for the apparent reasoning bias that historically has been said to act "irrationally" to interrupt logical processing (leading to the acceptance of conclusions that have prior belief values). The model accomplishes this without having to posit post hoc mechanisms or without having to violate its underlying assumption that the decisions people reach are based on logical operations applied to their understanding of the materials reasoned about. The Conversion Model claims that Long-Term Memory and normal language comprehension mechanisms participate in the encoding of the syllogisms' premises. The reasoner's decisions reflect his understanding of the materials—a personalized representation from whence rational decisions are made.

The Conversion Model traces its intellectual naissance to the theorizing of Henle (Henle, 1962; Henle & Michael, 1956). The model extends Henle's work by incorporating many of her tacit assumptions and careful observations. For example, it was the data by Henle and Michael (1956) which first systematically showed that the reasoner's belief in the real-world truth of the conclusions was irrelevant to his decisions. Using a questionnaire to assess students' beliefs, Henle found that the most frequently expressed attitude rarely corresponded to the most frequently accepted conclusion. In addition,

Henle's (1962) review of the literature guided our assumption that the reasoner's encoding of the premises was the key to his apparent irrationality. It is to Henle's credit that a model which embodied her speculations on a subset of concrete problems could account for decisions on a wide range of syllogisms. We, of course, take full responsibility for the shortcomings of the model. Some areas of difficulty for the model are described below, along with suggestions for how they might be approached by our program.

Encoding

Although the model emphasizes the reasoner's overall rationality, the very presence of a conversion operator may be viewed as an irrationality in an otherwise logical system. Why, e.g., should a student restrict his interpretation of quantified sentences in just the way we claim? Earlier, we suggested three pragmatic sources that give impetus to conversion: (a) ambiguity of the relational term, (b) communicative presupposition, and (c) an initial, simplifying assumption of symmetry. We also suggested that these sources of conversion are of a piece with the rules of normal English usage. We would argue that the presence of a conversion operation would only be irrational in those cases where it was used inappropriately. For example, conversion could be said to be irrational if it leads to an immediate inference that the reasoner knew to be false. Notice that when reasoners are confronted with such situations (e.g., "All horses are animals"), the evidence shows that they block conversion and use a more restricted interpretation (see Table 2). This selective and appropriate use of conversion (though not necessarily conscious) argues for its rational basis.

The fact that the conversion operator is part and parcel of English usage is illustrated by a sentence comprehension task. In one such study Revlin and Leirer (in preparation) asked students to verify quantified sentences against Euler diagrams under various conditions of time pressure. One particular source of the subjects' errors in pertinent here. The most frequent error when students saw sentences of the form "All A are B" was to accept as *true* diagrams where B was a subset of A—just the result that we would expect if students understood "All A are B" to mean "All B are A." Taken together, the foregoing data suggest the normative basis for conversion in the encoding of quantified relations.

Deduction

As the project to test the Conversion Model unfolded, we experienced a certain amount of disappointment because we had anticipated that the project would necessitate the discovery and construction of logical rules of analysis. These rules would have to be described if the reasoner's logical competence was to be accounted for—or so we thought. The model relies so heavily on the premise encoding, however, that the logical, data manipulation rules were not necessary for the model's predictions. We are still obliged to formulate such rules, however, since our intention is to present as complete a model as necessary; and certainly, we wish to account for the *logic* in logical thinking (cf. Siegler, 1976).

The operation of logical rules is not confined to a single stage in the model (we have avoided labeling Stage 2 a "deduction stage"): Logic inheres in the entire structure. Such rules are implicit in the reasoner's ability to gloss the input premises, in the kind of representation (or formalism) necessary for constructing a composite representation, and, of course, in the "read-off" mechanism that examines the composite representation and produces a candidate conclusion. It is a large order, therefore, to have to account for all of the logical rules (or data manipulation rules) that reasoners might bring to bear in reaching a conclusion. Our current efforts are concentrated on trying to express the immediate inference rules that might be applied to the initial encoding of the premises (since this is the cornerstone of the model). While the "read-off" rules might appear to be the more exciting finding, their nature is dependent on the representation posited for the initial encoding and on the type of concatenation rules that produce the composite representation. While Erickson's model (see Chap. 2) appears to have settled on the appropriate formalism for the quantified premises, the rules for selecting the appropriate diagram are not obvious—much remains to be done with both of our models.

Decision

The Conversion Model claims that the reasoner selects the conclusion that matches the COMP representation (Stage 4) and that the encoding of the potential conclusions is identical to the encoding of the premises (see Stage 3). We are currently exploring two alternative descriptions of the decision stage and the conclusion-encoding stage. First, it is entirely possible that the conclusions are encoded at the same level in the meaning stack as are the premises in the COMP stack. For example, as a result of repeated PASSES through the problem, the COMP stack may be at the level of [±Universal], [±Affirmative]; however, it is uncertain at what level of the conclusion's meaning stack the comparisons with the COMP stack are made. If the reasoner were popping the meaning stack for the conclusions while he does so for the COMP stack, then the conclusion meaning stack and the COMP stack would be at the same level, and the comparisons would be readily made. However, this would require large memory commitments since the reasoner would not only have to store the COMP stack, but he would also have to store individual stacks for each of the conclusions. We conjecture that the reasoner's encoding of the conclusions proceeds anew for each comparison, but that the level of encoding of the conclusions reaches only to the level in the COMP stack. Thus, in the example just given, the conclusions would only be encoded up to the features [±Universal], [±Affirmative]. We are currently examining this hypothesis using decision-time data since the encoding and comparison times should decrease with each succeeding PASS through the problem.

An alternative description of the encoding and comparison stages is that the reasoners' decisions are not the result of a simple comparison process but instead reflect an *entailment* match. In this case, the reasoner is said to fully encode the conclusions, but rather than comparing the encoding with the COMP stack—feature by feature—the reasoner tests whether the COMP representation *follows from* the conclusion. That is, the process is one of the induction from the conclusion rather than deduction from the premises (cf. Henle, 1971). We are currently exploring this possibility using complex, concrete materials since abstract sentences have too restrictive an interpretation to permit a differentiation between these alternative views of the encoding and comparison stages. While several questions of detail remain to be resolved, the Conversion Model appears to be sufficiently robust that these and other concerns do not pose special problems.

It is important, however, to raise a more general issue: What does performance on categorical syllogisms tell us about (a) human rationality in natural contexts, or (b) the general human capacity for rational decision-making? To answer the first part of the question requires a model of each candidate inference situation in order to compare it with the model offered for categorical reasoning. To our knowledge, no adequate structural descriptions exist for natural situations such as (a) class inclusion judgments in prose passages, (b) conversational implicature with class inclusion relations, (c) jury decision-making, (d) scientific thinking. Until researchers in these areas express their findings in terms of processing models, commonalities across situations will be obscured, and we will not be able to test the generality of anyone's findings.

To answer the second part of the question, concerning the general human capacity for rational decision-making, it is not necessary that the Conversion Model be able to account for decisions on any task other than categorical reasoning. Syllogisms serve as a task to assess human rational competence. As such, it permits us to posit a sufficient set of mechanisms that humans must possess to produce their decisions. As more knowledge is acquired about a variety of inference situations, we may find that similar mechanisms may be posited (the very presence of the Conversion Model suggests that it may serve as a normative model in this regard and prompt the analysis of new tasks in terms of its mechanisms). As a result, it is possible that a small set of processes—assembled in various ways—may be able to account for the decisions reached in a variety of natural inference situations. We are confident that as data from such situations become available and as the Conversion Model becomes more refined as a process model, both the components and extent of human rationality will be specified.

REFERENCES

Anderson, J., & Bower, G. *Human associative memory.* Washington, D.C.: Winston, 1973.

Chapman, L., & Chapman, J. Atmosphere effect re-examined. *Journal of Experimental Psychology,* 1959, **58**, 220–226.

Clark, H. Linguistic processes in deductive reasoning. *Psychological Review,* 1969, **76**, 387–404.

Cohen, M., & Nagel, E. *An introduction to logic.* New York: Harcourt, 1934.

Collins, A., & Quillian, M. Retrieval time from semantic memory. *Journal of Verbal Learning and Verbal Behavior,* 1969, **8**, 240–248.

Dickstein, L. Effects of instructions and premise order on errors in syllogistic reasoning. *Journal of Experimental Psychology: Human Learning and Memory,* 1975, **1**, 376–384.

Dickstein, L. Differential difficulty of categorical syllogisms. *Bulletin of the Psychonomic Society,* 1976, **8**, 330–332.

Erickson, J. A set analysis theory of behavior in formal syllogistic reasoning tasks. In R. L. Solso (Ed.), *Theories of cognitive psychology: The Loyola symposium.* Hillsdale, N.J.: Erlbaum, 1974.

Feather, N. Acceptance and rejection of arguments in relation to attitude strength, critical ability, and intolerance of inconsistency. *Journal of Abnormal and Social Psychology,* 1965, **69**, 127–136.

Frase, L. Validity judgments of syllogisms in relation to two sets of terms. *Journal of Educational Psychology,* 1966, **57**, 239–244.

Gordon, D., & Lakoff, G. Conversational postulates. *Papers from the Seventh Regional Meeting of the Chicago Linguistic Society.* Chicago: University of Chicago Press, 1971.

Gordon, R. Attitudes toward Russia on logical reasoning. *Journal of Social Psychology,* 1953, **37**, 103–111.

Grice, H. *The logic of conversation: William James lectures.* Cambridge, Mass.: Harvard University Press, 1967.

Haviland, S., & Clark, H. Acquiring new information as a process in comprehension. *Journal of Verbal Learning and Verbal Behavior.* 1974, **13**, 512–521.

Henle, M. On the relation between logic and thinking. *Psychological Review,* 1962, **69**, 366–378.

Henle, M. On the scholler of nature. *Social Research,* 1971, **38**, 93–107.

Henle, M., & Michael, M. The influence of attitudes on syllogistic reasoning. *Journal of Social Psychology,* 1956, **44**, 115–127.

Horn, L. *On the semantic properties of logical operators in English.* Unpublished doctoral dissertation, University of California, Los Angeles, 1972.

Janis, I., & Frick, P. The relationship between attitudes toward conclusions and errors in judging logical validity of syllogisms. *Journal of Experimental Psychology*, 1943, **33**, 73–77.

Janis, I., & Terwilliger, R. An experimental study of psychological resistances to fear arousing communications. *Journal of Abnormal and Social Psychology*, 1962, **65**, 403–410.

Johnson-Laird, P. N. Models of deduction. In R. Falmagne (Ed.), *Reasoning: Representation and process.* Hillsdale, N.J.: Erlbaum, 1975.

Kaufman, H., & Goldstein, S. The effects of emotional value of conclusions upon distortions in syllogistic reasoning. *Psychonomic Science*, 1967, **7**, 367–368.

Lakoff, G. Linguistics and natural logic. *Synthese*, 1970, **22**, 151–271.

Lefford, A. The influence of emotional subject matter on logical reasoning. *Journal of General Psychology*, 1946, **34**, 127–151.

McGuire, W. A syllogistic analysis of cognitive relationships. In M. Rosenberg & C. Hovland (Eds.), *Attitude organization and change.* New Haven: Yale University Press, 1960.

Meyer, D. On the representation and retrieval of stored semantic information. *Cognitive Psychology*, 1970, **1**, 242–299.

Morgan, J., & Morton, J. The distortion of syllogistic reasoning produced by personal convictions. *Journal of Social Psychology,* 1944, **20**, 39–59.

Morgan, W., & Morgan, A. Logical reasoning: With and without training. *Journal of Applied Psychology*, 1953, **37**, 399–401.

Parrott, G. *The effects of premise content on accuracy and solution time in syllogistic reasoning.* Unpublished Masters thesis, Michigan State University, 1967.

Parrott, G. *The effects of instructions, transfer, and content on reasoning.* Unpublished doctoral dissertation, Michigan State University, 1969.

Revlis, R. Syllogistic reasoning: Logical decisions from a complex data base. In R. Falmagne (Ed.), *Reasoning: Representation and process.* Hillsdale, N.J.: Erlbaum, 1975. (a)

Revlis, R. Two models of syllogistic reasoning: Feature selection and conversion. *Journal of Verbal Learning and Verbal Behavior*, 1975, **14**, 180–195. (b)

Revlis, R., Ammerman, K., Petersen, K., & Leirer, V. *Category relations and syllogistic reasoning.* In preparation.

Revlin, R., & Leirer, V. *The belief-bias effect in formal reasoning: The influence of knowledge on logic.* In preparation.

Sells, S. The atmosphere effect: An experimental study of reasoning. *Archives of Psychology*, 1936, **29**, 3–72.

Siegler, R. Where is the logic? *Contemporary Psychology*, 1976, **21**, 462–464.

Thistlethwaite, D. Attitude and structure as factors in the distortion of reasoning. *Journal of Abnormal and Social Psychology*, 1950, **45**, 442–458.

Wilkins, M. The effect of changed material on ability to do formal syllogistic reasoning. *Archives of Psychology*, 1928, **16**, 83.

Wilson, W. The effect of competition on the speed and accuracy of syllogistic reasoning. *Journal of Social Psychology*, 1965, **65**, 27–32.

Winthrop, H. Semantic factors in the measurement of personality integration. *Journal of Social Psychology*, 1946, **24**, 149–175.

THE NATURE OF DENIED PROPOSITIONS IN THE CONDITIONAL SENTENCE REASONING TASK: INTERPRETATION AND LEARNING

Herman Staudenmayer
New School for Social Research

Lyle E. Bourne, Jr.
University of Colorado

In this study we are investigating the effect of two forms of denial, denial by *negation* and denial by *affirmation*, on the inferences made in reasoning. When denial is by explicit negation, i.e., *not* is used, the affirmed (p and q) and denied ($\bar{p}$ and $\bar{q}$) logical classes of the antecedent and consequent, respectively, are linguistically represented by binary expressions, e.g., p and *not p*. But when denial is by affirmed alternatives, the linguistic representation of the logical classes can be binary or nonbinary, depending on the number of actual alternatives or elements representing the $\bar{p}$ and $\bar{q}$ classes. Thus, the nature of denial inherent in the materials used to represent the propositions,

The data for this chapter were collected at the Institute for the Study of Intellectual Behavior, University of Colorado. The work was supported by a research grant, MH-14314, and by a Research Scientist Award, 1-KS-MH37497, both from the National Institute of Mental Health, and a research grant, GB-340-77X, from the National Science Foundation. We would like to thank John Loder for his assistance in running subjects and the initial preparation of the data for analysis.

A part of this chapter was presented at the meeting of the American Psychological Association in Washington, D.C., September 1976.

Table 1. Always (A), Sometimes (S), and Never (N) Response Evaluations on the Eight Forms of the Conditional Argument for the BIC and COND When the Denied Propositions Represent the Logical p and q Classes, and Elements Within These Classes

Rule	Nature of $\bar{p}$ and $\bar{q}$	Affirming the antecedent	Denying the antecedent		Affirming the consequent		Denying the consequent		
		pq	$\bar{p}\bar{q}$	$\bar{p}q$	$\bar{p}\bar{q}$	qp	$\bar{q}\bar{p}$	$\bar{q}p$	$\bar{q}\bar{p}$
BIC	Class	A	N	N	A	A	N	N	A
	Elements	A	N	N	S	A	N	N	S
COND	Class	A	N	S	S	S	S	N	A
	Elements	A	N	S	S	S	S	N	A

at least to some extent, delineates the possible inferences that can be (or need be) made about the relations between representations of the classes of the antecedent and consequent propositions. How the nature of denial affects the processing strategies and the interpretation of conditionals is an empirical question. We address this question using the syllogistic sentence reasoning task (Taplin & Staudenmayer, 1973), first in an interpretation study and then, in a learning study.

In sentence reasoning, there are two common interpretations people make in evaluating conclusions of syllogisms based on the premise "If p, then q." These interpretations are the conditional (COND) and biconditional (BIC), defined in terms of logical truth tables. These interpretations are inferred, based on the pattern of evaluations of the eight forms of the argument presented in Table 1. A detailed description of the inference procedure is presented and discussed elsewhere (Staudenmayer, 1975; Taplin & Staudenmayer, 1973).

The considerations required for accurate evaluations change with the nature of denial for two forms of the argument, (a) denying the antecedent with a negative conclusion ($\bar{p}\bar{q}$: given "If p, then q," the subject is told that "$\bar{p}$ is true" and is asked if "$\bar{q}$ is true"), and (b) denying the consequent with a negative conclusion ($\bar{q}\bar{p}$: given "If $\bar{p}$, then $\bar{q}$," the subject is told that "$\bar{q}$ is true" and is asked if "$\bar{p}$ is true"). Specifically, when more than one alternative is used to represent each of the logical classes $\bar{p}$ and $\bar{q}$, a type of indeterminancy exists in the relation of the elements of one class to the elements of the other. Any element of one class (e.g., $\bar{p}$) can be paired with any element of the other ($\bar{q}$) in such a way that the conclusion to arguments involving both of these classes is indeterminate (see illustration in following paragraph). We shall refer to this as *within*-logical class indeterminancy. This consideration is sufficient for subjects to respond without evaluating what we shall refer to as *between*-logical class indeterminancy. This latter form of indeterminancy is exemplified in conditions in which the antecedent and consequent are represented by logical classes, as in the case with explicit negation. Given one logical class as a premise (e.g., $\bar{p}$), either the affirmed or the denied class of the other proposition (i.e., q and $\bar{q}$) can occur in the conclusion.

The distinctions we are making can be clarified with an illustration. As a first premise you are given the conditional sentence "If there is an A on the front, then there is a 1 on the back," which describes the relationship between vowels and numbers with respect to the front or back of hypothetical cards, modeled after Wason's (1966) original materials. To make our example hold for both the COND and the BIC, we will use the argument $\bar{q}\bar{p}$ because the considerations are the same for both rules. When explicit negatives *not A* and *not 1* are used to express the logical classes $\bar{p}$ and $\bar{q}$ respectively, the denied propositions logically represent the class of all things other than $\bar{p}$ and $\bar{q}$. Questions about the contingency between propositions in terms of truth table rules are based at the level of classes. Thus, given "There is not a 1 on the back" as a second premise, you are to evaluate the conclusion "There is not an A on the front" as either *always, sometimes*, or *never.* According to both the COND and BIC, you can never have an *A* on the front when there is *not a 1* on the back; therefore, it follows from simple noncontradiction that there must always be a *not A* on the front. The point is that this consideration of noncontradiction between arguments is necessary to make an evaluation of some forms of the argument so long as the logical $\bar{p}$ and $\bar{q}$ classes are not further delineated into elements.

When $\bar{p}$ and $\bar{q}$ each represent a set of elements, it is not necessary to consider this noncontradiction between arguments in evaluating the two forms of the argument involving $\bar{p}$ and $\bar{q}$. Instead, the evaluation can be made based on the indeterminancy of the relationships among the elements within each of the $\bar{p}$ and $\bar{q}$ classes. In terms of effort or difficulty of processing, it may be easier to evaluate these arguments when noncontradiction between arguments need not be considered. To illustrate, let the antecedent be represented by five vowels $\{A, E, I, O, U\}$ and the consequent by five numbers $\{1, 2, 3, 4, 5\}$. Letting $p = A$ and $q = 1$, $\bar{p}$ represents the set $\{E, I, O, U\}$, and $\bar{q}$ represents the set $\{2, 3, 4, 5\}$. The point about the indeterminancy of the relation between specific elements within these classes can again be explained with denying the consequent. As a second premise you are given "There is a 2 on the back" ($\bar{q}$) and asked to evaluate the conclusion "There is an E on the front" ($\bar{p}$). While E is one acceptable possibility because it represents $\bar{p}$, it is not the only possibility because I, O, and U also represent $\bar{p}$. Given one element of $\bar{q}$ you cannot uniquely specify which element in $\bar{p}$ will occur and, therefore, the indeterminate response is appropriate. The same is true if you are given $\bar{p}$ and asked to evaluate $\bar{q}$.

The patterns of response evaluations across the eight forms of the argument change when the denied propositions are interpreted to represent either the logical $\bar{p}$ and $\bar{q}$ classes or elements within these classes. The patterns are represented in Table 1 for both the BIC and the COND, with the nature of $\bar{p}$ and $\bar{q}$ designated as class and elements.

The use of specific alternatives to deny p and q raises another important consideration, the number of alternatives or elements in the p and q logical classes. When the antecedent and consequent propositions are binary, only one alternative represents $\bar{p}$, and only one represents $\bar{q}$. In the example sentence above, the antecedent might only be denied by an E and the consequent only by a 2. Formally, it is possible to equivalence the element and the class for both $\bar{p}$ and $\bar{q}$. However, psychologically there may be differences in interpretation since the instances or referents representing the $\bar{p}$ and $\bar{q}$ classes are specified in the binary alternative situation but unspecified in the situation using explicit negation. The importance of the size of the alternate classes has been demonstrated in categorical reasoning (Revlin & Leirer, Chap. 4) and in induction tasks (Wyer & Podeschi, Chap. 4).

EXPERIMENT 1: INTERPRETATION

This experiment explores how subjects interpret the sentence "If p, then q" in a sentence reasoning task when the antecedent and consequent propositions are explicitly denied with *not* or implicitly denied by affirmed alternatives. In addition, the nature of the alternatives representing $\bar{p}$ and $\bar{q}$ are manipulated so that the antecedent and consequent are analogous to binary and nonbinary dimensions.

One question we would like to consider is how subjects will interpret the antecedent and consequent when p and $\bar{p}$ and q and $\bar{q}$ are represented by specific binary values, respectively. Will the alternatives be interpreted as truth table classes? Or would they be interpreted as elements of the $\bar{p}$ and $\bar{q}$ logical classes, even though no other alternatives are explicitly present in the stimulus sequence?

A second question under consideration is how the nature of the denial of the propositions affects the truth table interpretation of the relations between the antecedent and consequent, BIC or COND. Using the explicit negative *not* in the conditional sentence reasoning task, Taplin and Staudenmayer (1973, Experiment 2) found more subjects interpreting the COND than the BIC. To date, there have been no studies using the sentence reasoning task with abstract material that use affirmed alternatives to deny p and q. Again, when alternatives are used for denial, the binary or nonbinary nature of the propositions must be considered.

Method

Subjects. The study sample consisted of 120 undergraduate students, recruited from the University of Colorado subject pool and run in groups of about 15; 40 subjects were assigned to each of three experimental conditions.

Stimulus materials and design. The eight forms of the argument were presented as syllogisms of the form:

Given: If there is an A on the front,
        then there is a 1 on the back.

And: There is an A on the front.

Evaluate: There is a 1 on the back.

These syllogisms were prepared for presentation as 2×2 slides. Three different forms of denial defined the three between-subject experimental conditions. In the Explicit Negation condition, denial was expressed as *not A* and *not 1*. In the Binary Alternative condition, denial was expressed with one specific alternative, e.g., $\overline{p} = E$, $\overline{q} = 2$. In the Nonbinary Alternatives condition, denial of each proposition was expressed by one of four alternatives, with a different alternative used for each denial of a proposition within one replication of the eight forms of the argument. For example, the eight forms shown as pairs of second premise and conclusion might be: $pq = A1$, $p\overline{q} = A2$, $\overline{p}q = E1$, $\overline{p}\,\overline{q} = I3$, $qp = 1A$, $q\overline{p} = 10$, $\overline{q}p = 4A$, $\overline{q}\,\overline{p} = 5U$.

Procedure. The nature of the task was explained by written instructions which the experimenter also read aloud to the subject before the experiment. A careful explanation was given for the meaning of the three response alternatives, *always, sometimes,* and *never.* All subjects worked 10 problems, each consisting of the 8 forms of the argument with order randomized for each problem. The content of p and q was changed for each problem, so that each of the five vowels and each of the five numbers served twice as the affirmed proposition, but never in the same pairing. The slides were presented at the rate of one about every 20 seconds. Subjects recorded their answers on each trial on a response sheet which was collected at the end of the session.

Results

Interpretation. Subjects were classified into two main categories, based on the pattern of responses to the eight forms of the argument presented in Table 1. The first category included those subjects who were consistent on at

Table 2. Classification of 40 Individuals Under Each Form of Denial as Interpretable or Uninterpretable According to Response Patterns in Table 1

Form of denial	Class		Elements		Uninterpretable
	BIC	COND	BIC	COND	
Explicit Negation[a]	5	23	–	–	12
Binary Alternative[b]	–	–	8	18	14
Nonbinary Alternatives[c]	–	–	13	13	14

[a]E.g., when p = A and q = 1, then $\overline{p}$ = not A, $\overline{q}$ = not 1.
[b]E.g., $\overline{p}$ = E, $\overline{q}$ = 2.
[c]E.g., $\overline{p}$ = (E, I, O, U), $\overline{q}$ = (2, 3, 4, 5).

least 6 of the 8 forms of the argument (for each form, at least 7 responses in one response category across 10 problems) and uniquely interpretable as BIC or COND. The second category included subjects who were inconsistent on more than two arguments and subjects who had a consistent pattern of responses other than the COND or BIC. The results for the three experimental conditions are presented in Table 2. The number of subjects who showed an uninterpretable pattern of responses was the same in all three conditions. The pattern of evaluations of the eight forms of the argument for individual subjects varied across the three conditions both in the interpretation of $\overline{p}$ and $\overline{q}$ as representing a class or elements and in the truth table meaning of the sentence, BIC or COND, as shown in Table 1. As expected, all of the subjects who had an interpretable truth table rule in the Explicit Negation condition interpreted *not p* and *not q* as representing the $\overline{p}$ and $\overline{q}$ classes, and all of the subjects in the Nonbinary Alternatives condition interpreted the explicit alternatives to be elements of $\overline{p}$ and $\overline{q}$. In the Binary Alternative condition, subjects did not interpret the one alternative representing $\overline{p}$ and $\overline{q}$, respectively, to be equivalent to those logical classes. Instead, they assumed there were other alternatives, even though they were not presented within any given problem. A simple explanation is that changing letters and numbers for each of the 10 problems induced this assumption. However, when the results for these individuals were analysed problem-by-problem, there was no indication that subjects started the problems interpreting the single alternatives as representations of the $\overline{p}$ and $\overline{q}$ classes and then switched to the many alternatives interpretation in later problems.

In evaluating the effect of the form of denial on the interpreted truth table meaning, COND or BIC, the class-elements distinction was ignored, and the overall comparison of the three conditions was significant, $\chi^2(2) = 6.40$, $p < .05$. The COND interpretation was more common among subjects in the Explicit Negation condition, $\chi^2(1) = 11.57$, $p < .001$, consistent with Taplin and Staudenmayer (1973). The same pattern occurred in the Binary Alternative condition, $\chi^2(1) = 3.85$, $p = .05$. In contrast, the number of COND and BIC interpretations were equal in the Nonbinary Alternatives condition.

Discussion

The failure of subjects to interpret binary alternatives as representing two mutually exclusive classes raises questions about experiments in which it has been assumed that logical classes like $\overline{p}$ and $\overline{q}$ could be represented by affirmed alternatives. Most notable among these are experiments that have used Wason's selection task with the conditional sentence "If there is a vowel in the front, then there is an even number on the back." The subject is presented with four cards having examples of a vowel (p), a consonant $(\overline{p})$, an even number (q), and an odd number $(\overline{q})$. The task is to turn over only those cards necessary and sufficient to prove the sentence according to the COND interpretation. A critical assumption is that subjects will interpret the particular letters and numbers to be equivalent to the logical classes. The correct solution is to turn over only those cards that have a determined alternative on the hidden side—namely, there is always a q on the other side of p, and there is always a $\overline{p}$ on the other side of $\overline{q}$. But the determinancy of the p and q solution holds only if the letters and numbers are interpreted as logical classes. If they are interpreted as elements within the classes, p still has a determined alternative on the other side, but $\overline{q}$ does not. Looking at the results of several studies (Bracewell & Hidi, 1974; Johnson-Laird & Wason, 1970; Wason & Evans, 1975), we note that many subjects selected only p as a solution to the selection task. It is possible that these individuals interpreted the letters and numbers as representing elements within the $\overline{p}$ and $\overline{q}$ classes rather than the classes themselves.

The finding of more COND than BIC interpretations with binary propositions again emphasizes the importance of the interpreted relations rather than of the stimulus properties. This distinction between the nature of the propositions and their interpretation has important consequences to some theoretical speculation by Wason and Johnson-Laird (1972) that has been offered to explain the predominance of the BIC in conditional reasoning. They formulated some very explicit hypotheses about how the nature of the propositions will influence interpretation based on their own work and that of Legrenzi (1970). Legrenzi was specifically interested in explaining why so many subjects interpreted Wason's card selection task according to the BIC.

His argument was that subjects prefer to interpret symmetrical, one-to-one relations between different antecedent and consequent events rather than the asymmetrical relations required for the COND. Legrenzi's test involved a pin-ball-like game in which a marble was rolled down on inclined plane and deflected either to the left or to the right, lighting up a red or green light, respectively. Most subjects interpreted the situation as BIC. If the marble deflected to the left, the red light would light up; if not, it rolled to the right, and the green light would light up.

Wason and Johnson-Laird (1972, p. 59) have generalized from these results the hypothesis that binary (antecedent and consequent) propositions are more likely to lead to the BIC interpretation. This hypothesis does not necessarily follow from the Legrenzi demonstration. Not only were the propositions binary, but the mappings were symmetrical because of the mechanics of the situation. With binary, abstract propositions these same two, one-to-one mappings can be made, but they are not the only possible ones. It is also possible to interpret asymmetrical relations like those described by the COND; in the Legrenzi example, the wiring of the apparatus could be such that when the marble rolled to the right, the red or the green light would light up. With abstract binary propositions in our experiment, the majority of subjects did interpret the asymmetrical relations. Furthermore, with nonbinary alternatives there were more BICs than with binary alternatives. Thus, the nature of propositions, binary or nonbinary, is not a good predictor of the interpretation of conditional sentences. Instead, it is the subject's interpretation of possible relations between propositions that determines the truth table interpretation.

EXPERIMENT 2: LEARNING AND PROCESSING

In this experiment we are concerned with the difficulty of learning the COND and BIC, and how the stimulus manipulations for denial in Experiment 1 affect the processing of each of these interpretations. In this context, difficulty is defined in terms of the complexity of processing the relations between the antecedent and consequent propositions as reflected by the number of errors made in evaluating the arguments. There are two possible factors that could explain why the COND is more difficult to process than the BIC, indeterminacy and asymmetry.

The evaluation of an argument is indeterminate when more than one conclusion follows the given premises. Typically, when the propositions in the sentence represent logical classes, either the affirmed or denied form of the proposition is a possible conclusion, and the indeterminacy is *between* classes. For the COND, denying the antecedent and affirming the consequent are arguments reflecting this type of indeterminacy. For the BIC, again with propositions representing logical classes, only one conclusion can follow from the premises on each argument, and thus, all the relations between the antecedent and consequent are determined.

When the propositions represent elements within the logical classes (namely, $\bar{p}$ and $\bar{q}$) a different type of indeterminancy is introduced *within* classes. Given an element from one of these classes, any one of the elements from the other class can occur. It is this type of indeterminancy which is manipulated independent of the interpretation, COND or BIC, in the condition that represents $\bar{p}$ and $\bar{q}$ with multiple alternatives.

While indeterminancy may be the cause of the difficulty of interpreting the COND, it seems unlikely since all of the subjects in Experiment 1 preferred to interpret the explicit alternatives in a manner leading to more indeterminate arguments.

This brings us to the second consideration, asymmetry. For the COND the relations between the antecedent and consequent are asymmetrical, i.e., p always implies q but q does not always imply p. Consequently, in evaluating the different arguments, people must differentiate between the different orders of the propositions as second premise and conclusion in the syllogisms. For the BIC, the relations between the propositions are symmetrical, and order is irrelevant to the evaluations.

We have also speculated about the nature of the processes involved in evaluating the $\bar{p}\bar{q}$ and $\bar{q}\bar{p}$ forms of the argument when instances of $\bar{p}$ and $\bar{q}$ are equivalent to these logical classes and when they are elements within them. One way to assess these processes is to measure the difficulty subjects have in learning forms of the argument under these conditions for both the COND and BIC interpretations. The relative difficulty of processing asymmetry and indeterminancy can be determined by using both class and elements representations for $\bar{p}$ and $\bar{q}$. For example, with elements the $\bar{p}\bar{q}$ and $\bar{q}\bar{p}$ arguments are indeterminate for the BIC, but they are still symmetrical in that every element within $\bar{p}$ can be paired with every element of $\bar{q}$, and vice versa. If indeterminancy is the source of processing difficulty, then there should be an increase in the number of errors on the $\bar{p}\bar{q}$ and $\bar{q}\bar{p}$ arguments for the BIC. On the other hand, if indeterminancy is not the source of difficulty, then these arguments should be no more difficult with elements than with classes.

A specific question arises from the findings of the Binary Alternative condition in the first experiment. None of the subjects interpreted the one alternative, representing $\bar{p}$ and $\bar{q}$, respectively, as representations of these logical classes. Instead, all subjects assumed there were other alternatives that could also represent the classes, even though they were never presented. Does this finding reflect a mere preference in interpretation? If so, it should be easily overcome with feedback which treats these elements as equivalent to the logical classes they represent. Or, is there a natural tendency not to interpret specific abstract alternatives as binary, mutually exclusive classes? If that is the case, learning to overcome the interpretation of binary propositions as elements within the logical classes should be difficult, if at all possible.

Method

Subjects. A total of 250 undergraduate students were recruited from the University of Colorado subject pool and run in groups of about 12; 25 students were assigned to each of 10 experimental conditions.

Design and procedure. The three types of stimulus materials defining the three ways of denying propositions in Experiment 1 were used. These were each presented to different groups of subjects who were given feedback according to either the COND or BIC. The pattern of feedback, based on class or elements, was also varied, but not factorially since feedback based on elements would be meaningless in the condition where denial was by the explicit *not*. Thus, two separate analysis of variance (ANOVA) designs were employed. In the first, two groups were given the explicit negation materials with feedback based on class, one group learning the BIC and the other the COND. In the second, eight groups were run defined by factorially combining feedback for the Nature of the Proposition (class or elements) with Rule (BIC or COND) with type of Alternatives (binary or nonbinary). In both analyses, each subject worked all eight forms of the conditional argument, randomized within each of 10 problems. The running procedure was the same as in Experiment 1, with one exception: Feedback was given after every trial.

Results

Denial by negation. The cell means for the average number of errors on the arguments for 25 subjects working 10 problems was presented in the upper portion of Table 3. The effect of Rule was significant, $F(1,48) = 20.98$, $p < .001$, $MS_e = 15.36$, with the BIC much easier to learn than the COND. The effect of Arguments was significant, $F(7,336) = 10.18$, $p < .001$, $MS_e = 1.22$, as was the Argument by Rule interaction, $F(7,336) = 9.85$, $p < .001$, $MS_e = 1.22$. Mean errors across arguments were low and stable (S.E. = .22) for the BIC, but higher and more variable (S.E. = 1.95) for the COND, as shown in Figure 1.

Denial by affirmation. The between-subject sources of variance were evaluated against $MS_e = 11.01$. Some means for levels of factors are presented in parentheses with the level names. Binary and Nonbinary Alternatives were not significantly different, $F(1,192) = 2.53$, $p = .11$, nor were any interactions involving Alternatives. Feedback based on the Nature of the Propositions was significant, $F(1,192) = 22.74$, $p < .001$, with learning of elements (0.93) easier

Table 3. Mean Errors on the Eight Forms of the Argument for Ten Experimental Conditions

Feedback pattern			Forms of the argument									
Rule	Nature of $\bar{p}$ and $\bar{q}$	Nature of propositions	Affirming the antecedent		Denying the antecedent		Affirming the consequent		Denying the consequent		Mean	S.E.
			pq	$p\bar{q}$	$\bar{p}q$	$\bar{p}\bar{q}$	qp	$q\bar{p}$	$\bar{q}p$	$\bar{q}\bar{p}$		
					Denial by Explicit Negation							
BIC	Class	Binary	.04	.12	.20	.12	.04	.08	.28	.04	.12	.22
COND	Class	Binary	.28	.64	1.92	2.44	2.28	2.08	2.36	3.28	1.91	1.95
					Denial by Affirmed Alternatives							
BIC	Class	Binary	.08	.36	.76	1.68	.12	.52	.76	2.00	.79	1.17
		Nonbinary	.00	.28	.40	1.40	.00	.40	.44	1.32	.53	.80
	Elements	Binary	.00	.32	1.44	.88	.92	1.48	.80	1.12	.87	1.28
		Nonbinary	.08	.16	.52	.60	.08	.40	.44	.56	.36	.53
COND	Class	Binary	.68	.96	2.32	3.60	2.60	2.24	4.08	6.72	2.90	1.46
		Nonbinary	.72	1.08	2.12	3.36	2.72	1.44	3.08	6.80	2.67	1.49
	Elements	Binary	.68	1.00	1.32	.44	1.64	1.36	3.24	.48	1.27	1.10
		Nonbinary	.32	.88	1.52	.60	1.64	.144	2.92	.44	1.22	1.22

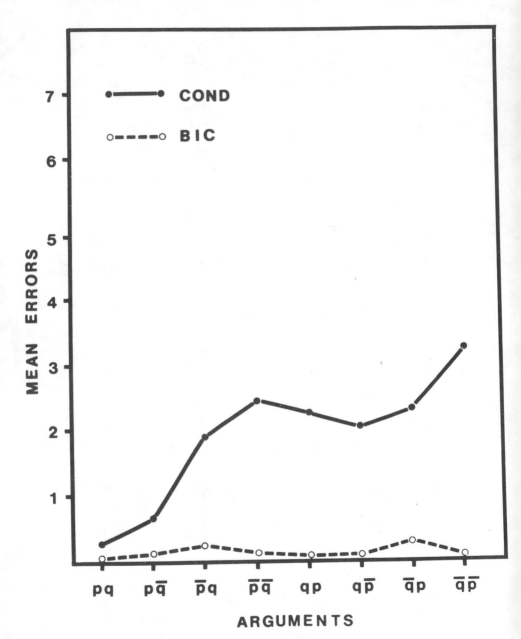

FIG. 1. Mean errors for the COND and BIC when denial is by the explicit *not* and feedback is based on treating *not p* and *not q* as representations of $\overline{p}$ and $\overline{q}$, respectively.

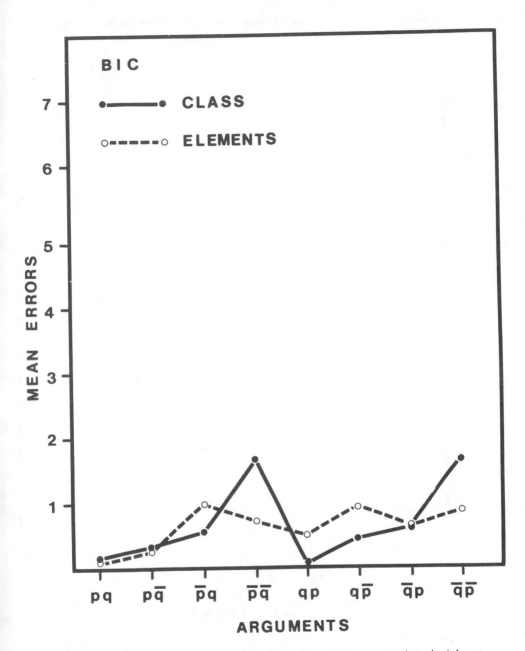

FIG. 2. Mean error for the BIC when alternatives expressing denial are treated as equivalent to the $\overline{p}$ and $\overline{q}$ classes in one feedback condition and as elements within these logical classes in another.

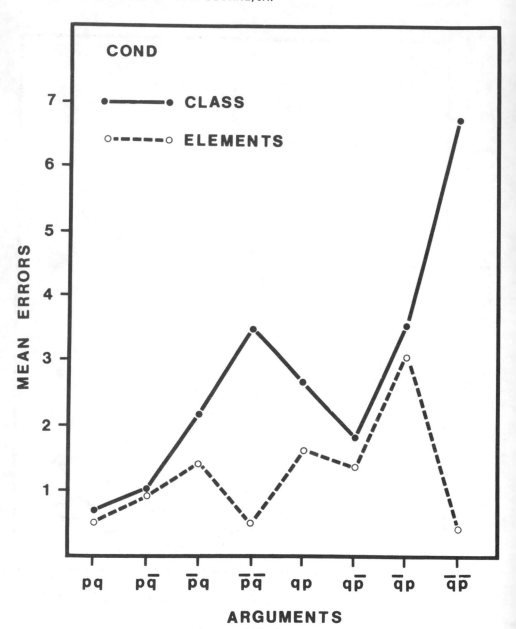

FIG. 3. Mean error for the COND when alternatives expressing denial are treated as equivalent to the $\overline{p}$ and $\overline{q}$ classes in one feedback condition and as elements within these logical classes in another.

than class (1.72). Rule was significant, $F(1,192) = 69.06$, $p < .001$, with the BIC easier (.64) than the COND (2.01). The Nature of the Propositions interacted with Rule, $F(1,192) = 20.23$, $p < .001$. The BIC was easy to learn for both class (.66) and elements (.61), but the COND was much harder with class (2.78) than elements (1.25). It is clear from this interaction that the significant main effect of the Nature of the Propositions is due primarily to the COND.

The within-subject sources of variance were evaluated against $MS_e = 1.79$. The main effect of Arguments was significant, $F(7,1344) = 51.57$, $p < .001$, as was the interaction with Rule, $F(7,1344) = 18.87$, $p < .001$, and with Nature of the Propositions, $F(7,1344) = 45.49$, $p < .001$. The three-way interaction of Arguments by Rule by Nature of the Propositions was also significant, $F(7,1344) = 21.56$, $p < .001$. The cell means from the ANOVA design are presented in the lower portion of Table 3, along with the mean and standard error for each experimental condition. Since the effect of stimulus Alternatives was not significant, the results from Binary and Nonbinary Alternatives were averaged to get a clear picture of the effects of feedback based on the Nature of the Propositions, class or elements, for the BIC and the COND.

The mean errors across arguments for learning the BIC are illustrated in Figure 2. Learning with feedback according to elements is fairly stable. However, learning with feedback according to class leads to a greater mean error on the two forms of the argument $\overline{p}\overline{q}$ and $\overline{q}\overline{p}$, that distinguish the two patterns of feedback, as shown in Table 1. This is the first indication that the interpretation of elements is more than a mere preference when denial is by affirmed alternatives. The effect is even more dramatic with the COND, as shown in Figure 3. The curves for feedback according to class and elements across arguments are again most disparate on the two forms of the argument, $\overline{p}\overline{q}$ and $\overline{q}\overline{p}$. However, only $\overline{q}\overline{p}$ has a different response under class and elements, reflecting the same indeterminancy of the mapping of elements within the $\overline{p}$ and $\overline{q}$ logical classes found in the BIC. This indeterminancy within the $\overline{p}$ and $\overline{q}$ classes is sufficient to make a *sometimes* response for the $\overline{p}\overline{q}$ argument for the COND with elements. For the COND with class feedback, the sometimes response reflects that $\overline{q}$ is possible as well as q given $\overline{p}$. In short, with elements the choice can be made because of the uncertainty of which elements within the class $\overline{q}$ will occur without considering that $\overline{q}$ may also occur. With class the uncertainty is about which class will occur, q or $\overline{q}$.

Discussion

The COND was invariably more difficult to process than the BIC. Moreover, the distribution of errors across the eight forms of the argument was homogeneous for the BIC but very heterogeneous for the COND. Two factors were proposed to account for the difficulty of the COND, indeterminancy and asymmetry. The results showed that within-class indeterminancy facilitates processing because it precludes the consideration of between-class indeterminancy and asymmetry. Thus, it is not indeterminancy per se which is the source of difficulty, and subjects are not bothered that some arguments do not have unique conclusions.

Between-class indeterminancy and asymmetry have in common the necessity to consider more than one logical class in evaluating an implication. Between-class indeterminancy must be considered in evaluating $\bar{p}q$, $q\bar{p}$, and $\bar{q}\bar{p}$ when feedback is based on elements, and $\overline{\bar{p}q}$ and $\overline{\bar{q}p}$ must be added to these when feedback is based on class. The difficulty of these arguments is shown in Figure 3 for the COND. When between-class indeterminancy is not a consideration for these arguments, as is the case for the BIC, these arguments are not more difficult, as shown in Figure 2. Asymmetry exists in two pairs of arguments, pq and qp, and $\overline{\bar{p}q}$ and $\overline{\bar{q}p}$. The latter pair of arguments are easiest when within-class indeterminancy is a relevant processing consideration and most difficult when it is not, as shown in Figure 3. With these pairs of arguments, the effect of asymmetry can be separated from the effect of between-class indeterminancy. In two of these arguments, qp and $\overline{\bar{p}q}$, the effects are confounded, but in the other two, pq and $\overline{\bar{q}p}$, only asymmetry is relevant. Since pq is virtually given in the task, it is not surprising that few, if any, errors are made on this argument. Thus, we focus on $\overline{\bar{q}p}$ to evaluate the effect of asymmetry. When asymmetry must be considered in evaluating the argument in the condition in which feedback is based on class, $\overline{\bar{q}p}$ is clearly the most difficult of all the arguments, as shown in Figure 3. But when asymmetry need not be considered in the condition in which feedback is based on elements, $\overline{\bar{q}p}$ is among the easiest arguments. In conclusion, there are two considerations that made the COND difficult to process, between-class indeterminancy and asymmetry.

These data argue against the traditional claim that students are simply unable to reason logically in a conditional reasoning task—such as the selection task (see Appendix in chapter 1). Rather, we have shown that the students' encoding of the materials in terms of the composition of the classes reasoned about have a significant impact on their evaluation of various arguments.

REFERENCES

Bourne, L. E., Jr. Knowing and using concepts. *Psychological Review*, 1970, **77**, 546–556.

Bracewell, R. J., & Hidi, S. E. The solution of an inferential problem as a function of stimulus materials. *Quarterly Journal of Experimental Psychology*, 1974, **26**, 480–488.

Johnson-Laird, P. N., & Wason, P. C. A theoretical analysis of insight into a reasoning task. *Cognitive Psychology*, 1970, **1**, 134–148.

Legrenzi, P. Relations between language and reasoning about deductive rules. In G. B. Flores D'Arcais & W. Levelt (Eds.), *Advances in psycholinguistics*. Amsterdam: North Holland, 1970.

Staudenmayer, H. Understanding conditional reasoning with meaningful propositions. In R. J. Falmagne (Ed.), *Reasoning: Representation and process*. Hillsdale, N.J.: Erlbaum, 1975.

Taplin, J. E., & Staudenmayer, H. Interpretation of abstract conditional sentences in deductive reasoning. *Journal of Verbal Learning and Verbal Behavior*, 1973, **12**, 530–542.

Wason, P. C. Reasoning. In B. Foss (Ed.), *New horizons in psychology*. Harmondsworth: Penguin, 1966.

Wason, P. C., & Evans, J. ST. B. T. Dual processes in reasoning? *Cognition*, 1975, **3**, 141–154.

Wason, P. C., & Johnson-Laird, P. N. *Psychology of reasoning: Structure and content*. Cambridge, Mass.: Harvard, 1972.

THE ACCEPTANCE OF GENERALIZATIONS ABOUT PERSONS, OBJECTS, AND EVENTS

Robert S. Wyer, Jr.
University of Illinois

Denise M. Podeschi
Washington University

Research and theory on the dynamics of human reasoning has given considerable attention to the factors that affect persons' judgments of the validity of statements of the form "All As are Bs;" "No Bs are As;:" "Some As are not Bs;" etc. This is evidenced by several chapters both in this volume (Erickson, Griggs, Revlin & Leirer) and elsewhere (Wason & Johnson-Laird, 1972). In everyday conversation, however, the statements we often make about classes of objects and events (e.g., "Businessmen are conservatives;" "College students like rock music") are less precise, in that the quantifiers of the categories described (*all, most, some*) are not always explicit. Despite this imprecision, we appear to understand the meaning of such statements, and we expect others to know what we mean when we utter them ourselves. For example, I may take exception to another's assertion that businessmen are conservative while knowing full well that many businessmen fit this

Portions of the research reported in this chapter were supported by National Science Foundation Grant SOC73-05684 to the first author. We would like to express our appreciation to Colleen Surber and Patrick Laughlin for their insightful comments on an earlier draft of the manuscript.

description; at the same time, I may agree with the assertion that college students like rock music despite the fact that several student friends of mine find rock intolerable, and that I know of some rock music that hardly any student likes. Persons' acceptance of generalizations appears to be based upon several implicit assumptions that vary with the type of relation being generalized and the types of categories being related. This chapter is concerned with an identification of certain of these assumptions.

The research to be described, and the conceptualization underlying it, were stimulated by the earlier research of Abelson and his colleagues (Abelson & Kanouse, 1965; Gilson & Abelson, 1965; Kanouse, 1971), and much of what we have to say here initially will serve only to clarify and extend upon the implications of this previous work. Two general questions will be addressed. The first concerns the extent to which a person's willingness to accept a generalization depends upon the nature of the categories described in it and the type of relation between these categories. The second concerns the manner in which the implications of different types of evidence are integrated, or combined, to arrive at an estimate of a generalization's validity.

GENERAL CONSIDERATIONS

Types of Evidence

In the typical situation to be considered in this chapter, a judge is presented three statements that bear upon a generalization of the form "As verb Bs," where A and B are two classes of elements (*tribes, bees,* etc.) and the verb describes an overt or covert reaction by As toward Bs. This evidence may be of two general types. One type, *inductive,* pertains to specific instances (or subclasses) of A and/or B (*Northern tribes, honeybees,* etc.) that are or are not related in the manner described in the generalization. The second type, *deductive,* pertains to more general categories (e.g., *primitive societies, buzzing insects*) to which A and/or B belong (i.e., to attributes of A or B). Thus, e.g., information that "Northern tribes buy bees" would be inductive evidence supporting the generalization "Tribes buy bees," while information that "Primitive societies buy bees" would be deductive evidence supporting this generalization.[1] The evidence presented may also differ in its

[1]The distinction between inductive and deductive evidence, which follows that made by Abelson and Kanouse (1966), should not be confused with a distinction between inductive and deductive *reasoning*. Similar reasoning processes could conceivably underlie the acceptance of generalizations based upon both types of evidence. For example, the conclusion "Tribes buy bees" could be inferred syllogistically from either (a) the premises "Tribes are primitive societies" and "Primitive societies buy bees," or (b) premises "Some tribes are Northern tribes" and "Northern tribes buy bees." The reasoning processes underlying these inference is, of course, a main concern of this chapter.

Table 1. Examples of Evidence of Different Types and Orientations Bearing Upon the Validity of the Generalization "Tribes Buy Bees"

	Case 1:	Case 2:
	Inductive, subject-specific evidence	Inductive, object-specific evidence
Subclass description	There are three types of tribes: Northern, Central, and Southern	There are three types of bees: bumblebees, honeybees, and sweat bees
Evidence	Northern tribes buy bees	Tribes buy bumblebees
	Central tribes buy bees	Tribes buy honeybees
	Southern tribes do not buy bees	Tribes do not buy sweat bees

	Case 3:	Case 4:
	Deductive, subject-specific evidence	Deductive, object-specific evidence
Category definition	Tribes are primitive, communal, agricultural societies	Bees are flying, buzzing, stinging insects
Evidence	Primitive societies buy bees	Tribes buy flying insects
	Communal societies buy bees	Tribes buy buzzing insects
	Agricultural societies do not buy bees	Tribes do not buy stinging insects

orientation; i.e., it may be specific to either the subject category as in the above examples; the object category (e.g., "Tribes buy honeybees;" "Tribes buy buzzing insects"); or both (e.g., "Northern tribes buy honeybees;" "Primitive societies buy buzzing insects").

The general type of stimulus materials presented in the situations to be initially considered here are shown in more detail in Table 1. Each set of inductive evidence is preceded by a statement that circumscribes the subclasses of the subject and object categories to which the evidence is specific, while each set of deductive evidence is preceded by a statement that specifies the attributes defining the category. Of the three pieces of evidence in each set, two (*confirming* evidence) support the generalization, whereas the third (*disconfirming* evidence) is inconsistent with it. (While in some studies to be described later in this chapter, the relative amounts of confirming and disconfirming evidence were varied, we will restrict our attention for the time being to this particular configuration.) In each case, judges are asked to consider the evidence presented and then to indicate the extent to which they would accept the generalization to which it pertains (in this example, "Tribes buy bees") on the basis of it.

In the four examples described in Table 1, the relative amounts of confirming and disconfirming evidence are the same. Nevertheless, these sets of evidence may have different effects on the acceptance of the generalization to which they pertain. These judgments are apt to be mediated by two general and rather obvious factors: (a) the judge's interpretation of the implications of the evidence for the number of members of A and/or B that are related in the manner specified in the generalization, and (b) the implicit quantifiers (*all, some,* etc.) that the judge assigns to A and B when interpreting the meaning of this generalization. The more universal the quantifiers assigned to A and B, the more instances of the relation are required for the generalization to be valid, and thus the less likely it is that the generalization will be accepted on the basis of a given amount of evidence. A judge's interpretation of the evidence, and the quantifiers he assigns to categories in the generalization, are likely to depend, in part, upon both the type of relation being evaluated and the types of categories entering into the relation. To give but one example, the evidence shown in Case 1 implies that some but not all tribes buy bees, while the evidence in Case 2 implies that tribes buy some but not all bees. Therefore, whether one or the other set of evidence will have greater effect may depend upon whether the implicit quantifier assigned to *tribes* is more or less universal than that assigned to *bees.* However, other factors may also be involved. To understand more clearly the nature of these factors, it will be helpful to consider in more detail the nature of the categories and relations described in a generalization and how they may affect the influence of evidence bearing upon them.

Characteristics of Categories

Types of category definitions. In the research discussed in this chapter, each class of elements described in a generalization is defined in terms of attributes (superordinate categories) that serve as criteria for membership in the class. For example, in Table 1, Case 3, *tribes* is defined as *primitive, agricultural, communal societies*, where primitive societies, agricultural societies, and communal societies are more general categories to which tribes belong. Note, however, that this definition, as stated, is ambiguous. On the one hand, it may be interpreted as *conjunctive* (i.e., as implying that tribes are primitive *and* agricultural *and* communal societies); to this extent, an object would have to belong to all three general classes in order to be a tribe. On the other hand, the definition may be interpreted as *disjunctive* (i.e., as implying that tribes are either primitive *or* agricultural *or* communal societies); in this event, an object would be classified as a tribe if it belonged to any one (or more) of the categories, without necessarily belonging to all three.

A. Case 3

(c̲= communal societies; p= primitive societies; a̲= agricultural societies)

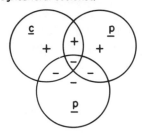

B. Case 4

(f̲ = flying insects; b̲= buzzing insects; s̲= stinging insects)

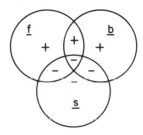

Fig. 1. Implications of deductive evidence presented in Cases 3 and 4, Table 1. Plus signs denote positive instances of the general proposition "Tribes buy bees," and minus signs denote negative instances.

The assumption that a judge makes about a category definition may affect his acceptance of a generalization on the basis of deductive evidence specific to this category. For example, consider the implications of the sets of deductive evidence shown in Table 1, Cases 3 and 4. These implications are summarized in the Venn diagrams shown in Figure 1. The effect of this evidence on the acceptance of the generalization depends upon which of the alternative combinations of attributes are assumed to define the category to which the evidence pertains. For example, if the definition of tribes is conjunctive (i.e., if tribes are defined as primitive *and* communal *and* agricultural societies), then a piece of confirming evidence (e.g., that primitive societies buy bees) does not necessarily mean that a tribe buys bees, whereas a piece of disconfirming evidence (that agricultural societies do not buy bees) is sufficient to conclude that no tribe buys bees and thus to render the generalization "Tribes buy bees" invalid. On the other hand, suppose the category definition is interpreted as disjunctive (as implying that tribes are primitive *or* communal *or* agricultural societies). Then a piece of confirming evidence *does* imply that at least some tribes buy bees, whereas a piece of disconfirming evidence does not necessarily mean that tribes do not buy them. It follows that the positive effect of confirming deductive evidence should be greater, and the negative effect of disconfirming deductive evidence should be smaller, to the extent that the definition of the category to which this evidence is specific is interpreted as disjunctive.

This analysis helps to conceptualize differences in the effect of deductive evidence pertaining to members of different types of categories. For example, Abelson and Kanouse (1966) reported that deductive evidence led to greater acceptance of a generalization if it was specific to the subject category than if it was specific to the object category. This would be expected if judges typically assumed that the definitions of subject categories, which invariably pertained to persons (tribes, foreigners, etc.), were more disjunctive than the definitions of object categories, which pertained to nonpersons (bees, cities, etc.).

Category homogeneity. A second potentially important characteristic of a category is its homogeneity, or the extent to which its members belong to the same or overlapping *sub*classes. (Specifically, the more overlapping the classes of a general category, or the more likely it is that the members of the category belong to more than one subclass, the greater the homogeneity of the category.) There are two reasons to suppose that the homogeneity of a category may affect the influence of inductive evidence pertaining to its subclasses. In the first place, it may affect the judge's perception of the implications of the evidence presented. To see this, consider the implications of the evidence presented in Table 1, Case 2, under two conditions: (a) when the subclasses (bumblebee, honeybee, and sweat bee) are mutually exclusive; (b) when these subclasses are overlapping. Venn diagrams exemplifying these two conditions are shown in Figure 2, assuming for convenience's sake that there are 30 members of each subclass. In the first (heterogeneous or nonoverlapping) subclass condition, the inductive evidence that tribes buy bumblebees and honeybees but not sweat bees implies that tribes buy 67% of all bees. However, in the second (homogeneous or overlapping subclass) condition, the evidence implies that tribes buy only 54% of all bees (i.e., only those bees that are bumblebees or honeybees but not sweat bees). Thus, a given mixture of confirming and disconfirming inductive evidence should lead

A. Mutually exclusive subclasses
(b = bumblebees ; h = honeybees ; s = sweat bees)

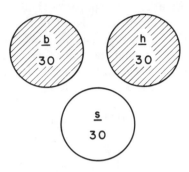

B. Overlapping subclasses

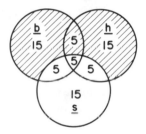

Fig. 2. Implications of inductive evidence shown in Table 1, Case 2 for the generalization "Tribes buy bees" under conditions in which the subclasses are (a) mutually exclusive, and (b) overlapping. Shaded areas indicate positive instances of the general proposition.

to greater acceptance when the category is interpreted as heterogeneous than when it is interpreted as homogeneous.

In the second place, category homogeneity may affect the implicit quantifier assigned to it. The nature of this effect (i.e., whether a more or less universal quantifier would be assigned to categories that are more heterogeneous) is not completely obvious on a priori grounds. Abelson and Kanouse (1966) found that inductive evidence specific to subject (person) categories led to less acceptance of a generalization than did inductive evidence specific to object (nonperson) categories. If, as Gilson and Abelson (1965) speculate, categories of persons are perceived to be more heterogeneous than categories of nonpersons, this would suggest that heterogeneous (person) categories are assigned more universal quantifiers. On the other hand, if person categories are, in fact, more heterogeneous, the evidence pertaining to them should have more positive implications for the validity of the generalization for reasons noted in the preceding paragraph. To this extent, inductive evidence should lead to greater acceptance of generalizations when it is subject (person)-specific rather than object (nonperson)-specific, contrary to Abelson and Kanouse's findings. Perhaps, in contrast to Gilson and Abelson's speculation, person categories are judged to be less heterogeneous than nonperson categories, and more universal quantifiers are attached to homogeneous than to heterogeneous categories. Then, both considerations descibted above (i.e., the implications of the evidence presented and the universality of the quantifiers assigned to subject and object categories) would imply less acceptance of generalizations based upon subject-specific than object-specific evidence, as Abelson and Kanouse's findings suggest. These matters will be considered in more detail in the pages to follow.

Type of Relation to be Generalized

Abelson and Kanouse (1966) identified two features of a relation that may affect the likelihood that a generalization about it is accepted. The relation may be either *manifest* (i.e., it may describe an observable action or behavior of A toward B such as *buys* or *kills*) or *subjective* (i.e., it may describe a feeling or affective reaction of A toward B such as *likes* or *fears*). The nature of this relation may affect the implicit quantifiers attached to the categories being related. A subjective relation between two elements may often be a necessary but not sufficient condition for a manifest relation between them. Consequently, e.g., tribes may be assumed to like more bees than they buy, and more tribes may be assumed to like bees than to buy them. To this extent, generalizations about subjective relations may be interpreted as pertaining to a larger number of instances than generalizations about manifest relations; alternatively, the implicit quantifiers of categories involved in subjective relations may be interpreted as relatively more universal. Therefore, a given amount of confirming evidence should have less positive effect on the acceptance of generalizations about subjective relations than on the acceptance of generalizations about manifest relations.

Both manifest and subjective relations may vary with respect to their implications for the favorableness of the subject's evaluation of the object. These implications may also be important to consider. Research on inferences based upon other types of information has frequently detected a positivity bias, i.e., a general tendency to infer a relation to be favorable rather than unfavorable (for a summary of this research, see Wyer, 1974; Zajonc, 1968). To the extent that this tendency generalizes to the conditions of concern here, judges may be more willing to accept generalizations about favorable relations (buy, like, etc.), independently of the implications of the evidence presented.

Inference Processes

The preceding analysis of the effects of inductive and deductive evidence assumes that a judge evaluates the implications of the evidence by applying principles of reasoning similar to those suggested by set theory (cf. Erickson, 1974). However, other principles may sometimes be involved. For example, judges in some instances may construe the separate implications of each piece and then may combine these implications according to an algebraic integration rule, such as summation (Fishbein & Hunter, 1964) or averaging (Anderson, 1965, 1971). For example, suppose judges receive evidence that tribes like buzzing and flying insects but not stinging insects and then are asked to estimate tribes' liking for bees. In such a case, they may arrive at their estimate by summing or averaging tribes' apparent liking for each of the individual attributes of bees, two of which (*buzzing* and *flying*) are favorable and one of which (*stinging*) is not. To this extent, the judges should infer that tribes have a moderately favorable opinion of bees and thus may accept the generalization that "Tribes like bees," regardless of whether *bees* is defined disjunctively or conjunctively. Note that a similar process seems intuitively less likely to underlie judges' inferences of manifest relations. While one's subjective reactions to an object may be a composite of one's reactions to individual attributes of the object, overt behavior must typically be directed toward an object as a whole. (E.g., if all bees are buzzing and flying and stinging, it is clearly possible to like bees without likeing stinging insects in general, provided other attributes of bees are favorable. However, it is *not* possible to buy bees without buying stinging insects.) Consequently, the acceptance of the generalization that tribes like bees may be more likely to be accepted than the generalization that tribes buy bees when part of the evidence is disconfirming.

IDENTIFICATION OF ASSUMPTIONS UNDERLYING JUDGES' USE OF INDUCTIVE AND DEDUCTIVE EVIDENCE

We have identified a large number of factors that may potentially affect the acceptance of generalizations. Certain of these factors pertain to the characteristics of the evidence presented: i.e., whether it is inductive or

Table 2. Description of Stimulus Materials Used in Experiment 1

	Subject	Object	Relation (verb)			
			Manifest favorable	Manifest unfavorable	Subjective favorable	Subjective unfavorable
		Replication 1				
Category	Tribes	Bees				
Subclasses (used in inductive evidence)	Punjabi Swahili Bengali	bumble honey sweat	buy	kill	like	dislike
Attributes (used in deductive evidence)	primitive communal agricultural	flying furry buzzing				
		Replication 2				
Category	Foreigners	American cities				
Subclasses	Italians Germans Frenchmen	Chicago New York Los Angeles	vacation in	bomb	like	dislike
Attributes	(persons with) accents (persons with) passports (persons with) travelers' checks	industrial busy populous				

Table 2. (cont'd)

	Subject	Object	Relation (verb)			
			Manifest favorable	Manifest unfavorable	Subjective favorable	Subjective unfavorable
		Replication 3				
Category	Urbanites	Magazines				
Subclasses	residents of New York City	Newsweek				
	residents of Chicago	Reader's Digest	read	destroy	like	dislike
	residents of Los Angeles	Saturday Evening Post				
Attributes	business-oriented	readable				
	active	paperbound				
	independent	lightweight				
		Replication 4				
Category	Students	Classes				
Subclasses	freshmen	history				
	sophomores	mathematics	attend	disrupt	like	dislike
	juniors	English				
Attributes	carry books	informative				
	sit in classrooms	formal				
	do homework	challenging				

deductive, whether it is specific to the subject or the object category of the proposition to be generalized, and whether it is confirming or disconfirming. Other factors pertained to characteristics of the generalization itself: i.e., whether the categories described in the generalization pertain to persons or nonpersons, whether the relation to be generalized is manifest or subjective, and whether this relation is favorable or unfavorable. The task of identifying the independent and combined effects of these factors, and understanding the reasons for these effects, is obviously complex. However, the preceding discussion suggests that the effects of these factors on the acceptance of generalizations may be a result of their mediating influence on judges' assumptions about (a) the implicit quantifiers of the categories in the generalization to which the evidence pertains, (b) the conjunctiveness of the definition of these categories, and (c) the heterogeneity of these categories. The series of experiments described below explored these possibilities. The first (Podeschi & Wyer, 1976, Experiment 1) replicated and extended upon the earlier study by Abelson and Kanouse, using a procedure that allowed a more detailed analysis of the independent and interactive effects of the type of evidence presented, the orientation of this evidence, and the type and favorableness of the relation described. Three subsequent experiments then attempted to validate several assumptions underlying the interpretation of the effects obtained in Experiment 1.

A Replication of Previous Findings

Method. Since the general procedure and stimulus materials used in this study were also applied in other experiments to be reported in this chapter, they will be described in some detail. Stimulus items were patterned after those used by Abelson and Kanouse (1966). Their general form is shown in Table 2. Four stimulus replications were constructed, each pertaining to a different pair of subject and object categories.

Three subclasses of each category were used in constructing inductive evidence, while three attributes (superordinate classes) were used in constructing deductive evidence. In addition, four verbs were selected to describe relations between the categories in each pair. One verb described a favorable manifest relation, a second described an unfavorable manifest relation, and the third and fourth described a favorable and an unfavorable subjective relation, respectively. The specific materials used in each stimulus replication are shown in Table 2.

Stimulus items representing each combination of evidence type and evidence orientation were constructed for each replication. In each item, two pieces of evidence supported the generalization to be evaluated while the third piece did not. Within each replication, all 16 combinations of evidence type

Table 3. Mean Acceptance of Conclusions Based Upon Inductive and Deductive Evidence as a Function of the Type and Evaluative Implications of the Relation Described

Type of evidence	Manifest relation		Subjective relation	
	Favorable	Unfavorable	Favorable	Unfavorable
	A. Initial experiment (Podeschi & Wyer, 1976)			
Inductive evidence				
Subject-specific	1.02	.55	.60	.12
Object-specific	1.38	.72	.72	.00
Deductive evidence				
Subject-specific	−.08	−.50	−.10	−.50
Object-specific	−.72	−.97	−.30	−.17
	B. Replication			
Inductive evidence				
Subject-specific	.41	−.38	.16	−.41
Object-specific	.91	.28	−.06	−.50
Deductive evidence				
Subject-specific	0	−.72	.03	−.22
Object-specific	−1.09	−.22	−.72	.56

(inductive vs. deductive), the orientation of the evidence (subject-specific vs. object-specific), the type of relation (manifest vs. subjective) and the evaluative implications of the relation (favorable vs. unfavorable) were represented. The 64 items were arranged randomly in a questionnaire. Judges were told to read the information provided and then to estimate the extent of their agreement with the generalization following the information along a 7-category scale from "strongly disagree" (assigned the value of −3) to "strongly agree" (+3).

Results. The mean agreement with generalizations based upon inductive and deductive evidence as a function of the three variables expected to affect it is shown in Part A of Table 3. Analyses of these data yielded seven significant main effects and interactions, including two triple interactions of (a) evidence type, evidence orientation, and relation type, and (b) evidence type, evidence orientation, and the evaluative implications of the relation. Since the results are discussed in detail elsewhere (Podeschi & Wyer, 1976, Experiment 1), only aspects germane to the issues of concern in this paper will be noted.

1. Generalizations were accepted more readily on the basis of one disconfirming and two confirming pieces of evidence when this evidence was inductive ($M = .65$) than when it was deductive ($M = -.42$). A comparison of Figures 1 and 2 suggests why this is so: Even if the category definition is interpreted as disjunctive, a greater proportion of positive instances of the relation described in the generalization is implied by inductive then by deductive evidence.

2. Generalizations were accepted less readily on the basis of inductive evidence when this evidence was specific to the subject than when it was specific to the object. However, they were accepted relatively more readily on the basis of deductive evidence that was specific to the subject. Both findings are consistent with results obtained previously by Abelson and Kanouse (1966). If our conceptualization of the factors underlying the effects of this evidence is valid, the first result suggests that either more universal quantifiers are implicitly assigned to subject than to object categories or subject categories are less heterogeneous, and thus the evidence presented has less positive implications (see Figure 2). The second finding suggests that the definition of a subject category is more apt to be interpreted as disjunctive than is the definition of an object category.

3. Generalizations about manifest relations were accepted more readily than generalizations about subjective relations when the evidence presented was inductive. This suggests that, as expected, subject and object categories are assigned less universal quantifiers when the relation between them is manifest than when it is subjective. In contrast, generalizations about manifest relations were not accepted more readily than generalizations about subjective relations when the evidence presented was deductive. In fact, they were accepted *less* readily than generalizations about subjective relations when this evidence was object-specific. This latter reversal is consistent with our speculation that the process of inferring the validity of subjective relations on the basis of object-specific deductive evidence may differ from that employed under other conditions. That is, judges in this case may estimate the subject's (A's) evaluative reactions to the object (B) by simply summing or averaging the evaluative implications of A's apparent reactions to each of B's three attributes. Since two of these three reactions are evaluatively similar to the overall reaction described in the generalization, judges should tend to accept this generalization. The magnitude of this acceptance is apt to be greather than it would be if a set-analytic process were evoked since, in this latter case, the disconfirming piece of evidence would have relatively more effect (see Figure 1).

There is a second indication that when deductive, object-specific evidence is presented about a subjective relation, persons invoke a different inference process than they do under other conditions. As shown in Table 3, generalizations describing favorable relations were typically accepted more readily than were generalizations describing unfavorable ones, suggesting a general positivity bias (Zajonc, 1968). However, when combining the implications of information in an impression formation task to arrive at evaluative judgments, information with favorable implications typically has *less* influence than information with unfavorable implications (Birnbaum, 1974; Hamilton & Zanna, 1972; Wyer & Watson, 1969). If this is so, and if a similar integration process is invoked in the present conditions, a judge should be more apt to infer that A dislikes B when A dislikes two of B's three attributes than to infer that A likes B when A likes two of B's attributes. This tendency may counteract the positivity bias detected in other conditions. Consistent with this interpretation, generalizations about unfavorable relations were accepted more readily ($M = -.17$) than generalizations about favorable ones ($M = -.30$) when deductive, object-specific evidence was presented, but in no other case.

Some qualification may need to be placed upon this latter interpretation, however. As part of a larger study to be described later in this chapter, the design of the initial experiment was conceptually replicated except that (a) the relative amounts of confirming and disconfirming evidence presented were varied, and (b) judgments were made along a scale from -5 to $+5$ rather than -3 to $+3$. The results of this study, averaged over stimulus information and amounts of confirming and disconfirming evidence (one disconfirming and two confirming pieces versus one confirming and two disconfirming pieces), are shown in Part B of Table 3. Analyses of these data yielded results that, with one exception, were similar in their implications to those described above. These results were not significantly contingent upon the relative amounts of confirming and disconfirming evidence. Note, however, that the reversal of the positivity bias under object-specific, deductive evidence conditions was much greater in the second study than in the first. Moreover, it extended to judgments of generalizations about manifest relations as well as subjective ones. It is not inconceivable that a process similar to the one described above is also involved in evaluating generalizations about manifest relations, contrary to our initial speculations. For example, if judges are told that tribes destroy buzzing and stinging but not flying insects, they may infer that tribes dislike two of bes' three attributes and thus dislike bees; this mediating inference may then affect their acceptance of a generalization that tribes manifest overt behavior that reflects this affective reaction (i.e., that they destroy bees). While this interpretation is plausible, the reason for detecting the effect in the second study but not in the first one remains a mystery.

Summary. The results described above would be consistent with our general conceptual analysis of the factors that underlie the acceptance of generalizations if several assumptions underlying it are valid. These assumptions pertain to the nature of the definitions of subject and object categories, the heterogeneity of these categories, and the implicit quantifiers assigned to them. A series of supplementary experiments were conducted both by Abelson and Kanouse and by the present authors to investigate certain of these assumptions. The nature of these experiments are described below.

Assignment of Implicit Quantifiers

Our interpretation of the effects of inductive evidence obtained in the preceding experiment requires two assumptions. One assumption is that subject categories are assigned more universal implicit quantifiers than object categories. The second is that less universal quantifiers are assigned to categories involved in generalizations about manifest relations than to those involved in generalizations about subject relations.

Two studies have obtained support for these assumptions using somewhat different procedures. Abelson and Kanouse (1966) asked judges to report the minimal evidence of a relation between instances of two categories, A and B, that would be necessary to justify a generalization of the form "As verb Bs." These estimates were reported along an "implicit quantifier" scale composed of alternatives such as all, most, some, etc. (Thus, if judges felt that the generalizations "Tribes buy bees" would be justified if some tribes bought a few bees, they chose the phrases *some* and *a few* along scales pertaining to the subject and object categories, respectively.) Judges believed that more evidence would be required about instances of the subject category to justify accepting the generalization than would be required about instances of the object category, suggesting that they are likely to assign more universal quantifiers to the former categories. Moreover, judges believed that less evidence would be required to justify generalizations about manifest relations than to justify generalizations about subjective relations, suggesting that they are apt to assign less universal implicit quantifiers to categories involved in manifest relations.

Similar conclusions may be drawn from a study by Podeschi and Wyer (1976, Experiment 2). Here, judges were asked to assume that someone had made a generalization of the form "As verb Bs" (e.g., "Suppose someone told you that tribes buy bees"), and then to estimate how likely it would be, given this generalization, that each of four statements containing different combinations of explicit quantifiers was true (specifically, statements of the form "All As verb all Bs;" "All As verb some Bs;" "Some As verb all Bs;" and "Some As verb some Bs"). Three other variables were manipulated: the type of relation (manifest vs. subjective), the evaluative implications of the relation (favorable vs. unfavorable), and the abstractness of the subject and object categories (whether they were familiar, such as tribes or bees, or whether they were abstract, being denoted by a letter of the alphabet). Two findings are of primary interest:

1. Response propositions were judged less likely to follow from the generalization when the relation described was manifest than when it was subjective, regardless of which explicit quantifiers were used in these propositions. This supports the assumption that manifest relations tend to be considered less universal than subjective ones.

2. When the subject and object categories of the generalization were concrete, statements of the form "All As verb some Bs" were judged more likely to follow from the stimulus generalization than were statements of the form "Some As verb all Bs," consistent with the assumption that object categories are assigned less universal quantifiers than subject categories. However, opposite results occurred when the categories involved were abstract. This contingency suggests that the relatively greater effect of object-specific than subject-specific inductive evidence, obtained by Abelson and Kanouse (1966) and replicated in the experiment reported earlier in this chapter, would not generalize to conditions in which the subject and object categories are abstractly described. One implication of this is that the difference in implicit quantifiers assigned to concrete subject and object categories is not simply a result of the position of these categories in the proposition being evaluated. Rather, the difference is due to the particular nature of these categories or the types of elements to which they pertain.

Effects of Category Definitions and Category Homogeneity

The different effects of deductive evidence specific to subject and object categories were assumed to result from differences in the interpretation of these categories as conjunctive or disjunctive. Two quite different approaches have been taken to investigate this possibility. The first (Podeschi & Wyer, 1976, Experiment 3) obtained indirect evidence for these differences in interpretation, using procedures that would *not* make salient to judges the fact that these differences were in question. Specifically, judges were presented stimulus items consisting of the definitions of the categories used in the first experiment described in this paper (e.g., "Tribes are primitive, communal, agricultural societies;" "Bees are flying, furry, buzzing insects"). In each case, they were told to assume that the definitional statement was definitively true and then, based upon this assumption, to estimate the likelihood that each of six response statements was true. Three of these latter statements pertained to the membership of the subclass in a superordinate category (e.g., "A tribe is a primitive society"), while the other three pertained to the membership of a superordinate category member in the subclass (e.g., "A primitive society is a tribe"). The differences between the judgments of the two sets of response statements were compared.

To see the implications of such differences, suppose judges are told to assume that "Tribes are primitive, communal, agricultural societies" and are than asked to estimate both the likelihood that "Tribes are agricultural societies" and the likelihood that "Agricultural societies are tribes." If judges treat the definition of tribes as conjunctive, they should estimate the first statement to be very likely to be true, and this estimate should typically be greater than their estimate of the likelihood that the second statement is true. However, if judges treat the definition as disjunctive, the first of these estimates should be relatively lower, and not necessarily much different, from the second. More generally, the greater the difference between the two estimates, the greater the likelihood that judges are treating the definition as conjunctive rather than disjunctive. If this reasoning is correct, and if definitions of subject categories are more apt to be treated as disjunctive than are definitions of object categories, differences between estimates analogous to those described above should be less when subject than when object categories are involved. This was, in fact, the case.

Unfortunately, however, neither this nor the preceding study (pertaining to the assignment of implicit quantifiers) provided any information as to *why* subject and object categories are assigned different implicit quantifiers, or why their defintions are interpreted differently. One possibility, noted earlier, is suggested by the fact that in all of the studies described to date, subject categories pertained to persons and object categories to nonpersons. If judges (themselves persons) make finer distinctions among members of their own species than among members of other species or among inanimate objects, they may be more apt to interpret the definitions of person categories as disjunctive for this reason. In addition, their greater sensitivity to differences among persons than to differences among nonpersons may lead them to require a greater amount of confirming evidence in order to justify accepting a generalization about members of the category as a whole. To this extent, categories of persons may be assigned more universal implicit quantifiers, as results also suggest. An additional reason why inductive evidence about subject (person) categories may lead to less acceptance of a generalization is that judges have a set to treat subclasses of persons as overlapping rather than as mutually exclusive. To this extent, disconfirming evidence pertaining to these subclasses should have greater effect, and the generalization should be less readily accepted for this reason.

In the other investigation into the effects of category definition, the type of category to which evidence pertained was manipulated independently of its position as the subject or object of the generalization. In addition, judges were given a set to consider the category definitions as either conjunctive or disjunctive (in the case of deductive evidence) or the subcategories as either overlapping or nonoverlapping (in the case of inductive evidence). If differences in the effects of subject-specific and object-specific deductive evidence are solely a result of differences in the interpretation of the definitions of the subject and object categories, this evidence should lead to greater acceptance of generalizations when the definitions are explicitly disjunctive than when they are explicitly conjunctive. On the other hand, the effects of evidence orientation and the type of category involved (person vs. nonperson) should be eliminated when the category definitions are explicit. Similar reasoning underlies a consideration of the effects of inductive evidence. That is, if differences in the effects of this evidence are mediated by differences in the perceived overlap of the subcategories of the class to which this evidence is specific, then the acceptance of generalizations based upon inductive evidence pertaining to these subclasses should be affected by a direct manipulation of judges' set to think of these subclasses as overlapping or nonoverlapping, while the effects of evidence orientation, controlling for this set, should be attenuated.

Method. Four stimulus replications were constructed, pertaining to generalizations about a different pair of categories. One category in each pair pertained to persons, and the other pertained to nonpersons. Then, for each pair, four verbs were selected that would meaningfully describe the four alternative types of relations (manifest favorable, manifest unfavorable, subjective favorable and subjective unfavorable) regardless of which category in the pair was the subject and which was the object. (E.g., in one case, the two categories selected were *scientists* and *apes*, and the four verbs were *copy, harm, love,* and *hate*; in another, the two categories were *hunters* and *snakes*, and the verbs selected were *seek, destroy, like,* and *dislike*.) In addition, three subclasses of each category were selected for use in presenting inductive evidence, and three superordinate categories (attributes) were selected to form definitions used in presenting deductive evidence.

Deductive evidence constructed from these materials was presented to subjects in a format similar to that used in the first experiment described (see Table 1), with one exception: In some instances, the definitions of the categories to which evidence pertained were made either explicitly conjunctive by connecting the attributes by *and* (e.g., "Scientists are thinking *and* inquisitive *and* problem-solving persons") or explicitly disjunctive by connecting the attributes by *or* (e.g., "Scientists are thinking *or* inquisitive *or* problem-solving persons"). A similar procedure was used in the case of inductive evidence to provide a set to consider the subcategories to which evidence pertained as overlapping or nonoverlapping: To provide a set to think of the subcategories as overlapping, the subcategory names were connected by *and* (e.g., "There are three kinds of scientists: physical *and* social *and* life"); to provide a set to think of the subcategories as nonoverlapping, they were connected by *or* ("There are three kinds of scientists: physical *or* social *or* life").

Table 4. Acceptance of Generalizations as a Function of Type of Evidence, Evidence Orientation, and Category Definition or Description

Category definition/ Subcategory description	Inductive evidence		Deductive evidence	
	Subject-specific	Object-specific	Subject-specific	Object-specific
Conjunctive	1.66	2.05	.98	1.15
Disjunctive	2.76	2.55	2.30	2.24

Finally, in some cases the person category was used as the subject of the generalization to be evaluated (e.g., "Scientists copy apes"), and in other cases the person category was used as the object (e.g., "Apes copy scientists"). The design, therefore, allowed the effects of evidence orientation (subject-specific vs. object-specific), the type of category to which it pertained (person vs. nonperson), and the type of category definition or subcategory description (conjunctive vs. disjunctive) to be isolated.

As in the first experiment, each set of evidence consisted of two confirming pieces and one disconfirming piece. This evidence was presented in eight 32-item questionnaires, each administered to a different group of four judges. In four of the questionnaires, items were introduced by conjunctive definitions or subcategory descriptions, while in the other four, items were introduced by disjunctive definitions or subcategory descriptions. The 32 items in each form were further subdivided into two sets of 16. In one set of items, the person category was used as the subject of the generalizations, while in the other set, the nonperson category was used as the subject. The 16 items in each subset, in combination with the 4 questionnaire forms, comprised a graeco-latin-square design consisting of 4 stimulus replications, 4 verbs (manifest favorable, manifest unfavorable, subjective favorable and subjective unfavorable) and 4 configurations of evidence (subject-specific inductive, subject-specific deductive, object-specific inductive and object-specific deductive). Thus, all 16 combinations of evidence configuration and verb were represented in each questionnaire; however, no verb or evidence configuration was presented more than once in any given questionnaire within a given stimulus replication. Judges read each set of stimulus information under instructions to assume that it was true and this to indicate, along a scale from −5 to +5, how strongly they would agree with the generalization following it.

Results. Data relevant to the major concerns of this study are shown in Table 4, pooled over the type of category (persons vs. nonperson) to which evidence pertained. Their implications are summarized below:

1. On the basis of *deductive* evidence, generalizations were accepted significantly[2] more readily when the category definition was disjunctive (M = 2.27) than when it was conjunctive (M = 1.02). On the other hand, controlling for the type of definition, their acceptance did not significantly depend upon either the position of the category to which the evidence was specific (subject vs. object) or whether the category pertained to persons or to nonpersons ($F < 1.0$). In combination, these data support the hypothesis that the different effects of subject-specific and object-specific deductive evidence are primarily a result of differences in the assumptions judges make about the disjunctiveness of the definitions of subject and object categories, and that these differences are eliminated when the nature of their definitions is made explicit.

2. On the basis of *inductive* evidence, generalizations were accepted more readily when the subcategories were described disjunctively (and thus were expected to be interpreted as nonoverlapping) than when the subcategories were described conjunctively (and thus conveyed the impression of being more overlapping). However, as with deductive evidence, the effects of evidence orientation and category type (person vs. nonpersons) were not significant, nor did these effects interact with the type of subcategory description. If the description of the subcategories affects the apparent homogeneity of the category to which they belong, these data suggest that generalizations are accepted more readily when the category to which the evidence pertains is less homogeneous. This is consistent with the implications of Figure 2. However, it may also indicate that homogeneous categories (those whose subcategories are relatively overlapping) are assigned more universal implicit quantifiers than heterogeneous categories. To this extent, it follows that categories of persons, which in other studies reported here and elsewhere appear to be assigned more universal quantifiers, are interpreted as more homogeneous than are categories of nonpersons. This latter conclusion differs from that drawn by Gilson and Abelson (1965).

Summary and Conclusions

Reasonably clear conclusions may be drawn from the series of studies described in this section concerning the effects of different types of evidence on the acceptance of generalizations, and also the reasons for these effects. These conclusions may be summarized briefly.

1. Deductive evidence leads to greater acceptance of generalizations to the extent that the definition of the category to which it is specific is interpreted

---

[2] Unless otherwise noted, this and other results described are significant at $F(1,30) > 4.17$, $p < .05$.

as disjunctive rather than conjunctive. Categories of persons are typically assumed to have more disjunctive definitions than categories of nonpersons; as a result, the acceptance of generalizations based upon a given configuration of deductive evidence is greater when the evidence is specific to a category of persons than when it is specific to a category of nonpersons.

2. The effect of inductive evidence on the acceptance of generalizations is largely a function of the universality of the implicit quantifiers assigned to the categories to which this evidence is specific. The assignment of these quantifiers is in turn partly a function of the nature of the relation described in the generalization being evaluated. That is, categories are assigned less universal quantifiers when the relation to be generalized is manifest than when it is subjective, and thus generalizations about manifest relations are more likely to be accepted on the basis of inductive evidence pertaining to them. The assignment of quantifiers appears also to depend upon the homogeneity of the category to which the evidence pertains. Specifically, when the category is more homogeneous (i.e., its subcategories are more overlapping), a more universal implicit quantifier is assigned to this category, and thus generalizations are accepted less readily on the basis of inductive evidence specific to the category. Categories of persons are assigned more universal quantifiers than categories of nonpersons; as a result, generalizations are accepted less readily on the basis of inductive evidence specific to categories of persons than inductive evidence specific to nonpersons.

3. There appears to be a general tendency to accept generalizations about relations that have positive evaluative implications (i.e., relations that suggest a favorable reaction by members of the subject category toward members of the object category).

4. The conclusions drawn above may apply only when judgments are based on the implications of the information presented for the number of subject and object category members that are related in the manner described. This may not be the case when judges evaluate a proposition about a subject's affective reaction to an object based upon evidence pertaining to the subject's reactions to specific attributes of the object. Here, they may invoke a process akin to that detected in other research on the manner in which evaluative judgments of persons are formed on the basis of adjectives describing their attributes (Anderson, 1965; Birnbaum, 1974). Specifically, judges may base their inferences on a composite (sum or average) of the subject's apparent affective reactions to each of the object's attributes (cf. Wyer, 1975; Wyer & Hinkle, 1976). To this extent, the orientation of the evidence presented and the relation described in the generalization may not only affect the interpretation of the generalization and of the implications of specific pieces of evidence presented, but may also affect the process of combining or integrating the implications of this evidence.

This latter possibility raises an entirely new set of questions that so far have not been addressed. It is to these questions that we turn next.

INFORMATION INTEGRATION PROCESSES

Several restrictions were placed upon the nature of the evidence presented in the preceding studies. For one thing, the relative amounts of confirming and disconfirming evidence were held constant. Moreover, the evidence in each set presented was of only one type (either inductive or deductive) and was specific to only one category (either the subject or the object). As a result, several questions of importance in developing a general understanding of the effects of evidence on the acceptance of generalizations were unanswered. One general question pertains to the manner in which different types and amounts of evidence are combined, or integrated, in arriving at a judgment. We now consider two aspects of this question. One concerns the manner in which inductive and deductive evidence combine to affect judgments. The second deals with the manner in which subject-specific and object-specific evidence combine to affect the acceptance of generalizations to which the evidence pertains. Let us consider these matters in turn and present some preliminary data bearing upon each.

Integration of Inductive and Deductive Evidence

Our interpretation of the process underlying the acceptance of generalizations has been based largely upon a set-theoretic conceptualization. According to this conceptualization, judges use the configuration of evidence presented to estimate the frequency with which members of subject and object categories are related in the manner described in the generalization, and this estimate provides a basis for accepting the generalization. Such a formulation implies that the effects of different pieces of evidence may often be highly interactive. This would particularly be the case if these pieces are of different types. For example, the implications of a piece of inductive evidence (e.g., "Tribes buy bumblebees") may often be either redundant or inconsistent with the implications of deductive evidence accompanying it (e.g., "Tribes buy flying insects;" "Tribes do not buy buzzing insects"), and it, therefore, may have less influence than it would have if it were considered either alone or in other informational contexts.

There are, however, other plausible interpretations of the manner in which judges use evidence to estimate the validity of a generalization. For instance, when confronted with several pieces of evidence, they may first consider the implications of each piece separately, and then they may combine these implications in some algebraic fashion (by summing or averaging) to arrive at a judgment. Anderson (1965, 1971) has proposed a general model of information integration of the form

$$J = \frac{\Sigma \, w_i s_i}{\Sigma \, w_i} \tag{1}$$

where s_i, the "scale value" of the ith piece of information, is a function of the implications of the information for the judgment to be made (J), and w_i is the weight or importance attached to the information. This model has often been applied successfully in describing the manner in which judges estimate their affective reactions to persons on the basis of information about their attributes (for a summary of this research, see Anderson, 1971; Wyer, 1974). As we have already noted, such a model may describe the acceptance of generalizations about subjective (affective) relations based upon object-specific deductive evidence (i.e., evidence about the object's attributes). It would also account for other results reported if one assumes that the weight (w_i) of evidence of different types and with different implications varies with the orientation of the evidence and the type of relation being evaluated.

In a recent study we obtained information bearing upon the relative utility of a set-theoretic formulation and an algebraic formulation in describing how evidence is used to evaluate generalizations. Sets of evidence were constructed in such a way that the combined effects of inductive and deductive evidence could be determined. The relative amounts of confirming and disconfirming evidence in each set were also systematically varied. Since the design is rather complex, let us first describe it briefly before turning to the results and their implications for the issues at hand.

Method. The materials constructed for use in this study were a refinement of those used in the first study reported in this chapter (see Table 2). They differed in two respects. First, the subcategories of tribes (replication 1), American cities (replication 2), and magazines (replication 3) were clearly *subclasses* of the category to which they pertained instead of specific instances of the category. (E.g., the three descriptions of American cities were changed from Chicago, New York, and Los Angeles to *eastern, midwestern,* and *western*; the three descriptions of magazines were changed from *Newsweek, Reader's Digest,* and *Saturday Evening Post* to *sports, news,* and *fashion*). Second, the verbs used to describe the four types of relations (manifest favorable, manifest unfavorable, subjective favorable, and subjective unfavorable) were systematically varied so that a particular verb appeared in no more than one replication.

Three general evidence presentation conditions were constructed. In Condition 1, which was a partial replication of the first study reported in this paper, the three pieces of evidence presented were either all inductive (I) or all deductive (D). However, the relative numbers of confirming (+) and diconfirming (−) pieces of evidence were systematically varied. Specifically, the sets consisted either of two pieces of confirming and one piece of disconfirming evidence (I+I+I− or D+D+D−) or one piece of confirming and two pieces of disconfirming evidence (I+I−I− or D+D−D−). In the other two conditions, the evidence presented was partly inductive and partly deductive. In Condition 2, this evidence consisted of either (a) one piece of inductive evidence and two pieces of deductive evidence (I+D+D− or I+D−D−), or (b) one piece of deductive and two pieces of inductive evidence (D+I+I− and D+I−I−). In Condition 3, the four sets of evidence were of the types I+I+D−, I+I−D−, D+D+I−, and D+D−I−. In each case, the evidence was preceded by either a definition of the subject or object category to which evidence pertained, a description of the three subcategories into which it was partitioned, or both. Thus, e.g., the set of I+D+D− subject-specific evidence bearing upon the generalization "Tribes buy bees" in Condition 2 was:

Altogether there are three kinds of tribes: Northern, Central, Southern.
Tribes are primitive, communal, agricultural societies.

Northern tribes buy bees.
Communal societies buy bees.
Agricultural societies do *not* buy bees.

Four 32-item questionnaires were prepared in each condition. In 16 items, evidence consisted of 2 confirming pieces and 1 disconfirming piece; in the reamining 16, evidence consisted of 1 confirming and 2 disconfirming pieces. The 16 items in each of these subsets, in combination with the 4 questionnaire forms, comprised a graeco-latin square design consisting of the 4 stimulus replications, 4 verbs (manifest favorable, manifest unfavorable, subjective favorable, and subjective unfavorable), and 4 combinations of evidence orientation (subject-specific or object-specific) and evidence configuration. Thus, all 16 combinations of verb and evidence configuration were represented in each questionnaire; however, no verb or evidence configuration pretaining to a given replication was presented more than once within the 16-item subset.

Sixteen introductory psychology students participated in each of the three experimental conditions. Within each condition, four judges completed each of the four questionnaire forms. After reading each set of evidence, judges recorded their agreement with the generalization to which it pertained along a scale from −5 ("strongly disagree") to +5 ("strongly agree").

To explore the manner in which inductive and deductive evidence combine to affect inferences, two orthogonal analyses were performed. In the first, the

Table 5. Mean Acceptance of Generalizations Based Upon Disconfirming Inductive and Deductive Evidence as a Function of the Type of Confirming Evidence Accompanying it and the Type and Favorableness of the Relation to be Generalized

Type of evidence	Manifest relation		Subjective relation	
	Favorable	Unfavorable	Favorable	Unfavorable
Disconfirming inductive evidence (I–)				
Confirming evidence of same type (I+I+)	2.94	2.31	2.47	1.41
Confirming evidence mixed (I+D+)	.91	.12	.62	1.12
Confirming evidence of different type (D+D+)	2.09	1.75	1.87	1.44
Disconfirming deductive evidence (D–)				
Confirming evidence of same type (D+D+)	.75	.84	1.97	1.97
Confirming evidence mixed (I+D+)	1.38	1.44	2.12	.50
Confirming evidence of different type (I+I+)	1.78	1.78	.91	1.59

effect of a single piece of disconfirming evidence (either I— or D—, as denoted previously) was investigated as a function of the configuration of confirming evidence accompanying it. In the second, the effect of a single piece of confirming evidence (I+ or D+) was investigated as a function of the configuration of disconfirming evidence accompanying it. We will present the results of each analysis in turn, and then consider their implications for the information integration processes underlying the judgments made.

Effects of disconfirming evidence in different contexts. The first analysis involved data pertaining only to those six configurations containg two pieces of confirming evidence and one piece of disconfirming evidence (in Condition 1, I+I+I— and D+D+D—; in Condition 2, I+D+I— and I+D+D—; and in Condition 3, D+D+I— and I+I+D—). These configurations could be arranged in a 2 X 3 design involving the type of disconfirming evidence presented (I— or D—) and the type of confirming evidence accompanying it (both pieces similar in type to the disconfirming piece, one piece similar and one piece dissimilar to the disconfirming piece, or both pieces dissimilar to the disconfirming piece). An analysis of judgments as a function of these and other experimental variables yielded a significant interaction of the type of disconfirming evidence, the type of confirming evidence, the type of relation being generalized, and the favorableness of this relation, $F(2,45) = 4.56, p < .05$. Data relevant to this interaction are shown in Table 5. Two aspects of these data are of particular interest.

1. When the disconfirming piece of evidence was inductive, generalizations were accepted more readily when the two confirming pieces were either both inductive or both deductive than when they were of different types. This was also true when the disconfirming evidence was deductive and the relation to be generalized was subjective and unfavorable. This suggests that in these instances disconfirming evidence may have greater influence when the confirming evidence is of different types, and thus its implications are harder to assimilate.

2. When the disconfirming evidence was deductive, generalizations about manifest relations were accepted less readily when the confirming evidence presented was also deductive than when it was inductive. However, generalizations above favorable subjective relations were accepted more readily in the former condition than in the latter.

Effects of confirming evidence in different contexts. The six configurations containing two pieces of disconfirming evidence (in Condition 1, I+I—I— and D+D—D—; in Condition 3, I+I—D— and D+D—I—; and in Condition 2, I+D—D— and D+I—I—) were arranged in a manner analogous to the configurations containing two pieces of confirming evidence. Data were then analyzed as a function of the type of confirming evidence presented (I+ or D+), the type of disconfirming evidence accompanying it (both pieces of the

Table 6. Mean Acceptance of Generalizations as a Function of Similarity in Type of Confirming Evidence to Disconfirming Evidence, Evidence Orientation, and Type of Relation

	Subject-specific evidence		Object-specific evidence	
	Manifest relation	Subjective relation	Manifest relation	Subjective relation
Confirming and disconfirming evidence similar in type (I+I−I−, D+D−D−)	−2.05	−2.39	−1.78	−2.09
Disconfirming evidence mixed (I+I−D−, D+I−I−)	−1.59	−1.59	−1.09	−1.48
Disconfirming evidence and confirming evidence different in type (I+D−D−, D+I−I−)	− .73	−1.30	−1.81	−1.20

same type as the confirming piece, one piece of the same and one of a different type, or both pieces of a different type) and other experimental variables. Overall, generalizations were accepted more readily when the confirming piece was inductive than when it was deductive ($p < .05$), independently of the type of disconfirming evidence accompanying it. However, this difference was significantly greater when the evidence was subject-specific ($M = -1.29$ and -1.93 for inductive and deductive evidence conditions, respectively) than when it was object-specific ($M = 1.52$ and -1.64, respectively), $F(1,45) = 4.11$, $p < .05$. This suggests that the relatively greater power of confirming inductive evidence than confirming deductive evidence is most apparent when it pertains to the subject of the generalization being evaluated.

These data do not mean that the effect of confirming evidence per se is independent of the nature of the disconfirming evidence accompanying it. In fact, a significant interaction occurred involving the similarity of the type of confirming evidence to that of the disconfirming evidence, evidence orientation, and the type of relation being judged, $F(2,45) = 4.38$, $p < .05$. Data relevant to this interaction are shown in Table 6. In three of four cases, the influence of the disconfirming evidence increased with its similarity in type to the confirming evidence. (Alternatively, confirming evidence had relatively *less* influence when it was of the same type as the disconfirming evidence accompanying it.) However, an exception to this tendency occurred when object-specific evidence about a manifest relation was presented; here, the two pieces of disconfirming evidence had substantial effect when they were both different from as well as both similar to the type of confirming evidence presented.

Implications for information integration. Neither a set-theoretic conceptualization nor an algebraic formulation seems able by itself to account for the data obtained in this study. To see this, let us consider the implications of the data for each formulation in turn.

1. Implications for a set-theoretic conceptualization. First, consider the data in Table 5, which shows the effect of disconfirming inductive and disconfirming deductive evidence in various contexts. Since disconfirming inductive evidence is not inconsistent with any of the three sets of confirming evidence, there is no reason to expect discounting. However, the evidence that generalizations were accepted less readily when the confirming evidence was mixed (both inductive and deductive) than when it was all of the same type suggests that either the confirming evidence was discounted under the former condition or that the disconfirming evidence was discounted under the latter condition.

When the piece of disconfirming evidence is deductive, somewhat different considerations arise. Here, disconfirming deductive evidence (e.g., "Tribes do not buy buzzing insects") is consistent with confirming deductive evidence ("Tribes buy flying insects"); however, it would be inconsistent with confirming inductive evidence (e.g., "Tribes buy bumblebees") unless the definition of *bee* is interpreted as disjunctive. Thus, in this case, discounting processes may be operative if a set-analytic reasoning process underlies judgments. The results obtained when the relation to be generalized is manifest would be explained if judges tend to discount disconfirming deductive evidence when it is accompanied by confirming inductive evidence. Unfortunately, however, this reasoning would not account for the results obtained when the relation being considered is subjective. These data again suggest that factors not taken into account by a set-theoretic formulation must be operating.

Data pertaining to the effect of confirming evidence when presented in different contexts are also not readily explained on the basis of a set-theoretic formulation. For one thing, such a formulation would predict different degrees of discounting of evidence in different contexts. However, the difference between the effect of confirming inductive evidence and the effect of confirming deductive evidence did not depend on the nature of the evidence accompanying it. Moreover, the specific type of discounting suggested by the data in Table 6 would also be hard to account for. For example, the generalization "Tribes buy bees" was accepted less readily on the basis of evidence that either (a) northern tribes but not central or southern tribes buy bees (I+I−I−), or (b) primitive societies but not communal or

Table 7. Effects of Inductive and Deductive Evidence Upon the Acceptance of Generalizations When Presented in Different Contexts

Context evidence	Inductive evidence			Deductive evidence		
	I+	I−	Difference (D)	D+	D−	Difference (D)
I+I−	2.28	−2.18	4.46	.69	−1.15	1.84
D+I−	.69	−1.63	2.32	1.79	−1.73	3.52
I+D−	1.52	−1.15	2.67	1.36	− .89	2.25
D+D−	1.36	−1.73	3.09	1.38	−1.98	3.36

agricultural societies buy bees (D+D−D−) than on the basis of evidence that either (c) northern tribes buy bees, but communal and agricultural societies do not (I+D−D−) or (d) primitive societies buy bees, but central and southern tribes do not (D+I−I−). It is quite possible that the disconfirming evidence was discounted to a greater degree in the latter two cases than in the former two. However, there is no reason to predict this on the basis of a set-theoretic analysis alone.

2. Implications for an algebraic formulation of integration. When applying an algebraic formulation of the form described by Equation 1, it is typically assumed that the scale value of each piece of information (s_i) and often its absolute weight (w_i) are unaffected by the type and implications of the information accompanying it. Such a model, however, cannot account for the results reported here unless one assumes that at least one of the two parameters pertaining to each piece varies idiosyncratically with the evidence configuration in which the piece is contained, and also that it depends upon the type of relation being evaluated. Many of these contingencies are evident from the data reported in Tables 5 and 6. Perhaps a clearer indication of the assumptions required in order to apply such a model may be gained by ignoring differences in the effects of evidence due to its orientation and to the type of relation being judged and reorganizing the data in the manner described in Table 7. This table shows the effect of differences in the implications of single pieces of inductive evidence (I+ and I−) and deductive evidence (D+ and D−) when accompanied by each of four different configurations of other evidence. These data suggest two conclusions:

(a) The effect of adding inductive evidence is greater when the other evidence available is of a single type (I+I− or D+D−; $D = 3.68$) than when it is mixed (D+I− or I+D−; $D = 2.50$). This suggests that the combined influence (weight) of one piece of confirming and one piece of disconfirming evidence is less when these pieces are of the same type than when they are of a different type. On the other hand, the effect of adding deductive evidence is not appreciably different when the other evidence available is of the same type (D = 2.65) than when it is mixed (D = 2.88). Thus, in this case, the combined weight of confirming the disconfirming pieces of evidence does not depend upon whether those pieces are the same type or different types.

(b) The effects of adding inductive evidence is greater when the confirming evidence already available is inductive (D = 3.48 for I+I– and I+D– context conditions combined) than when this latter evidence is deductive (D = 2.70 for D+I– and D+D– conditions combined). However, the effect of adding deductive evidence is less in the former conditions (D = 2.05) than in the latter (D = 3.44). Thus, the relative weight attached to confirming inductive and confirming deductive evidence appears to depend upon whether the other information available is either inductive or deductive.

While the experimental design precluded statistical tests of the differences described above, the magnitude of these differences is sufficient to suggest that they be taken seriously. To this extent, they indicate that an algebraic model cannot account for these data unless one assumes that the absolute weight (w_i) of a given type of evidence, as well as its relative weight, varies with the type of evidence presented with it. The nature of this variation may often be difficult to predict a priori. To this extent, an averaging formulation is, of course, of limited utility even if valid.

Integration of Subject-Specific and Object-Specific Evidence

In considering how evidence combines to affect the acceptance of generalizations, a question also arises as to how evidence is used when it pertains to both the subject and object simultaneously. In considering this question, two possibilities seem plausible. Compare the implications of a set of inductive evidence specific to both tribes and bees (e.g., "Northern tribes buy bumblebees; Central tribes buy honeybees; Southern tribes do *not* buy sweat bees") with the implications of a set of inductive evidence specific only to tribes (e.g., "Northern tribes buy bees; Central tribes buy bees; Southern tribes do *not* buy bees"). Each piece of evidence in the first set has less general implications for the proposition "Tribes buy bees" than the corresponding piece in the second set. Thus, one might expect a piece of confirming evidence to have less positive effect on the acceptance of a generalization when it is specific to both the subject and the object than when it is specific to only one. However, by the same token, a piece of disconfirming evidence should have less negative effect when it is both subject-specific and object-specific. Therefore, whether the first or second set of evidence described above will lead to greater acceptance of the generalization depends upon whether the effect of making confirming evidence both subject-specific and object-specific is greater or less than the effect of making disconfirming evidence both subject- and object-specific. These and other possibilities were explored in a study described briefly below.

Method. Stimulus items were constructed from the same materials used in the preceding experiment. Four 32-item questionnaire forms were again prepared, each form completed by a different group of 4 subjects. The items in each questionnaire represented all combinations of five variables: the relative amounts of confirming and disconfirming evidence (two pieces of confirming and one piece of disconfirming evidence vs. one piece of confirming and two pieces of disconfirming evidence), the type of subject-specific evidence (inductive vs. deductive), the type of object-specific evidence (inductive vs. deductive), the type of relation described in the generalization being evaluated (manifest vs. subjective), and the favorableness of this relation (favorable vs. unfavorable). The 16 items at each level of the first variable (amount of evidence) were varied over questionnaire forms in a manner analogous to that used in previous experiments, so that no verb or type of evidence from the same stimulus replication occurred more than once in any given questionnaire. Each item was introduced by two statements relevant to the types of evidence being presented. For an example, an item consisting of subject-specific inductive evidence and object-specific deductive evidence bearing upon the generalization "Tribes buy bees" was:

Altogether there are three kinds of tribes: Northern, Central and Southern.
Bees are flying, furry, buzzing insects.

Northern tribes buy flying insects.
Central tribes buy furry insects.
Southern tribes do *not* buy buzzing insects.

As in other experiments, judges responded to each item by recording their agreement with the generalization to which the evidence pertained along a scale from −5 ("strongly disagree" to +5 ("strongly agree").

Results. Judgments, pooled over stimulus replications, were analyzed as a function of the five experimental variables described below. This analysis revealed significant[3] main effects of the amount of evidence, the favorableness of the relation being judged, and the type of object-specific evidence presented (inductive or deductive), as well as several interactions involving these variables. The effects of object-specific evidence were similar to those

[3] Here and elsewhere, results reported in this study were significant at $F(1,15) > 4.50$, $p < .05$.

Table 8. Separate and Combined Effects of Subject-Specific and Object-Specific Evidence

Object-specific evidence presented	Subject-specific evidence presented		
	None	Inductive	Deductive
A. 2 confirming, 1 disconfirming piece			
None	–	2.28	1.59
Inductive	2.28	2.50	2.64
Deductive	1.17	2.03	2.09
B. 1 confirming, 2 disconfirming pieces			
None	--	--2.39	−2.05
Inductive	−1.97	-- .58	−1.27
Deductive	−1.91	−1.72	−1.53

obtained in previous studies reported. Specifically, this evidence led to greater acceptance of generalizations when it was inductive (M = .82) than when it was deductive (M = .21). Moreover, inductive evidence led to greater acceptance of generalizations about manifest relations (M = 1.16) than of generalizations about subjective relations (M = .49), while deductive evidence led to relatively little acceptance of generalizations regardless of whether the relation was manifest (M = .19) or subjective (M = .24). However, parallel effects involving the type of subject-specific evidence were not obtained. In fact, no effects involving the type of subject-specific evidence were significant. This suggests that when evidence is specific to both the subject and the object of a generalization, the implications of the object-specific evidence dominate those of the subject-specific evidence.

A better feel for the effect of presenting evidence specific to both the subject and the object categories rather than to only one of the categories may be gained by comparing the data collected in this experiment with those obtained in Condition 1 of the preceding experiment, in which only one type of evidence was presented at a time. The acceptance of generalizations is shown in Table 8 as a function of the amount and type of evidence pertaining to the subject and the amount and type of evidence pertaining to the object. These data show clearly that the acceptance of generalizations was greater when evidence pertained to both subject and object categories then when it was specific to only one of these categories. This tendency occurred regardless of the relative amounts of confirming and disconfirming evidence presented. Thus, persons appear to attach relatively greater weight to confirming evidence (or less weight to disconfirming evidence) when this evidence pertains to both subject and object categories simultaneously. The reason for this is unclear.

DIRECTIONS FOR FUTURE RESEARCH

The studies reported in this chapter, in combination with those performed earlier by Abelson and his colleagues, provide valuable insight into the manner in which persons use information to evaluate generalizations of the type typically encountered in everyday conversation. In particular, they help to understand and predict contingencies in the acceptance of generalizations as a function of the type of relations to which they pertain, the nature of the categories of elements being related, and various characteristics of the evidence itself. However, at the same time, this research leaves several important questions unanswered concerning the precise manner in which evidence of different types and orientations is combined to arrive at an estimate of a generalization's validity. As we have noted, neither a set-theoretic formulation of the reasoning underlying the use of this evidence nor an algebraic model of information integration appears adequate by itself to account for the results reported. It seems likely that different integration processes are invoked at different times, depending upon the nature of the evidnece presented and the type of relation being evaluated. In any event, a more rigorous investigation of these processes and the conditions in which they occur is necessary in order to develop a more complete conceptualization of the reasoning process underlying the acceptance of generalizations.

Despite these latter ambiguities, the factors that underlie the acceptance of generalizations are sufficiently well understood to consider seriously their implications for a variety of interesting questions associated with belief and attitude formation and change. Although space precludes a detailed consideration of these matters, two lines of research may be worth noting. First, knowledge of the different types of evidence that are most apt to lead to the acceptance of generalizations may be applied in the construction of persuasive communications. The potential fruitfulness of such an effort was demonstrated by Kanouse and Abelson (1967). By constructing alternative persuasive communications differing in both the type of evidence presented (inductive or deductive) and the type and favorableness of the relation to which it pertained (either manifest or subjective, and either favorable or unfavorable), they showed that subjects' beliefs in a target proposition were most influenced by communications containing the same sort of evidence that led to the greatest acceptance of generalizations under the more artificial conditions constructed by Abelson and Kanouse (1966) and in the studies reported in this chapter. (Specifically, messages containing inductive evidence supporting positive manifest relations and deductive evidence supporting negative subjective relations were more influential than messages of other types.) Additional possibilities along these lines are worth pursuing.

A perhaps more intriguing application of the findings reported in this chapter and elsewhere, noted by Kanouse (1971), is based upon the general notion that persons' judgments about themselves and their environment can be altered by simply making salient to them different subsets of previously formed cognitions that have implications for the judgments. One way of doing this is simply to ask persons questions designed to elicit the recall of different subsets of judgment-related cognitions before they make the target judgment. Similar techniques have been applied effectively in social psychological research of a variety of types (cf. Henninger & Wyer, 1976; Salancik, 1974; Salancik & Conway, 1975). To see the implications of this possibility in the context of the research discussed in this chapter, consider an exampled suggested by Kanouse (1971). Suppose a judge is told that urbanites destroy *Reader's Digests* and is asked whether urbanites hate magazines. The answer to this question may be mediated by two different lines of reasoning. First, the judge may reason that if urbanites destroy *Reader's Digests*, they are likely to destroy magazines in general, and that if they destroy magazines, they are likely to hate magazines. Alternatively, he may reason that if urbanites destroy *Reader's Digests*, they are likely to hate *Reader's Digests*, and that if they hate *Reader's Digests*, they are apt to hate magazines. However, the findings reported by Abelson and Kanouse (1966) and replicated in the studies reported in this paper suggest that judges should be more apt to infer that urbanites destroy magazines given that they destroy *Reader's Digests* (i.e., to accept a generalization based upon inductive evidence about a manifest relation) than to infer that urbanites hate magazines given that they hate *Reader's Digests* (to accept a generalization based upon inductive evidence about a subjective relation). They, therefore, should be more apt to conclude that urbanites hate magazines if the first line of reasoning is used than if the second is used. To test this prediction, Kanouse and Gross (cited in Kanouse, 1971) asked judges explicitly to make one or the other type of mediating judgment before reporting their judgment of the generalization to be evaluated (e.g., their estimate of the likelihood that urbanites hate magazines). As expected, judges were more likely to accept the generalization if they had previously been asked whether, e.g., urbanites destroy magazines than if they had previously been asked whether, e.g., urbanites hate *Reader's Digests*. The application of the results obtained in the studies reported here to this "Socratic method" of social influence may be well worth pursuing.

REFERENCES

Abelson, R. P., & Kanouse, D. E. The subjective acceptance of verbal generalizations. In S. Feldman (Ed.), *Cognitive consistency: Motivational antecedents and behavioral consequents.* New York: Academis Press, 1966.

Anderson, N. H. Averaging versus adding as a stimulus-combination rule in impression formation. *Journal of Experimental Psychology*, 1965, **70**, 394–400.

Anderson, N. H. Integration theory and attitude change. *Psychological Review*, 1971, **78**, 171–206.

Birnbaum, M. H. The nonadditivity of personality impressions. *Journal of Experimental Psychology*, 1974, **102**, 543–561.

Erickson, J. L. A set analysis theory of behavior in formal syllogistic reasoning tasks. In R. Solso (Ed.), *Theories in cognitive psychology: The Loyola Symposium.* Hillsdale, N.J.: Erlbaum, 1974.

Fishbein, R., & Hunter, R. Summation versus balance in attitude organization and change. *Journal of Abnormal and Social Psychology*, 1964, **69**, 505–510.

Gilson, C., & Abelson, R. P. The subjective use of inductive evidence. *Journal of Personality and Social Psychology*, 1965, **2**, 301–310.

Hamilton, D. L., & Zanna, M. P. Differential weighting of favorable and unfavorable attributes in impressions of personality. *Journal of Experimental Research in Personality*, 1972, **6**, 204–212.

Henninger, M., & Wyer, R. S. The recognition and elimination of inconsistencies among ayllogistically related beliefs: Some new light on the "Socratic effect." *Journal of Personality and Social Psychology*, 1976.

Kanouse, D. E. *Language, labeling and attribution.* Morristown, N.J.: General Learning Press, 1971.

Kanouse, D. E., & Abelson, R. P. Language variables affecting the persuasiveness of simple communications. *Journal of Personality and Social Psychology*, 1967, **7**, 158–163.

Podeschi, D. M., & Wyer, R. S. Acceptance of generalizations based upon inductive and deductive evidence. *Journal of Personality and Social Psychology*, 1976, **34**, 496–509.

Salancik, J. R. Inference of one's attitude from behavior recalled under linguistically manipulated cognitive sets. *Journal of Experimental Social Psychology*, 1974, **10**, 415–427.

Salancik, J. R., & Conway, M. Attitude inferences from salient and relevant cognitive content about behavior. *Journal of Personality and Social Psychology*, 1975, **32**, 829–840.

Wason, P. C., & Johnson-Laird, P. N. *Psychology of reasoning: Structure and content.* Cambridge, Mass.: Harvard University Press, 1972.

Wyer, R. S. *Cognitive organization and change: An information-processing approach.* Hillsdale, N.J.: Erlbaum, 1974.

Wyer, R. S. Some informational determinants of one's own liking for a person and beliefs that others will like this person. *Journal of Personality and Social Psychology*, 1975, **31**, 1041–1053.

Wyer, R. S., & Hinkle, R. L. Informational factors underlying inferences about hypothetical persons. *Journal of Personality and Social Psychology*, 1976, **34**, 481–495.

Wyer, R. S., & Watson, S. F. Context effects in impression formation. *Journal of Personality and Social Psychology*, 1969, **12**, 22–33.

Zajonc, R. B. Cognitive theories in social psychology. In G. Lindzey & E. Aronson (Eds.), *Handbook of social psychology*, Vol. 1 (2nd ed.). Reading, Mass.: Addison-Wesley, 1968.

REASONING AND THE REPRESENTATION OF TEXT

THE ROLE OF INFERENCE IN MEMORY FOR REAL AND ARTIFICIAL INFORMATION

George R. Potts
University of Denver

The contention that remembering represents an active process of reconstruction has become one of the basic axioms of cognitive psychology. Subjects do not passively store and later retrieve sensory experiences. Instead, incoming information is restructured to fit one's existing world knowledge. To answer a question, this stored information must be actively decoded, again drawing heavily on one's existing knowledge. Thus, memory should not be thought of as an isolated system which can be studied independently from other cognitive capacities. Remembering must, instead, be conceptualized as an exercise in problem solving which is inseparable from a person's general reasoning capabilities. Given this view, it seems unreasonable to expect that one could ever come to appreciate fully the richness and complexity of the act of remembering by performing experiments in which subjects are merely required to regurgitate information which was presented to them. One should

This work was supported in part by Grant No. BNS 76-80008 from the National Science Foundation. I would like to thank Lance Rips and Ed Shoben for their helpful comments on an early draft of this paper.

also examine subjects' ability to answer questions about information which was not actually presented. Thus, it should not be surprising that the process of drawing inferences has been receiving increased attention among researchers in the field of memory.

Experiments examining memory for inferences have fallen into one of two classes. In one class, the researcher defines an artificial body of information which the subject attempts to learn during the experimental session. After studying the information, subjects are asked a series of questions. Some of these questions test information which was actually presented; others test information which was not presented but which could be deduced from the presented information. Comparison of performance on these two types of questions can provide a measure of the nature and extent of subjects' constructive activity. In the second class, the semantic memory experiments, no new information is presented during the experimental session. Instead, the researcher measures the time required to answer a question about information which is already stored as part of subjects' generalized world knowledge. These reaction times are used to test hypotheses about the form in which information has been encoded and stored during a person's routine interactions with the perceptual world.

Though both of these lines of research have been fruitful (and have multiplied), they have, with few exceptions, remained relatively independent. This chapter represents an attempt to confront the results obtained in the two paradigms and, where necessary, to reconcile the differences between them. Such an attempt is important for two reasons.

First, both lines of research have their own inherent limitations. Experiments relying solely on an analysis of information stored as part of one's existing world knowledge are unavoidably correlational in nature. Hence, it is virtually impossible to demonstrate convincingly that a particular effect obtained in such a paradigm is not confounded by one or more important extraneous variables. Indeed, examination of the semantic memory literature reveals that it is composed of a very small number of basic results and a seemingly endless list of possible confounding factors, any of which could have accounted for the basic results. Attempts to eliminate a particular confound can always be challenged on the grounds that the manipulations employed, while reducing or eliminating one confound, may have unintentionally introduced or accentuated another. Use of an artificial body of information learned expressly for a particular experiment, on the other hand, enables much better control over extraneous variables. Unfortunately, subjects often develop rather specialized strategies for dealing with such information. Hence, one can never be sure that such studies reflect the operation of the same psychological processes as do experiments which use real information.

In view of the limitations of both these paradigms, it would seem that the most reasonable and productive approach lies in the coordination of the two types of experiments. The use of such converging operations should help make it possible to begin to determine whether a particular effect is due to the artificiality of experiments using artificial information, a confound in experiments using real information, or whether it is a theoretically important effect worthy of further examination.

The second reason for attempting a coordination of the results obtained using real and artificial information arises from the fact that most inferences occurring during text processing do not consist of merely reorganizing the presented material. Inferences usually arise out of the interaction between new information and one's existing world knowledge. The investigation of this interaction should be a high priority issue for researchers interested in text processing. As a first step in such an investigation, it is important to determine the degree to which experiments employing real and artificial information yield the same basic results and to reconcile any important differences.

This chapter begins with a description of some basic results arising out of the semantic memory literature and experiments using artificial information. A theoretical position is then described which accounts for these results. Finally, some preliminary experiments designed to test this position are described.

AN EMPIRICAL DATA BASE

Real-World Set Inclusion Relations

One of the most basic semantic memory results is the finding that when attempting to verify true real-world set inclusion relations, reaction time is a direct function of semantic distance. The greater the semantic distance between the terms of a relation, the longer the reaction time. Thus, e.g., the time required to verify a remote relation such as "A collie is an animal" is longer than the time required to verify a less remote relation such as "A collie is a dog" (Collins & Quillian, 1969). For false sentences, an effect in the opposite direction is obtained.

The effect obtained with true relations was originally interpreted as support for Quillian's (1969) notion of *cognitive economy*. According to this position, people do not store deducible information. Inferences are deduced only when required by a test on the information. Naturally, the more complex an inference, the longer it will take to answer a question about it. The fact that an opposite effect is obtained for false sentences would seem to pose a problem for such a model. As it turns out, however, though not explicitly predicted by the model, this effect is not inconsistent with it (see Collins & Quillian, 1972, and Collins & Loftus, 1975, for discussions of this point).

However, the methodological problems arising from the use of information stored as part of one's existing world knowledge are nowhere more apparent than in this study of the effect of inferential distance. Numerous confounds have been uncovered which would invalidate this result as evidence for the principle of cognitive economy. Conrad (1972) noted that inferentially remote relations are not encountered as frequently as are less remote relations. She suggested that frequency rather than inferential distance was the controlling variable. Other researchers (e.g., Landauer & Freedman, 1968; Landauer & Meyer, 1972; Meyer, 1970; Wilkins, 1971) noted that the object nouns of inferentially remote set inclusion sentences (e.g., *animal*) tend to describe larger sets than do the object nouns of less remote sentences (e.g., *dog*). These researchers argued that set size, not inferential distance, was the controlling variable. Finally, Rips, Shoben, and Smith (1973) noted that the terms of inferentially remote relations tend to be rated by subjects as being less similar than the terms of less remote relations. They argued that similarity, not inferential distance, was the controlling factor. As noted previously, experiments can be and have been run to test the relative importance of each of these factors; however, one can never be sure that these control experiments did not introduce a new set of confounds. Such is the nature of correlational studies. Because of this, it would be very informative to examine the effects of inferential distance using artificial information. We have done this, and the distance effects we observed were very different from the results described above.

Artificial Linear Orderings

The experiments in question involved presenting subjects with a series of paragraphs to study. Each paragraph described a linear ordering of four (Potts, 1972, 1974) or six (Potts, 1974; Scholz & Potts, 1974) terms. A four-term ordering (which will be characterized as $A > B > C > D$) can be described in terms of six pairwise relationships. Three of these pairs $(A > B, B > C, C > D)$ describe relations between adjacent elements in the ordering and will be referred to as *adjacent pairs*. These adjacent pairs are necessary to the establishment of the ordering. The remaining three pairs $(A > C, B > D,$ and $A > D)$ describe relations between nonadjacent elements in the ordering and will be referred to as *remote pairs*. Since the relations employed were transitive, these remote pairs could be deduced from some subset of the adjacent pairs. The 15 pairwise relations comprising a six-term ordering can be classified in a similar manner. Each paragraph presented the adjacent pairs necessary to establish a single ordering. A sample paragraph describing a four-term ordering is presented below (from Potts, 1974).

In art class, Sally showed her nature painting to the teacher. Her teacher felt that certain parts of the picture were drawn better than others. The teacher said her tree was better than her grass, her sky was better than her bird, and her bird was better than her tree. Upon hearing his, Sally decided to drop art and major in psychology. (p. 433)

Though only the adjacent pairs were presented, subjects were tested for their knowledge of all the pairs. Interestingly, even though the remote pairs were never presented, proportion correct was higher and reaction time shorter on these remote pairs than on the adjacent pairs. This was the case for both true and false sentences, and constitutes strong evidence that subjects were making and storing inferences while studying.

Though this result clearly contradicts Quillian's (1969) assumption that subjects draw inferences only at the time of test, the discrepancy between this data and results obtained using real set inclusion relations is bothersome. One possible explanation for the discrepancy is that experiments employing artificial information tap a different set of psychological processes than do semantic memory experiments which test subjects' generalized world knowledge. This would clearly be an unhappy state of affairs, for it would severely limit the generality of both lines of research. It would also make it very difficult to examine the processes involved in incorporating new information into one's existing world knowledge. A second, and less troublesome, possibility is that the strategies used to deal with linear orderings (e.g., "A horse is larger than a collie") do not correspond to the strategies used to deal with set inclusion relations (e.g., "A collie is a dog"). To distinguish between those two possibilities, it would be desirable to examine performance on real linear orderings and on artificial set inclusion relations.

Real Linear Orderings and Artificial Set Inclusions

Moyer (1973) was the first to report the semantic memory analog to our linear ordering experiments using artificial information. He showed subjects various pairs of animal names and asked them to indicate which animal was larger. He found that, just as in our linear ordering experiments using artificial information, the larger the difference in size between a pair of animals, the shorter the reaction time. This basic result has since been replicated several times (e.g., Banks & Flora, 1977; Paivio, 1975).

Similarly, Frase (1969, 1970) has examined proportion correct on artificial set inclusion relations and has obtained results similar to the typical semantic memory results. In these experiments, subjects learned a series of paragraphs each describing a five-term set inclusion relation $(A > B > C > D > E)$. A sample paragraph is given below:

The Fundalas are outcasts from other tribes in Central Ugala. It is the custom in this country to get rid of certain types of people. The hill people of Central Ugala are farmers. The upper highlands provide excellent soil for cultivation. The farmers of this country are peace loving, which is reflected in their art work. The outcasts of Central Ugala are hill people. There are about fifteen different tribes in this area. (Frase, 1969, p. 2)

The relation described by this paragraph can be characterized as an ordering:

Fundalas ⊂ outcasts ⊂ hill people ⊂ farmers ⊂ peace loving

Frase observed an interaction between truth value and inferential distance similar to the one obtained in a typical semantic memory experiment. For true sentences, proportion correct on the inferred remote pairs was lower than proportion correct on the adjacent pairs which were actually presented. For false sentences, proportion correct on the remote pairs was higher than proportion correct on the adjacent pairs. It should be noted, however, that in these experiments using artificial set inclusion relations, overall proportion correct is very low, much lower than proportion correct in the semantic memory experiments. This difference turns out to be an important diagnostic; a possible explanation will be presented later.

EXPLANATION FOR THE DISTANCE EFFECTS

Linear Orderings

The most widely accepted explanation for the distance effect obtained with linearly ordered information is that proposed by Moyer (1973). He argues for the existence of an "internal psychophysics" whereby subjects store actual perceptual representations of information. According to this position, the process involved when comparing two items stored in memory (e.g., "Which is larger, an elephant or a horse?") is analogous to the process of making an actual comparison between two stimuli. It is well established that when making such a perceptual comparison, the more discrepant the two terms, the more discriminable the difference between them and the easier the comparison. A variety of process models can be attached to this model to enable precise quantitative predictions, but the basic notion is quite simple.

This position can be easily extended to account for our work on linquistically derived artificial linear orderings. One needs only to argue that subjects arrange the terms of the ordering along an internal interval scale and that the ease of comparing two terms is a direct function of the distance separating those two terms on the scale. Support for such an explanation can be found by examining a subject's note-taking behavior in our experiments using artificial linear orderings. In these experiments, 73% of the subjects who took notes did so by listing the terms in an array from left to right or from top to bottom. Further, Griggs and Shea (in press) have demonstrated that increasing the described distance between two terms (e.g., "A is much larger than B") serves to decrease reaction time to the pair.

Set Inclusion Relations

As noted previously, interpretation of the semantic memory experiments using set inclusion relations is very difficult due to the large number of confounds inherent in such designs. Possible explanatory factors include cognitive economy, frequency, set size, and semantic similarity. This latter factor is attributed to Rips et al. (1973) and will be discussed in detail shortly.

Since the use of artificial information enables much better control over extraneous variables, it should be easier to develop a satisfactory explanation for the obtained interaction between inferential distance and truth value of the question. The most incisive explanation for the error profile obtained using artificial set inclusion relations has been given by Griggs (1976a). A similar explanation was proposed recently by Carroll and Kammann (1977). A detailed discussion of this position can be found in Griggs' chapter in this volume, but I will summarize his major points.

Griggs noted that the interaction between inferential distance and truth value was obtained even when subjects were allowed to refer to the paragraph while responding to the test questions. On the basis of this result, Griggs concluded that this interaction reflected not memory errors, but two different logical errors which subjects make when dealing with set inclusion relations. (a) Subjects tend to assume erroneously that the relations are symmetrical (i.e., if told that "all A are B," they tend to respond true to the sentence, "all B are A"). This accounts for the very low proportion correct on false statements of adjacent relations. This kind of "invalid conversion" (Johnson, 1972) error has also been observed by several other researchers studying syllogistic reasoning (e.g., Ceraso & Provetera, 1971; Chapman & Chapman, 1959; Johnson, 1972; Revlis, 1975; Woodworth & Sells, 1935). (b) Subjects fail to assume transitivity (i.e., if told that "All A are B" and "All B are C," they tend to respond *false* to any sentence, true or false, employing the pair of terms A and C). This accounts for the fact that as inferential distance increases, performance on true sentences decreases while performance on false sentences increases.

Although this explanation accounts nicely for the data and may well be correct, it leaves a very important question unanswered. Specifically, it does not address the question of why subjects make these maladaptive logical errors when dealing with artificial set inclusion relations. It also leaves open the question of why such errors are not found in experiments dealing with real set inclusion relations. In the theoretical discussion which follows, we will argue that subjects do, indeed, make logical errors when dealing with real set inclusion relations; we will further argue that the logical errors obtained when dealing with artificial set inclusion relations result from the generalization of strategies used for dealing with real information. To make these points, we must first make some assumptions about the nature of the representation of real information.

PROCESSING REAL AND ARTIFICIAL RELATIONS

Assume that our world knowlede (semantic memory) constitutes a multidimensional space. Knowledge about a particular lexical item is represented by the position of that item in this space. For example, our knowledge about the lexical item *lion* includes knowledge of its size and ferocity relative to other lexical items. The dimensions can be dichotomous as well as continuous; e.g., *lion* could be given a +1 on the dimension of furriness and a −1 on the dimension of wingedness. Note, of course, that furriness might actually represent a continuous dimension. Indeed, it may well be that there are very few, if any, truly dichotomous variables. Even something as seemingly dichotomous as the presence of wings could be graded according to the salience of the wings in the concept under consideration. Though *lion* would certainly anchor the scale at the "no wings" end, *chicken* might be much lower on the scale than *eagle*.

Given the above representation, comparing two items on a particular single dimension (e.g., size, ferocity, etc.) is relatively easy. Once the relevant dimension is identified, the items in semantic memory fall into an ordering on this dimension just as the items in an artificial linear ordering form a linear array. The farther apart two terms are, the more discriminable the difference between them and the easier the comparison. This principle accounts for the distance effects obtained for both real and artificial linear orderings.

The terms of an artificial set inclusion relation can also be arranged into a linear array, and it should be possible for subjects to use the same response strategy used in dealing with linear orderings. Thus, one might expect performance on the two kinds of material to be identical. Instead, subjects make a large number of errors when dealing with set inclusion relations. Why? The answer can be found by examining the difficulties inherent in dealing with a real set inclusion relation. Such a relation cannot be represented by a single ordering, for each term enters into many different, nonoverlapping set inclusion relations (i.e., a dog is both a mammal and a pet). Hence, one cannot think of terms being ordered on a single *is a* relation. Instead, membership in a particular class is defined by having a particular value on each of a set of critical dimensions. It is easy to see why making such a decision would be very difficult compared to simply isolating a single dimension and making a comparison. As it turns out, however, in most cases subjects do not have to go through such a decision process. Rips et al. (1973) have noted that there is a confound between "similarity" (i.e., Euclidian distance in a multidimensional space) and the relation of set inclusion. In general, when asked to verify the truth of a statement "An X is a Y," the statement tends to be true if X and Y are similar and false if X and Y are dissimilar. This confound has been carried into semantic memory experiments where true items tend to be sentences such as "A dog is an animal," and false items tend to be sentences such as "A tree is an animal." In such cases, Rips et al. (1973) note, subjects do not need to evaluate the actual logical relation, they merely need to make a similarity judgment and respond *true* if the terms are similar and *false* if the terms are dissimilar. It follows that the more similar two terms, the easier to respond *true*; the more dissimilar, the easier to respond *false*. This accounts for the observed interaction between truth value and inferential distance.

The relationship of this position to Griggs' notion of logical errors becomes clear when one notes that the two key characteristics of a similarity relation are (a) symmetry (i.e., "X is similar to Y" imples that "Y is similar to X"), and (b) a lack of transitivity (i.e., "X is similar to Y and Y is similar to Z" does not necessarily imply that "X is similar to Z"). Thus, Griggs' hypothesis that subjects make logical errors when dealing with artificial set inclusion relations is equivalent to the hypothesis that subjects respond to such relations as though they were similarity relations.

The only problem with the above analysis is that it is not clear what "similarity" means in the context of an artificial set inclusion relation. This can be given meaning by arguing that subjects represent (store) an artificial set inclusion relation in the same form as they represent an artificial linear ordering—namely, they arrange the terms of the relation in an imaginary array. Support for this position has been provided by Griggs (1976a) who reported that subjects were unable to determine whether a remote set inclusion sentence had actually been presented or whether they had deduced the information themselves. (For a more detailed discussion of these data, see Griggs' chapter in this volume.) Once the artificial information, be it a linear ordering or a set inclusion, is encoded into an array, subjects use the information just as they have learned to use real information. If the information represents a linear ordering, they evaluate the relative positions of the terms and respond correctly. If the information represents a set inclusion relation, on the other hand, they make the logical error of treating it as though it were a similarity relation. If the two terms are close together in the array, subjects tend to respond *true*; if the two terms are far apart, subjects tend to respond *false*.

Given that subjects make the same logical error with both real and artificial information, why do their responses yield a large number of overt errors when dealing with artificial information but only a particular reaction time profile when dealing with real information? The answer to this question is simple. As noted previously, there is a confound in semantic memory experiments so that the correct response to a sentence involving two similar terms is usually *true*, and the correct response to a sentence involving two dissimilar terms is usually *false*. Hence, the strategy of responding *true* to similar terms and *false* to dissimilar terms does not yield a large number of errors. In the experiments using artificial information, on the other hand, the false items are simple reversals of the true items. For every true sentence "All X are Y," there is a corresponding false sentence "All Y are X." Hence, there is no confound between truth value and similarity, and any attempt to respond on the basis of similarity results in a large number of errors.

In short, the present hypothesis suggests that subjects use very similar strategies in dealing with real and artificial information. Why do subjects make such seemingly maladaptive logical errors when dealing with an artificial set inclusion relation? The errors results from their erroneous tendency to treat the relation as a similarity relation. This is simply a strategy which has been carried over from their treatment of real set inclusion relations. With such relations, though still technically a logical error, responding on the basis of similarity is not at all maladaptive and does not lead to errors.

Semantic Features or Multidimensional Space?

At this point, it must be noted that I have taken some liberties with the theoretical position of Rips et al. (1973). In that study, they did speak of similarity in terms of Euclidian distance in multidimensional space. The space was derived by obtaining independent measures of rated similarity and then scaling these ratings to generate a multidimensional space. However, in a later study (Smith, Shoben, & Rips, 1974), the authors made it clear that they viewed the use of multidimensional spaces as an analytic tool and not as a psychological model for the representation of information. The psychological model they favored was a Semantic Feature Model.

According to this Semantic Feature model, information about a concept is stored as a set of semantic features. Set inclusion is determined by a set of *defining features* for a particular superordinate category. Thus, a particular exemplar such as *horse* will be classified as a *mammal* if it has the defining features, hair and milk production. In addition to this small set of defining features, however, there is also a fairly large set of *characteristic features* for a superordinate category. These characteristic features tend to be associated with the category in question. For example, a particular exemplar is likely to be a *mammal* if it has warm blood, bears live young, has four legs, etc. The more characteristic features an exemplar has, the more likely it is to belong to the superordinate category in question.

To determine class inclusion precisely, a subject would have to verify that a particular exemplar has all of the defining features of the superordinate category in question. This could be a very difficult decision to make. Smith et al. (1974) argued that, in general, subjects do not need to make such an evaluation. Typically, subjects make their decision on the basis of a preliminary scan of overlapping features. If a particular exemplar shares a large number of features with a particular superordinate category, subjects indicate that the exemplar is a member of the category. If an exemplar has very few overlapping features, subjects indicate that the exemplar is not a member of the category. Only when an intermediate number of overlapping features are detected do subjects go on to evaluate the defining features.

The distance effect obtained with linearly ordered information can also be explained in terms of an analysis of semantic features. Presume that a particular term is associated with a number of features pertaining to a single dimension such as size. Such an item might be coded as being the largest (or smallest) of all possibilities. It might be coded as being basically large (or basically small). Finally, it might also have some analog information indicating exactly how large (or small) it is. According to such a model, the more similar the two terms are on the relevant dimension, the more defined the information necessary to order them correctly, and the longer the reaction time. For a detailed discussion of models of this type, see Banks, Fujii, and Kayra-Stuart (1976).

If one argues that an artificial set inclusion relation is represented in the same form as an artificial linear ordering, then such a relation can be thought of as also having a set of features which indicate its placement in that ordering. Though a distinction between defining and characteristic features is not possible with such a relation, it is still reasonable to argue that subjects respond on the basis of overall feature overlap (i.e., similarity) when dealing with such relations.

The major point to be made from this discussion is that the semantic feature and multidimensional space models are interchangeable with regard to the present theoretical position. In both cases it is argued that set inclusion relations are evaluated in terms of the overall similarity of the two terms in question rather than on the basis of a careful evaluation of the necessary conditions for inclusion in the relevant class. Similarly, linear orderings are evaluated in terms of the particular value of the terms on the relevant dimension or relevant set of features. At present, the choice of a representation must be left to the whim of the theoretician. Currently, the semantic feature model seems to be the more popular of the two among semantic memory theorists. The multidimensional space model does seem to be worthy of consideration, however, and attempts to differentiate the two alternatives empirically should prove to be enlightening.

PRELIMINARY TESTS OF THE MODEL

Though the testing of the present model is just beginning, some of the preliminary results are provocative. Two such results are described below. For a more detailed description of this work, see Potts (1976).

Reaction Times for Artificial Set Inclusion Relations

In general, the overall error rate obtained when dealing with artificial set inclusion relations has always been too high to enable a meaningful analysis of reaction times. However, one would expect that some proportion of subjects do not make errors on these relations. The reaction time profile for these subjects is of considerable interest.

According to the present analysis, the reaction time profile for real set inclusion relations and the error profile for artificial set inclusion relations are both due to subjects' tendency to respond erroneously on the basis of similarity. For artificial relations, the set of false sentences is constructed by reversing the order of the terms in the true sentences, and, therefore, there is no relation whatsoever between similarity and truth value. This is why any attempt on the part of subjects to respond on the basis of similarity will invariably lead to a large number of errors. It follows from this that any subjects who do not make errors must not be responding on the basis of similarity. They must instead be evaluating the relations correctly. Since the present model argues that artificial linear orderings and set inclusion relations are stored in the same form, it follows that subjects who do not make logical errors on the set inclusion relations should have a reaction time profile similar to that obtained using linear orderings. Specifically, for both true and false sentences, reaction time should decrease with increases in inferential distance.

To test this prediction, a group of 19 college undergraduates studied two paragraphs, each of which described a five-term set inclusion relation (e.g., "All Fundalas are outcasts"). A second group of 18 college undergraduates studied two paragraphs, each of which described a five-term linear ordering (e.g., "The Fundalas are more numerous than outcasts"). The paragraphs were identical except for the relation used (*all are* vs. *are more numerous than*). The information in each paragraph was tested using a set of 20 test sentences. Four sentences described true adjacent pairs, six described true remote pairs. For each true sentence (e.g., $A > B?$) there was a corresponding false sentence which was constructed by reversing the order of the terms in the true sentence (e.g., $B > A?$). Subjects studied the first paragraph and then

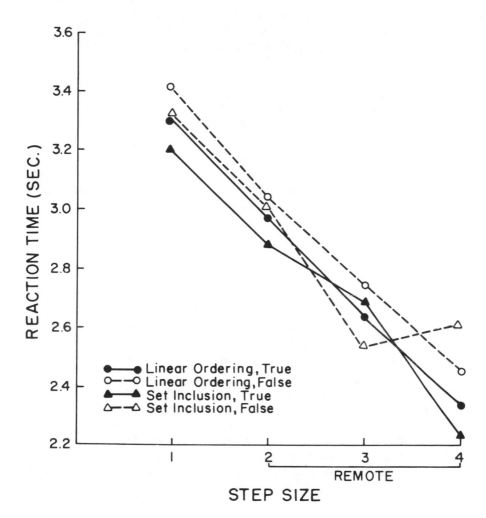

Fig. 1. Reaction time as a function of remoteness (step size) and truth value for subjects who do not make logical errors.

responded to the set of test sentences pertaining to that paragraph. They then studied and responded to the second paragraph. This cycle was repeated until subjects had responded to each paragraph three times. After each set of 20 test sentences, subjects were given feedback telling them how many errors they had made.

In analyzing the reaction times, only the last four trials (two on each paragraph) were scored. Figure 1 presents the mean reaction time correct as a function of inferential distance (step size) for the 6 set inclusion and 17 linear ordering subjects who scored 80% or better on both adjacent and remote pairs in both true and false sentences. As can be seen, performance on linear orderings and set inclusion relations is virtually identical. Reaction time to remote pairs was significantly shorter than reaction time to adjacent pairs for both true and false set inclusion relations and both true and false linear orderings. Thus, as predicted by the present model, subjects who do not make errors on the artificial set inclusion relations show the same reaction time profile as subjects who learn artificial linear orderings.

Responses to a Similarity Relation

If subjects do indeed respond to an artificial set inclusion relation as though it were a similarity relation, then one would expect that the use of similarity as a relation should yield the same results as the use of a set inclusion relation. Of course, it must be kept in mind that not all subjects respond to set inclusion relations in this way. Hence, the set inclusion profile will almost certainly reflect a mixture of strategies.

To test these predictions 55 college undergraduates were randomly divided into three groups. One group ($n = 19$) learned two paragraphs describing a five-term set inclusion relation. A second group ($n = 18$) learned a pair of linear orderings, while a third group ($n = 18$) learned a pair of similarity relations. Again, the paragraphs given to each group were identical except for the actual relation used. An example of each of the paragraphs representing each of the three types of relation is given below.

Linear ordering

The Fundalas of Central Ugala are more numerous than outcasts. The outcasts of Central Ugala are more numerous than hill people. The hill people of Central Ugala are more numerous than farmers. The farmers of Central Ugala are more numerous than pacifists.

Set inclusion

All the Fundalas of Central Ugala are outcasts. All the outcasts of Central Ugala are hill people. All the hill people of Central Ugala are farmers. All the farmers of Central Ugala are pacifists.

Similarity

The Fundalas of Central Ugala are similar to outcasts. The outcasts of Central Ugala are similar to hill people. The hill people of Central Ugala are similar to farmers. The farmers of Central Ugala are similar to pacifists.

The procedure was virtually identical to the one employed in the previous experiment except that no feedback was given after each paragraph. It was impossible to give feedback in this experiment because the similarity relation does not lend itself to a clear breakdown into true and false sentences (e.g., given that "A is similar to B and B is similar to C," is the sentence "C is similar to A" true or false?). Once again, three trials were given on each of the two relations. It was hoped that subjects' response strategies would become stereotyped and that individual subjects could be classified according to the response strategy they were using.

Since remote sentences describing a similarity relation cannot be classified as true or false, the data in all conditions will be described in terms of subjects' tendency to respond *true*. Figure 2 presents the probability (averaged over subjects and trials) of saying *true* to forward (e.g., A > B?) and backward (e.g., B > A?) test sentences as a function of the type of relation and inferential distance (step size). Table 1 presents the number of subjects responding consistently (over 80%) *true* or *false* as a function of type of pair (adjacent vs. remote) and relation. Of major interest are the tendency to assume symmetry and the tendency to fail to assume transitivity for the three relation types.

An indication of the tendency to assume symmetry can be obtained by examining the difference in the tendency to respond *true* to forward and backward sentences. If subjects assume symmetry, then responses to forward and backward sentences should be identical; if subjects assume nonsymmetry, then the response to a backward sentence should be exactly the opposite of the response to the corresponding true sentence. Examination of Figure 2 reveals that for a similarity relation, the proportion of *true* responses is virtually identical for forward and backward sentences. Hence, as one would expect, subjects are clearly assuming symmetry for these relations. This conclusion is supported by the individual subjects' data in Table 1. The proportion of similarity subjects consistently responding *true* or *false* is the same for forward and backward sentences. Linear ordering subjects, on the other hand, show no such tendency to assume symmetry. They consistently respond *true* to forward sentences and *false* to backward sentences. This can also be seen clearly in the individual subjects' data. For set inclusion subjects, the tendency to assume symmetry is intermediate between these two extremes. This should lead one to question whether this is due to a certain

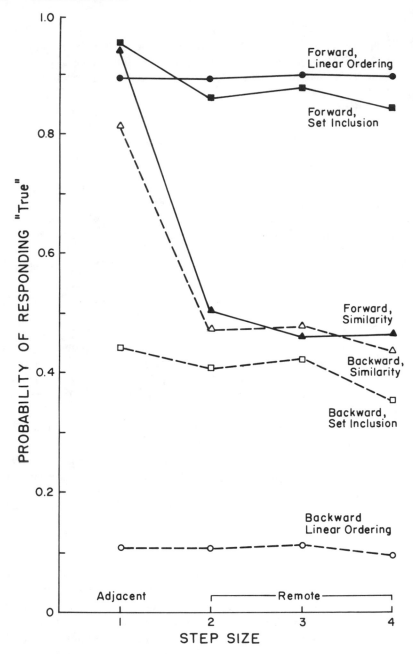

Fig. 2. Probability of responding *true* as a function of type of relation, re-moteness (step size), and truth value. (Adapted from Potts, 1976).

Table 1. Number of Subjects Responding Consistently (over 80%) as a Function of Type of Pair and Relation (From Potts, 1976)

Type of pair	Type of Relation								
	Set inclusion			Similarity			Linear ordering		
	T	F	(?)	T	F	(?)	T	F	(?)
Adjacent, forward (e.g., A — B)	18	0	(1)	17	0	(2)	15	0	(3)
Remote, forward (e.g., A — C)	15	1	(3)	9	9	(1)	15	0	(3)
Adjacent, backward (e.g., B — A)	4	8	(7)	14	2	(3)	0	15	(3)
Remote, backward (e.g., C — A)	3	9	(7)	9	10	(0)	0	16	(2)

Note. — T = subjects responding *true*, F = subjects responding *false*, ? = subjects not meeting the criterion of consistency.

proportion of the subjects responding according to symmetry and a certain proportion assuming nonsymmetry. Such a result would constitute strong evidence for the present theoretical position. Unfortunately, the data are not that clear. Most subjects consistently respond *true* to both adjacent and remote forward sentences. For backward sentences, more subjects respond *false* than *true*. Most interesting, however, is the large number of subjects whose responses are not consistent on these sentences. This would seem to indicate uncertainty on the part of subjects regarding how to respond to the false sentences.

An indication of the tendency to assume transitivity can be obtained by examining the difference in the tendency to respond *true* to adjacent and remote pairs. A large difference would indicate a failure to assume transitivity. Examination of Figure 2 indicates that responses to the similarity relation show such a difference. It is interesting that the proportion of *true* responses to remote sentences is near 50%. This should lead one to wonder whether half of the subjects assume transitivity (i.e., respond the same to adjacent and remote sentences), and half do not. Examination of Table 1 reveals that this is indeed the case. All subjects consistently respond *true* to adjacent similarity sentences; on remote similarity sentences half of the subjects consistently respond *true*, while the other half consistently respond *false*. For linear ordering subjects, on the other hand, there is virtually no difference in the tendency to respond *true* to adjacent and remote pairs. Hence, these subjects clearly assume transitivity. For set inclusion subjects, there is also very little difference in the responses to adjacent and remote pairs, though the small observed difference did turn out to be significant. Thus, the present experiment found little (but some) evidence for the contention that subjects fail to assume transitivity for these relations. It must be noted, however, that this experiment is unusual in this respect. The experiments reported by Griggs in this volume as well as other experiments we have performed have all found a much greater difference in performance on adjacent and remote pairs for these relations. It is unclear why this difference was not found in the present experiment.

A RESPONSE TO GRIGGS' CRITICISMS

At the end of his chapter, Griggs expresses several objections to the model proposed in this chapter. His basic disagreement seems to be with my contention that subjects construct an ordering to represent artificial set inclusion information and that logical errors arise as subjects attempt to use the ordering to answer questions. This is in contrast to his contention that the representation of artificial set inclusion relations consists of "a subset of the presented adjacent pairs."

There are two pieces of evidence that might lead one to favor the ordering explanation that I have proposed. First, there is Griggs' (1976b) finding that, when given a recognition task with artificial set inclusion relations, subjects cannot distinguish between inferences and information which was actually presented. This replicates the recognition results I have reported with linear orderings (Potts, 1973) and suggests that, rather than storing the presented information, subjects are using that information to construct an integrated representation of the information. Second, there is my finding (Potts, 1976) that subjects who do not make logical errors demonstrate identical reaction time profiles for linear orderings and set inclusion relations; for both true and false sentences, reaction time decreases with increases in inferential distance. Griggs' notes having observed the same effect. This would seem to contradict the contention that set inclusion subjects were simply storing the adjacent pairs.

However, Griggs argues correctly that these facts do not conclusively eliminate his model. As Griggs notes, the recognition results could be explained by arguing that the presentation conditions were set up in such a way as to cause massive interference (e.g., Reitman & Bower, 1973), or by arguing that the test procedure was insensitive (Anderson & Bower, 1973). The reaction time profile for subjects who do not make errors can be explained by arguing that subjects who do not make logical errors construct an ordering, while subjects who do make errors simply store pairs.

Though the question of whether subjects deal with artificial set inclusion relations by constructing an ordering or merely by storing pairs is an interesting one, it is not critical to the model I have proposed. The basic characteristic of the position I have proposed here is that subjects erroneously treat both real and artificial set inclusion relations as similarity relations. The notion that subjects represent artificial set inclusion relations in the form of a unified ordering represents a resonable and parsimonious assumption which accounts nicely for the present data; however, it is not essential to the primary proposition. Even if one assumes that subjects store individual pairs, it is still quite reasonable that, when they are forced to answer questions about information which was not presented, they make the logical error of treating the relations as similarity relations. Hence, the present model does not rise or fall on the assumption that subjects represent artificial set inclusions in the form of an ordering. At present, this merely seems to be a viable and parsimonious explanation. To make a convincing case for this, however, it is necessary to examine Griggs' objections in detail.

1. Griggs' potentially most damaging criticism is that "it seems implausible that subjects would form a line representation without employing transitivity." Why, Griggs agrues, should subjects assume transitivity in forming a linear array but not use that property in responding to the questions? The answer, I believe, lies in the fact that transitivity is not a necessary property of a similarity relation. If told that "A and B are similar" and that "B and C are similar," what can subjects deduce for sure about the relation between A and C? Actually, nothing. However, in arguing that subjects "construct an ordering," I am proposing that subjects conclude that A and C are less similar than either A and B or B and C. Making such an assumption, which I feel is reasonable thought not logically necessary, will lead to an array "A – B – C" on the dimension of similarity. Though such an array is constructed, it does not necessarily have the property of transitivity in that there is no assurance that subjects will say that A and C are similar. In fact, the performance of individual subjects on a similarity relation, which was described in the previous section, indicated that approximately half of the subjects assumed transitivity, and half did not.

The viability of this explanation hinges on the assumption that if subjects are told that A and B are similar and that B and C are similar, they will view the terms A and C as being less similar than either of these presented pairs. Is this assumption reasonable? To test this question, I conducted an informal experiment on nine subjects (secretaries and clinical psychology graduate students and faculty). These subjects were given the following information:

> Assume that JAL, MEP, TOC, and CAZ represent four different concepts.
> Assume the following relations hold:
>> a JAL is similar to a CAZ
>> a MEP is similar to a JAL
>> a CAZ is similar to a TOC

If subjects adopt the strategy of representing the information as a linear array, this array would be characterized as:

$$MEP - JAL - CAZ - TOC$$

After reading the relations (which were left in front of them), subjects were asked three questions. Each of the first two questions consisted of presenting two pairs of terms and asking subjects to indicate which pair was more similar. The two sets of alternatives were:

1. JAL − CAZ and JAL − TOC
2. MEP − CAZ and MEP − JAL

Eight of the nine subjects chose JAL − CAZ as the answer to the first question, and seven of the nine subjects chose MEP − JAL as the answer to the second question.

For the last question, subjects were asked "Of all four terms, which two are the most dissimilar to each other?" Six of the nine subjects indicated that the pair MEP − TOC was the most dissimilar pair of terms.

These data clearly confirm our hypothesis that, in dealing with similarity relations, most subjects do indeed make assumptions which lead to an ordered array of terms even though such assumptions are not logically necessary.

2. Griggs argues that a distinction between defining and characteristic features is not possible when dealing with artificial logical relations. This is, of course, quite true. Indeed, their insistence on the existence of such a distinction has been one of the most hotly debated assumptions of the Smith et al. (1974) model. I, for one, am not convinced of its usefulness. Without that assumption, the Smith et al. feature model would merely argue that set inclusion decisions are made on the basis of an overall comparison of overlapping features. Such a model is functionally equivalent to the argument that subjects respond on the basis of overall distance in a multidimensional space. I merely intended to point out that isomorphism.

3. Griggs states that his recognition data do not support the present model. He contends that the fact that subjects incorrectly recognized true deducible sentences as "OLD" indicates that they recognized the transitivity of the relation and used this property in answering the question. If this is the case, why should they not also indicate that the sentence is *true*. The answer, I think, lies in the fact that not every subject falsely recognizes true remote sentences as OLD, just as not every subject incorrectly responds *false*. Given that the information is represented as an array ordered on the dimension of similarity, subjects have no idea whether a true remote sentence was presented any more than they know whether it was true. It is quite likely that subjects who indicate that a sentence is OLD do also indicate that it is *true*. To test this, it would be necessary to give the same subjects both a recognition and a verification task on the same ordering.

More problematic is the fact that subjects do not incorrectly identify false sentences as OLD. Theoretically, if they are treating the relations as symmetrical (as similarity relations are), then they should make such errors. However, to account for this, one would need only to assume that subjects remembered something about the direction in which the array was constructed. Though not the ultimate in elegance, this does not seem to be an unreasonable assumption.

4. Griggs describes a result reported in Potts (1976) in which the terms were nonsense syllables, and no logical errors were observed. He argues that this result does not contradict his proposal that there are two distinct classes of subjects, one of which stores an ordering and makes no errors, the second of which stores pairs and does make errors. He is correct; it was never argued that this result did contradict the model. This result merely constituted another verification that, when subjects do not make errors on set inclusion relations, the resulting reaction time profile is identical to that obtained when linear orderings are used. Griggs proposes one possoble explanation for the absence of logical errors in that particular experiment, but it is only one of many possible explanations. These possibilities are discussed in Potts (1976).

5. Griggs cites a recent article by McCloskey and Glucksberg (1976) as evidence against the Rips et al. (1973) similarity model. McCloskey and Glucksberg included highly related false sentences in the test sequence and, contrary to the predictions of the similarity model, did not observe either the elimination of the distance effect or high error rate among true sentences. Though this is a very provocative piece of research, it is certainly not conclusive. Models are not eliminated on the basis of a single contradictory result, especially when that result constitutes a confirmation of the null hypothesis in an area containing as many pitfalls as that of semantic memory. One serious potential problem with the McCloskey and Glucksberg result is that it is not clear that there were enough highly related false sentences to

lead to the predicted effects. Only further work will tell how serious a challenge to the similarity model this result really is.

In closing, I would like to reiterate that I still do view the present interpretation as "speculative." My primary hope is that it will serve to accentuate the need for an integration of the semantic memory literature and work employing artificial information, and to provide one basis for such an integration.

REFERENCES

Anderson, J. R., & Bower, G. H. *Human associative memory.* Washington, D.C.: Winston, 1973.

Banks, W. P., & Flora, J. Semantic and perceptual processes in symbolic comparisons. *Journal of Experimental Psychology: Human Perception and Performance*, 1977, in press.

Banks, W. P., Fujii, M., & Kayra-Stuart, F. Semantic congruity effects in comparative judgments of magnitudes of digits. *Journal of Experimental Psychology: Human Perception and Performance*, 1976, **2**, 435–447.

Carroll, M., & Kammann, R. The dependency of schema formation on type of verbal material: Linear orderings and set inclusions. *Memory & Cognition*, 1977, **5**, 73–78.

Ceraso, J., & Provitera, A. Sources of error in syllogistic reasoning. *Cognitive Psychology*, 1971, **2**, 400–410.

Chapman, L. J., & Chapman, J. P. Atmosphere effect re-examined. *Journal of Experimental Psychology*, 1959, **58**, 220–226.

Collins, A. M., & Loftus, E. F. A spreading-activation theory of semantic processing. *Psychological Review*, 1975, **82**, 407–428.

Collins, A. M., & Quillian, M. R. Retrieval time from semantic memory. *Journal of Verbal Learning and Verbal Behavior*, 1969, **8**, 240–247.

Collins, A. M., & Quillian, M. R. Experiments on semantic memory and language comprehension. In L. W. Gregg (Ed.), *Cognition in learning and memory.* New York: Wiley, 1972.

Conrad, C. Cognitive economy in semantic memory. *Journal of Experimental Psychology*, 1972, **92**, 149–154.

Frase, L. T. Structural analysis of the knowledge that results from thinking about text. *Journal of Educational Psychology Monograph*, 1969, **60** (6, Part 2).

Frase, L. T. Influence of sentence order and amount of higher level test processing upon reproductive and productive memory. *American Educational Research Journal*, 1970, **7**, 307–319.

Griggs, R. A. Logical processing of set inclusion relations in meaningful text. *Memory & Cognition*, 1976, **4**, 730–740. (a)

Griggs, R. A. Recognition memory for deducible information. *Memory & Cognition*, 1976, **4**, 643–647. (b)

Griggs, R. A., & Shea, S. L. Integrating verbal quantitative information in linear orderings. *Memory & Cognition*, in press.

Johnson, D. M. *Systematic introduction to the psychology of thinking.* New York: Harper & Row, 1972.

Landauer, T. K., & Freedman, J. L. Information retrieval from long-term memory: Category size and recognition time. *Journal of Verbal Learning and Verbal Behavior,* 1968, 7, 291–295.

Landauer, T. K., & Meyer, D. E. Category size and semantic-memory retrieval. *Journal of Verbal Learning and Verbal Behavior,* 1972, 11, 539–549.

McCloskey, M., & Glucksberg, S. *Semantic memory: Test of a feature comparison model.* Paper presented at the meeting of the American Psychological Association, Washington, D.C. September 1976.

Meyer, D. E. On the representation and retrieval of stored semantic information. *Cognitive Psychology,* 1970, 1, 242–300.

Moyer, R. S. Comparing objects in memory: Evidence suggesting an internal psychophysics. *Perception and Psychophysics,* 1973, 13, 180–184.

Paivio, A. Perceptual comparisons through the mind's eye. *Memory & Cognition,* 1975, 3, 635–647.

Potts, G. R. Information processing strategies used in the encoding of linear orderings. *Journal of Verbal Learning and Verbal Behavior,* 1972, 11, 727–740.

Potts, G. R. Memory for redundant information. *Memory & Cognition,* 1973, 1, 467–470.

Potts, G. R. Storing and retrieving information about ordered relationships. *Journal of Experimental Psychology,* 1974, 103, 431–439.

Potts, G. R. Artificial logical relations and their relevance to semantic memory. *Journal of Experimental Psychology: Human Learning and Memory,* 1976, 2, 746–758.

Quillian, M. R. The teachable language comprehender: A simulation program and theory of language. *Communications of the ACM,* 1969, 12, 459–476.

Reitman, J. S., & Bower, G. H. Storage and later recognition of exemplars of concepts. *Cognitive Psychology,* 1973, 4, 194–206.

Revlis, R. Two models of syllogistic reasoning: Feature selection and conversion. *Journal of Verbal Learning and Verbal Behavior,* 1975, 14, 180–195.

Rips, L. J., Shoben, E. J., & Smith, E. E. Semantic distance and the verification of semantic relations. *Journal of Verbal Learning and Verbal Behavior,* 1973, 12, 1–20.

Scholz, K. W., & Potts, G. R. Cognitive processing of linear orderings. *Journal of Experimental Psychology,* 1974, 102, 323–326.

Smith, E. E., Shoben, E. J., & Rips, L. J. Structure and process in semantic memory: A feature model for semantic decisions. *Psychological Review,* 1974, 81, 214–241.

Wilkins, A. J. Conjoint frequency, category size, and categorization time. *Journal of Verbal Learning and Verbal Behavior,* 1971, 10, 382–385.

Woodworth, R. S., & Sells, S. B. An atmosphere effect in formal syllogistic reasoning. *Journal of Experimental Psychology,* 1935, 18, 451–460.

DRAWING INFERENCES FROM SET INCLUSION INFORMATION GIVEN IN TEXT

Richard A. Griggs
University of Florida

The processing of artificial knowledge structures described in meaningful text has been the subject of many recent studies (e.g., Brockway, Chmielewski, & Cofer, 1974; Griggs, 1976a; Potts, 1976, Chap. 6 in this volume; Tzeng, 1975). The label *artificial* is employed to distinguish this line of research from semantic memory research in which the structure of existing world knowledge is studied (e.g., Collins & Wuillian, 1972; Smith, Shoben, & Rips, 1974).[1] In artificial knowledge studies, the processing of arbitrary information learned during an experimental session is investigated. Linear ordering and set inclusion relational structures are usually employed in these

The research reported in this chapter was partially supported by NIMH Grant No. PHS RO1 MH 16817 to Frank Restle, Indiana University, and by a research grant to the author from the Social and Behavioral Sciences Council, University of Florida. I wish to express my appreciation to Larry Osterman and Don Keen for their comments on earlier drafts of this chapter.

[1] See Potts' chapter in this volume for a more detailed contrast of these two approaches.

studies because their transitivity property permits inference making. This allows investigators to address the question of whether inferences are made during study and, therefore, incorporated into the memory representation for the relation or whether they are deduced at time of test. The main queries posed by these studies concern the memory representations for these set-theoretic relations and the processing of the representations to answer questions about the relational information.

This chapter is concerned with some recent conflicting findings about drawing inferences from such structured paragraphs of text. For paragraphs describing artificial linear ordering relations, subjects respond faster and more accurately to questions about information they have to deduce from the paragraph than to questions about information presented in the paragraph. This result has not been observed for paragraphs describing set inclusion relations. Subjects do not appear even to make the permitted inferences. A series of experiments investigating the processing of set inclusion information and attempting to resolve the above conflict will be described. First, the experimental work leading to the conflicting results for the two similar relations will be briefly presented; next, experiments investigating the conflict will be discussed; and finally, some recent theoretical explanations concerning the representation and processing of a set inclusion relation will be evaluated.

BACKGROUND

The first experiments on processing set inclusion information that are relevant to this discussion were conducted by Frase (1969, 1970). In his experiments, Frase employed paragraphs that contained sentences which asserted subset relations between five sets. The following is a sample five-term set inclusion paragraph similar to those employed by Frase and by subsequent researchers:

> All the Fundalas are outcasts from other tribes in Central Ugala. These people are isolated from the other tribes because it is the custom in this country to get rid of certain types of people. All the outcasts of Central Ugala are hill people. The hills provide a most accommodating place to live. All the hill people of Central Ugala are farmers. The upper highlands provide excellent soil for cultivation. All the farmers of this country are peace loving people which is reflected in their artwork. All together, there are about fifteen different tribes in this area.

If the sets are letter-coded so that they are (A) Fundalas, (B) outcasts, (C) hill people, (D) farmers, and (E) peace loving people, then the four primary sentences of the paragraph all "All A's are B'S", "All B's are C's," "All C's are D's," and "All D's are E's"—a series of universal affirmative statements. The extraneous sentences are included to make the paragraph seem more natural and are ignored in all analyses. Thus, the basic text structure of the paragraph is a series of subset relations, a set inclusion.

The five-term inclusion can be described in terms of ten pairwise relationships. Four of these pairs (AB, BC, CD, DE) describe relations between adjacent sets in the inclusion and are referred to as adjacent pairs. The remaining six pairs describe relations between nonadjacent pairs (AC, AD, AE, BD, BE, CE) and are referred to as *remote* pairs. Only the adjacent pairs are presented in the paragraph.

Frase employed an incidental learning task. Subjects read paragraphs in order to decide if the statement typed at the top of each paragraph was a valid conclusion from the text or, in other experiments, underlined the information in the paragraph that was needed to verify the conclusion at the top of the paragraph. This task was followed by a free recall test which was sometimes followed by a validity judgment test. On free recall tests subjects were asked to write down all the assertions they could recall and all the inferences they could generate. For each paragraph the validity judgment test consisted of 20 universal affirmative assertions. Ten were valid—the four adjacent sentences given in the text and the six valid remote inferences. Ten were invalid—the 10 valid assertions but with the relations reversed, e.g., "All B's are A's" is the invalid counterpart of "All A's are B's." Subjects indicated for each assertion whether it was a valid or invalid conclusion from the text.

In general, Frase found memory for adjacent pairs to be superior to memory for remote pairs. Recall of presented, adjacent information was superior to recall of deducible, remote information. However, even the recall of adjacent pairs was poor. In Frase (1970), e.g., recall of adjacent pairs was only 35% of possible recall, and recall of remote pairs was only 15%. The number of assertions recalled was a decreasing function of *step size* (the number of adjacent pairs that have to be related to each other to produce an assertion). An assertion of Step Size 4 (e.g., "All A's are E's") was less likely to be recalled than an assertion of Step Size 3 (e.g., "All A's are D's"), and so on. Thus, as inferential distance increased, recall decreased.

The validity test results were different. No significant difference between proportion correct on remote pairs and adjacent pairs was observed. Frase (1969), however, did observe an interaction of validity by step size. If only valid test statements are considered, subjects did better on presented information (Step Size 1) than on deducible information (Step Size > 1). If only invalid sentences are considered, subjects did better on deducible information.

Potts (1972, 1974, 1975; Scholz & Potts, 1974) has found very different results for a similar transitive relation, the linear ordering relation. Potts investigated the processing of paragraphs describing linear ordering relations such as A > B > C > D, where A', B, C, and D symbolically represent the terms of the ordering and ">" some comparative adjective describing the dimension on which the terms are ordered. His procedure was very straightforward. In brief, subjects, who knew they were going to be tested, studied a paragraph describing one or more linear orderings and then were given a True-False test on the information in the paragraph. An example of a four-term linear ordering paragraph used by Potts is the following:

> In a small forest just south of nowhere, a deer, a bear, a wolf, and a hawk were battling for dominion over the land. It boiled down to a battle of wits, so intelligence was the crucial factor. The bear was smarter than the hawk, the hawk was smarter than the wolf, and the wolf was smarter than the deer . . . . Each of the battles was decided in its own way and tranquility returned to the area (Potts, 1972, p. 730).

As in Frase's experiments, the adjacent pairs were presented, and transitivity allowed remote pairs to be deduced. The adjacent and remote pairs comprising the ordering were the true test statements; false test statements were constructed by reversing the order of terms in each true statement.

Potts has found that performance (both proportion correct and response latency) is superior on deducible, remote information. In fact, performance is a function of inferential distance, i.e., the farther apart the two terms are in the ordering, the better the performance. This is a very robust result and is the case for both true and false sentences. Potts' explanation of these results is that subjects make the permissible inferences during study and integrate these with the presented order information to construct a more general semantic representation of the ordering. Specifically, an integrated representation with spacing of terms along a mental continuum by either analog or linear transformations has been implicated. This general semantic representation is stored, not a set of the order relations. This agrees with recent findings in sentence memory experiments which support the constructivist theory of language comprehension (e.g., Bransford, Barclay, & Franks, 1972; Bransford & Franks, 1971; Cofer, 1973). Briefly, constructivist theory proposes that humans actively transform linguistic input into a cognitive structure which is a function of the input information, context of the situation, and prior knowledge. (For more detail, see Bransford & McCarrell, 1974.) Frase's results did not indicate such a constructive encoding process. Performance on deducible information was not better than performance on presented information.

MORE EXPERIMENTAL EVIDENCE FOR
DIFFERENTIAL PERFORMANCE

Frase's experiments differed from Potts' in several ways. Potts used a True-False test, while Frase administered a free recall test followed by a validity judgment test. Frase employed an incidental learning task, while Potts used a study/test paradigm giving subjects either limited or a self-paced amount of time to read and study each paragraph. Frase also inserted extraneous information between successively presented adjacent pairs whereas Potts did not. Thus, the observed differences could have been brought about by these procedural differences or by differential processing of the two set-theoretic structures.

Griggs (1976a) looked at both types of set-theoretic material in the same experimental conditions, thereby removing procedural differences. In Experiment 1, extraneous material was inserted between the presented adjacent pairs in both types of paragraphs. A self-paced study/True-False test paradigm was employed. Subjects (college undergraduates) were instructed to respond *true* to a sentence if it was presented in the paragraph or was a valid conclusion from the information in the paragraph and to respond *false* if it was not presented and was not a valid conclusion from the information in the paragraph. No feedback was given.

Mean proportion correct as a function of step size for both linear orderings and set inclusions is given in Table 1. In general, Potts' linear ordering results were replicated. A distance effect was observed. Proportion correct on remote pairs was significantly greater than proportion correct on adjacent pairs for both true and false statements. Frase's set inclusion results were also replicated. No significant distance main effect was observed, but a truth value main effect and a truth value by inferential distance interaction were observed. For true statements, subjects performed better on adjacent pairs.

Table 1. Mean Proportion Correct as a Function of Step Size for Linear Orderings and Set Inclusions

Step size	Linear orderings		Set inclusions	
	True	False	True	False
1	.82	.82	.76	.47
2	.86	.84	.67	.59
3	.88	.87	.65	.61
4	.92	.88	.74	.70

Note. – Data from Experiment 1, Griggs (1976a).

For false statements, subjects performed better on remote pairs. Overall level of performance on set inclusions (.630) was much lower than that on linear orderings (.848). Performance on false adjacent test statements was especially poor (.465).

The extraneous material did not seem to affect the linear ordering results, but it could be the source of difficulty with the set inclusion material. In Experiment 3, Griggs (1976a) attempted to determine whether the set inclusion error profiles still appeared if the extraneous material was removed. Subjects studied paragraphs which contained only the adjacent pairs in the inclusion in a chained order (AB, BC, CD, DE) and no extraneous material whatsoever.[2] Study was self-paced, and the experimental conditions were the same as in Experiment 1 except for the deletion of the extraneous material.

The results of this experiment were essentially the same as those for Experiment 1. Mean proportion correct as a function of step size is given in Figure 1. The overall level of performance was low (.688), and a truth value by step size interaction was observed. Thus, even when the adjacent pairs of an inclusion are presented in a chained order with no extraneous material between the presented pairs (or even in the paragraph), subjects have difficulty with set inclusion information.

ERRONEOUS LOGICAL PROCESSING OF SET INCLUSION INFORMATION

One hypothesis to account for these set inclusion error profiles is that the difficulty with set inclusion material is not in memory but in the subjects' logical processing of the set inclusion information. It is possible that the set inclusion statements are sometimes being interpreted to mean that the two sets described, A and B, for example, are equivalent. Using such an interpretation one would deduce that "All B's are A's." Such erroneous symmetric deductions would help account for the poor performance of false adjacent statements. This error of "invalid conversion" (Johnson, 1972) is fairly common in syllogistic reasoning studies (e.g., Ceraso & Provitera, 1971; Chapman & Chapman, 1959) and is the key feature of Revlis' model of syllogistic reasoning (1975; see also Chap. 3 in this volume).

A conversion operation may help to explain the poor performance of false statements but certainly will not account for the decreasing step size function for true test statements and the increasing step size function for false test statements. Subjects are failing to assume transitivity, and this failure is an increasing function of step size. Thus, the erroneous logical processing

---

[2] This is the only experiment to be reported in which we did not employ paragraphs containing extraneous material.

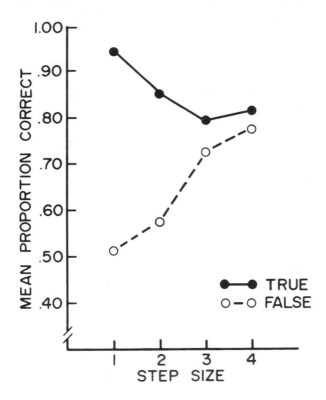

Fig. 1. Mean proportion correct as a function of step size for set inclusion paragraph containing no extraneous material. Data are from Experiment 3, Griggs (1976a).

hypothesis proposes that two errors in subjects' logical processing account for the set inclusion results: (a) Subjects make invalid symmetric inferences, and (b) subjects fail to make many valid transitive inferences, and this failure is an increasing function of inferential distance.

Griggs (1976a) examined this logical processing hypothesis by presenting the questions and the paragraph simultaneously. In Experiment 4, the study and test phases were combined into one phase. Thus, there was no memory load, and the subject merely had to calculate answers to the questions with the paragraph in front of him. The procedure employed was very similar to Frase's incidental learning task described earlier. Each subject was tested on only one paragraph and was instructed to process as much of the paragraph as necessary in order to answer each question. The order of the test sentences was randomized for each subject.

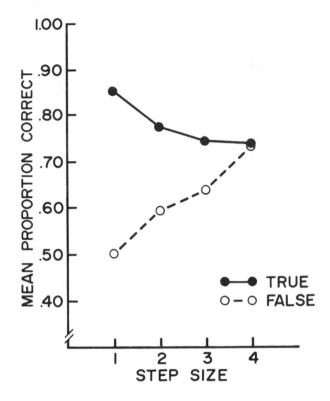

Fig. 2. Mean proportion correct as a function of step size for true and false test statements presented simultaneously with the set inclusion paragraph. Data are from Experiment 4, Griggs (1976a).

Mean proportion correct as a function of step size is given in Figure 2. The same pattern of True-False differences observed for set inclusions in the two experiments already discussed was observed in this experiment in which the subject had the study paragraph in front of him at all times. Performance on true test statements was better than in previous experiments, but performance on false statements was still very poor. These results suggest that the major source of difficulty is not memory retrieval but rather erroneous logical processing.

If subjects are making erroneous symmetric deductions, then this faulty interpretation should be prevented if actual counterexamples to the erroneously deduced equivalency are included in the study paragraphs. In a syllogistic reasoning study, Ceraso and Provitera (1971) presented one group of college students with traditional sentence-type syllogisms, while another group received modified syllogisms with explicit premises to restrict interpretations of the premises. That is, the premises were modified so that only one interpretation of a quantifier was possible. Ceraso and Provitera found that subjects performed consistently better when given modified syllogisms.

A similar approach was used by Griggs (1976a, Experiment 5) to test the logical processing hypothesis. In a self-paced study/True-False test paradigm, paragraphs were used that contained the adjacent pairs that established a set inclusion, and counterexample statements which destroyed the equivalency between adjacent sets in the inclusion. For example, if the statement "All A's are B's" was in the paragraph, then a counterexample statement such as "Some B's are not A's" was also in the paragraph. Hence, subjects who studied the paragraph should be prevented from inferring "All B's are A's." A paragraph employed by Griggs (1976a) was the following:

> All the Fundalas are outcasts from other tribes in Central Ugala. These people are isolated from the other tribes because it is the custom in this country to get rid of certain types of people. There are four other tribes of outcasts in Central Ugala. All the outcasts of Central Ugala are hill people. The hills provide a most accommodating place to live. The hill people called Kandali are not outcasts. All the hill people of Central Ugala are farmers. The upper highlands provide excellent soil for cultivation. There are, however, several tribes of farmers which are not hill people. All together, there are about fifteen different tribes in this area.

The insertion of counterexamples in the paragraph dramatically improved performance on false test statements. Figure 3 shows mean proportion correct as a function of step size. Subjects performed better on false test statements than on true statements. Proportion correct, however, remained a decreasing function of step size for true test statements, and the interaction between truth value and step size was again observed. Thus, as predicted by the erroneous logical processing hypothesis, the insertion of counterexamples improved performance on false test statements but did not affect the interaction between truth value and step size. Conversion errors account partially for the set inclusion error profiles, but not entirely.

Subjects do not appear to make transitive inferences with set inclusions as they do with linear orderings. To encourage subjects to do so, Griggs (1976a, Experiment 6) told them in preliminary instructions that transitive inferences were valid and provided examples of such inferences. To prevent conversions, instructions that these were invalid were also given. Dickstein (1975) employed a similar strategy successfully in a syllogistic reasoning study. He

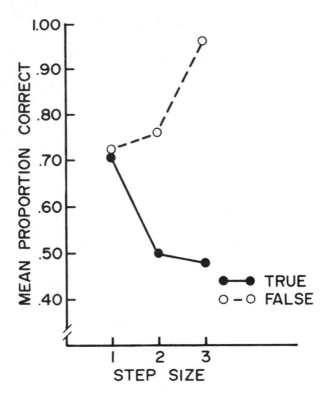

Fig. 3. Mean proportion correct as a function of step size for set inclusion paragraphs containing counter-examples. Since four-term set inclusions are employed, there are only three step sizes. Data are from Experiment 5, Griggs (1976a).

found that instructions designed to reduce conversion errors significantly improved performance on syllogisms.

The instructions that transitive inferences were valid and conversions invalid clearly eliminated the True-False differences that had been observed in all the previous experiments. Proportion correct on true statements was not significantly different from proportion correct on false statements. The step size function for true statements is an increasing function; the step size function for false statements increased but then becomes almost flat over the last three step sizes. The functions are given in Figure 4. Performance on deducible information was superior to performance on presented information for both true and false statements. These results are similar to those reported

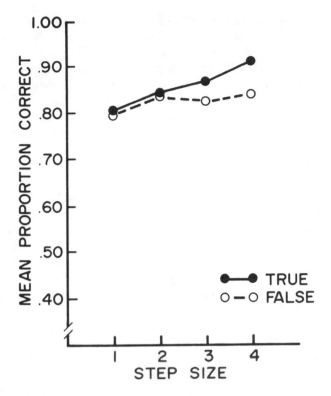

Fig. 4. Mean proportion correct as a function of step size for set inclusion paragraphs with pre-study instructions about transitivity and conversion errors. Data are from Experiment 6, Griggs (1976a).

earlier for linear orderings in Griggs (1976a). Thus, college students can be trained to educe and operate correctly on set inclusion structures; i.e., if subjects are instructed about transitivity and how to use it with set inclusion information, they can and will employ it.

RECALL OF SET INCLUSION INFORMATION

Based on the results of Frase (1969, 1970) and Griggs (1976a), it seems clear that after studying set inclusion paragraphs, most subjects come away with memory mainly for the presented information. Further evidence supporting this conclusion was provided by Griggs (1977). This experiment employed a self-paced study/test paradigm with set inclusion paragraphs, but used a recall test instead of a True-False test. In contrast to Frase (1969,

1970), subjects knew they were going to be tested on the set inclusion information. Subjects studied four different set inclusion paragraphs and then were instructed to recall in any order the pairwise relations that had been presented in each paragraph (reproductive recall) and all relations that could be deduced from the information in the paragraph (productive recall). They were told to structure their recall in universal affirmative sentences, each relating two sets. An example of a permissible deduction was given. The title of each paragraph was provided on the recall sheet for that paragraph, and subjects were allowed as much time as they wanted for recall.

As in Frase (1969, 1970), recall measures were adjusted for guessing by subtracting incorrect recall from correct recall. This procedure changed the recall scores only slightly. Using a scoring method in which recall having the correct relation, whether the universal quantifier was employed or not, was scored as correct, reproductive recall (50% of possible correct recall) was superior to productive recall (30% of possible recall), but note that even reproductive recall was poor. In addition, subjects often failed (44% of the time) to generate deductions in recall although the information necessary to permit such deductions had been recalled.

Subjects seem to have stored only the material which was actually presented and to have made few deductions at time of test. This is indicated by the small amount of productive recall and the finding that many deductions were not produced in recall even with instructions to do so and when the information necessary to permit them was recalled. This supports the hypothesis that college students studying set inclusion paragraphs do not make the allowable transitive inferences, integrate them with the presented assertions into a large semantic structure, and then store this structure in memory, as they appear to do for linear ordering information. As pointed out by Frase (1975), the set inclusions relation appears to create special difficulties for the integration of presented and deducible information into a more general sementic structure.

RECOGNITION MEMORY FOR SET INCLUSION INFORMATION

Griggs (1976b) investigated set inclusion performance using a self-paced study/test paradigm with a Bransford and Franks type recognition test (see Bransford & Franks, 1971). If subjects do not make the transitive inferences and do not store a general set inclusion structure, then when they are required to decide if the test sentences have actually been presented, the typically observed inability in Bransford and Franks' recognition studies to differentiate OLDS (sentences that have actually been presented) and NEWS (sentences expressing information that could be inferred from the information in the presented sentences) should not be observed. Subjects should be able to differentiate between true adjacent and true remote sentences. Thus, the set inclusion structure, even though transitive, could provide evidence contrary to constructivist theory.

Each subject studied and was tested on only one set inclusion paragraph. Study time was self-paced, and study and test were separated by a short arithmetic task. Subjects were instructed to respond *yes* to a test statement if that sentence had actually been presented and *No* if it had not been presented in the paragraph.

Surprisingly, the predictions based on previous set inclusion studies were not confirmed. Subjects were very inaccurate in deciding whether true remote sentences had actually been presented, but very accurate in their decisions on false remote sentences. For true sentences, proportion correct for adjacent sentences (.74) was significantly higher than proportion correct for remote sentences (.33). The opposite was found for false sentences. Proportion correct on remote sentences (.90) was significantly higher than proportion correct on adjacent sentences (.74).

Since the remote pairs were not presented, a simple response bias for saying *Yes* might account for the low proportion correct on true remote sentences. This bias might be the result, e.g., of an "atmosphere" effect (Chapman & Chapman, 1959; Woodworth & Sells, 1935). The word *all* supposedly suggests a universal affirmative atmosphere, and statements are accepted because of this general atmosphere. However, this response bias should have also affected the proportion correct for false adjacent and remote sentences, since the correct answer to these was *No*. No such effects were observed.

Subjects found it very difficult to decide between information that was actually presented and information that had not been presented but was deducible from presented information. The same pattern of recognition results was observed by Potts (1973) for linear ordering paragraphs except that all the proportions correct were slightly higher. Thus, the set inclusion results are consistent with constructivist theory and Potts' linear ordering research, but inconsistent with the predictions based upon earlier set inclusion work.

A possible explanation for the above inconsistency is an interaction between type of test and universal quantification. Statements like "All A's are B's" may not be as plausible as statements like "A's are B's," and, therefore, not as likely to be accepted as true. Thus, the truth value by inferential distance interaction observed in set inclusion studies could be a function of plausibility. Subjects may be very cautious in drawing inferences from long chains of set inclusion statements because it is so easy for the universe of discourse to shift greatly during such a chain. When the test is concerned with truth value, subjects might reject remote sentences as true, but when the test is concerned only with occurrence, the quantifier may not interfere. Thus, the quantifier may be important on a True-False test but not on a recognition test.

Griggs and Osterman (in preparation) investigated this interaction hypothesis. In a self-paced/True-False test paradigm, performance on paragraphs and test statements which did not contain universal quantifiers was compared to performance on paragraphs and test statements that did. Mean proportion correct as a function of inferential distance for both types of set inclusion statements is given in Table 2. The only significant effects were truth value and the truth value by distance interaction. Deleting the universal quantifiers from the study paragraphs and test sentences did not change error profiles for set inclusions. Thus, the type of test by universal quantification interaction hypothesis was not supported.

A TENTATIVE RESOLUTION

Potts (1976 and in Chap. 6 of this volume) proposes a possible explanation to resolve this apparent conflict for set inclusions with different types of tests and to explain the error profiles obtained with artificial set inclusion structures. Potts hypothesizes that subjects create a representation for a set inclusion that is functionally equivalent to that for a linear ordering, i.e., they arrange the terms of the inclusion in a linear array. Subjects, however, erroneously respond on the basis of similarity (proximity in the array) and do not evaluate the actual relation between the terms in the test statement. Since the similarity relation is symmetric and nontransitive, the set inclusion results follow. The recognition results of Griggs (1976b) support this hypothesis since they suggest that subjects do integrate the set inclusion information into some more general semantic structure, such as an array, and base their recognition responses on this array and not some set of the presented pairs. Thus,

Table 2. Mean Proportion Correct as a Function of Step Size for Set Inclusions With and Without Universal Quantifiers

Step size	With quantifiers		Without quantifiers	
	True	False	True	False
1	.88	.44	.81	.36
2	.72	.56	.72	.57
3	.68	.72	.77	.72

Note.—Since four-term set inclusions were employed, there are only three step sizes.

according to Potts' explanation, subjects process the set inclusion information into a linear array, but then, when answering questions, most subjects process the memory representation incorrectly, resulting in the typically observed set inclusion results. The data for subjects who process the representation correctly, on the other hand, should be comparable to that observed in linear ordering studies. Thus, if data on individual subjects are considered, two types of subjects are found—those who process the representation correctly and those who do not.

Granted there are mainly two types of subjects in the set inclusion studies. There are subjects who do well on the task, but they are few in number. I do agree with Potts, however, that these good subjects probably represent the set inclusion in an order arrangement and then process it correctly resulting in reaction time profiles like those for linear orderings. Potts (1976) reports some supporting findings. For subjects who made few logical errors, mean reaction time to deducible remote pairs was significantly shorter than reaction time to the adjacent presented pairs. Where available, individual subject reaction time data have also been analyzed for some of the previously discussed set inclusion studies (Griggs, 1976a). These reaction time analyses also reveal profiles for good subjects that are similar to those for linear orderings, i.e., decreasing functions of inferential distance.

It is fairly easy to propose a tentative explanation for how good subjects could arrive at such an order representation. As Erickson (1974 and Chap. 2 in this volume) proposes, subjects might simplify the interpretation of a universal affirmative sentence and choose only one interpretation. They might interpret such a statement as a Venn diagram representation in which A is a *proper* subset of B. If a subject did this for a series of these statements, a set of concentric circles representing the sets in the paragraph and the given subset relations would result. Going from this representation to an order representation would be direct and plausible.

These good subjects, however, are not our main concern. The primary problem is how the majority of the subjects (those who perform poorly) represent the set inclusion information. If Potts' proposal, a linear array (an imaginary line with the terms ordered on it), is correct, then how do subjects arrive at this representation? It is illogical that they would use transitivity to do this if they do not use transitivity to process the representation when answering questions. They could interpret each universal affirmative statement to mean the two described sets are similar, but why would they place consecutively mentioned sets to the right on a line if they were employing similarity and not transitivity? Sets A and B could be similar and sets B and C similar, but sets A and C are not necessarily similar. A possibility is that subjects merely position the items on a line in the order or input. Griggs (1976a, Experiment 3), however, found the typical set inclusion error profiles for a mixed presentation order (not **AB**, **BC**, **CD**, **DE**). Thus, it seems very implausible that subjects would form a line representation without employing transitivity.

Falmagne (1975) clearly makes the same point in explaining the logic is *not* absent from such processes as syllogistic reasoning and transitive inference, but rather is present in constructing the representation of the information in these tasks. Falmagne points out that "in order for a subject to select the appropriate representation—the straight line—in a transitive inference task, he must be aware of the formal similarity between the terms of the problem and the properties of the line, namely, in this case, transitivity . . . . A crucial step in this process is the choice of the straight line as the vehicle for inference. The import of this point appears if one realizes that the subject was entirely free to choose to map the information onto a circle, for example" (pp. 254–255).

Potts suggests an alternative formulation in terms of Smith, Shoben, and Rips' (1974) semantic feature comparison model as to how subjects process real set inclusion relations. This seems completely inappropriate for artificial set inclusions. What are the defining and characteristic features for the arbitrary sets that would allow Smith et al.'s two-stage processing model to fit the set inclusion data? It would appear to be impossible to identify such features because the material is fictional, and the only features to be used would be from the experimental paragraphs.

GENERAL DISCUSSION

Potts' tentative explanation lacks force unless a plausible path from the input set inclusion paragraph to the internal order representation can be mapped out for the typical subject in these experiments. It seems highly unlikely that subjects could construct a "line" representation without employing transitivity. If a subject uses transitivity to construct the representation, it is improbable that he would abandon it during testing. When given instructions about transitivity and its validity, subjects do employ it correctly in processing set inclusion information (Griggs, 1976a).

A more satisfactory explanation of the set inclusion results could be expressed in terms of two general types of subjects—(a) subjects who assume transitivity and employ it properly, and (b) subjects who do not assume transitivity. The first type of subject constructs and stores a representation which preserves the correct subset information. Such a representation is functionally equivalent to that for a linear ordering. The second type of subject stores some (or all) of the presented adjacent pairs of the set inclusion. These subjects not only fail to assume transitivity, but also make invalid conversion errors.

This explanation fits the available data rather well except for the contradictory recognition results of Griggs (1976b). These recognition results, however, are not completely consistent with Potts' explanation either. Since subjects incorrectly identified true deducible statements as OLD and did not identify false sentences as OLD, it can be inferred that subjects made the transitive inferences during the study period and integrated this deduced information with the presented information into a more general representation (e.g., a linear array). Thus, during testing they no longer knew which set inclusion statements were actually presented.

This interpretation indicates that subjects are employing transitivity to construct the representation. The results are also consistent with the argument that subjects are using transitivity to process the integrated representation during testing. If subjects understand that transitive inferences are consistent with the overall integrated structure, then they should display a tendency to identify these inferences as OLD, and they do. Subjects should not incorrectly identify false sentences as OLD, and they do not. Thus, they are obviously not processing the representation as a similarity relation, as Potts proposes they are for a True-False test. If Potts' explanation of the set inclusion results is correct, then why would subjects display differential modes of processing the same representation for different types of tests?

The recognition results are contradictory for another reason. On the True-False test, subjects are instructed to respond *true* if the sentence was presented or is deducible from the information presented and *false* if it was not presented and is not deducible from the presented information. This means subjects are saying that deducible remote sentences were presented on recognition tests, but not on True-False tests.

A possible explanation for the seemingly paradoxical recognition results is that they are due to the experimental procedure employed. The original Bransford and Franks (1971) recognition experiment has been criticized for arranging conditions in such a manner as to cause massive forgetting of the particular presented information (Reitman & Bower, 1973) and for using an insensitive test procedure (Anderson & Bower, 1973). It is possible that the ability to differentiate OLD and NEW sentences would be found if a more sensitive forced-choice test procedure were employed. There is in fact some evidence that subjects do *not* make false recognitions in the Bransford and Franks integration paradigm if the forced-choice procedure is employed instead of the usual Yes-No procedure (Anderson & Bower, 1973, pp. 351–352; Griggs & Keen, in preparation). Lawson (1977) has obtained similar results for artificial linear ordering information: subjects were able to discriminate true implications from presented sentences when a sentence classification task similar to a forced-choice procedure was employed. Thus, the possibility at least exists that the set inclusion results are an artifact of the test procedure employed and are not indicative of the represenation stored by the subject.

Potts reports an additional set inclusion experiment which might be interpreted as being inconsistent with the present explanation of set inclusion performance, but it really is not. Potts (1976, Experiment 3) employed abstract terms (nonsense syllables) as set names and provided subjects with feedback on performance after each set of test questions. Subjects studied and were tested on nine paragraphs containing no extraneous material. The first paragraph presented, however, was not an artificial paragraph but a *real* set inclusion paragraph (i.e., composed of sentences like "All collies are dogs," etc.). Potts only analyzed performance on the last eight paragraphs which all contained abstract set inclusion information. Performance was very good—an overall proportion correct of .958 was obtained. The reaction time profiles for these subjects were similar to those for subjects in another condition of this experiment—those who studied only abstract linear ordering paragraphs. Reaction time to the remote pairs was significantly shorter than reaction time to the adjacent pairs.

Potts concludes that when logical errors are eliminated, the reaction time results for set inclusions are very similar to those for linear orderings. The important question, however, is why the logical errors are eliminated, and Potts does not address this problem. Potts' experiment is comparable to Griggs' set inclusion experiment with pre-study transitivity instructions (1976a). Instead of explicit instructions about transitivity, Potts employed a real set inclusion example as his first paragraph. This real paragraph performs the same function as the instructions. After working through the transitive inferences in the real problem, subjects probably worked through the subsequent artificial, abstract set inclusion paragraphs in the same way during study, resulting in an integrated representation and the observed performance. It is reasonable to predict this since subjects do not make transitivity errors with real set inclusion information. Note that performance does not significantly improve over trials (i.e., performance is just as good on the second paragraph as it is on the ninth), so it is not the feedback on the artificial paragraphs that is important here.

What Potts really demonstrated is that subjects can be induced to process artificial set inclusion information as they process artificial linear ordering information. This is essentially what Griggs (1976a) demonstrated through the use of instructions. Thus, Potts' results are consistent with both Potts' explanation of performance on artificial set inclusion information and the explanation proposed in this chapter.

CONCLUSIONS

In summary, it appears that most subjects perform differently on True-False tests for artificial linear orderings and set inclusions unless given special prestudy instructions about transitivity or prior study and test on a real set inclusion relation. For linear orderings, subjects perform better on deducible remote pairs than on presented adjacent pairs irrespective of truth value. Based upon this result, it is assumed that the presented and deducible order information is integrated into a more general semantic representation (such as a linear array of the terms), and this representation is what is stored in memory. For set inclusions, however, a truth value by inferential distance interaction is found. For true statements, performance is better on adjacent pairs; for false statements, performance is better on remote pairs. These set inclusion results do not dictate that an integrated representation be assumed.

Potts (1976 and Chap. 6 in this volume), however, proposes such a representation for artificial set inclusions. To explain the error profiles, he also assumes this representation is processed incorrectly as a similarity relation. I propose an alternative representation of the artificial set inclusion information—a subset of the presented adjacent pairs. In addition, I feel that most subjects commit conversion errors and do not assume transitivity. Both explanations reasonably account for most of the existing data, and no data are currently available that will clearly distinguish between them.

Potts also proposes that subjects may respond to real set inclusion questions in the same way, i.e., on the basis of similarity (Smith et al., 1974). Subjects do not make a large number of errors, however, in semantic memory experiments. Supposedly, this is due to a confound in these experiments; i.e., the correct response to a statement describing two similar terms is usually *true*, and the correct answer to a statement involving two dissimilar terms is usually *false*. Hence, subjects would be correct most of the time if they responded according to similarity. Potts is attempting to generalize his explanation to the processing of both artificial and real set inclusions and to account for both types of experiments using similar psychological principles.

As Potts admits, however, the Smith et al. feature comparison model is not "universally" accepted as the explanation of semantic memory data (e.g., Glass & Holyoak, 1975). A recent test of this model by McCloskey and Glucksberg (1976) is relevant to Potts' argument about why subjects do not make many errors on real information by responding according to similarity. They included highly related false sentences in their test of the feature comparison model. The data did not confirm the predictions of the model. In particular, a high error rate for highly related false sentences was not observed. Therefore, Potts' argument that both real and artificial set inclusions are processed according to similarity was not supported.

Potts' attempt, however, to relate these two lines of research is a step in the right direction since, for the most part, these lines have developed relatively independently of one another. It should also be pointed out that Potts only considers his interpretation to be "speculative." Further work is definitely needed not only to clarify both lines of research but also to integrate them.

REFERENCES

Anderson, J. R., & Bower, G. H. *Human associative memory*. Washington, D.C.: Winston, 1973.

Bransford, J. D., Barclay, J. R., & Franks, J. J. Sentence memory: A constructive versus interpretive approach. *Cognitive Psychology*, 1972, **3**, 193–209.

Bransford, J. D., & Franks, J. J. The abstraction of linguistic ideas. *Cognitive Psychology*, 1971, **2**, 331–350.

Bransford, J. D., & McCarrell, N. S. A sketch of a cognitive approach to comprehension: Some thoughts about understanding what it means to comprehend. In W. Weimer & D. Palermo (Eds.), *Cognition and the symbolic processes*. New York: Halsted Press, 1974.

Brockway, J., Chmielewski, D., & Cofer, C. N. Remembering prose: Productivity and accuracy constraints in recognition memory. *Journal of Verbal Learning and Verbal Behavior*, 1974, **13**, 194–208.

Ceraso, J., & Provitera, A. Sources of error in syllogistic reasoning. *Cognitive Psychology*, 1971, **2**, 400–410.

Chapman, L. J., & Chapman, J. P. Atmosphere effect re-examined. *Journal of Experimental Psychology*, 1959, **58**, 220–226.

Cofer, C. N. Constructive processes in memory. *American Scientist*, 1973, **61**, 537–543.

Collins, A. M., & Quillian, M. R. Experiments on semantic memory and language comprehension. In L. W. Gregg (Ed.), *Cognition in learning and memory*. New York: Wiley, 1972.

Dickstein, L. S. Effects of instructions and premise order on errors in syllogistic reasoning. *Journal of Experimental Psychology: Human Learning and Memory*, 1975, **1**, 376–384.

Erickson, J. R. A set analysis theory of behavior in formal syllogistic reasoning tasks. In R. L. Solso (Ed.), *Theories in cognitive psychology: The Loyola Symposium*. Hillsdale, N.J.: Erlbaum, 1974.

Falmagne, R. J. Overview: Reasoning, representation, process, and related issues. In R. J. Falmagne (Ed.), *Reasoning: Representation and process*. Hillsdale, N.J.: Erlbaum, 1975.

Frase, L. T. Structural analysis of the knowledge that results from thinking about text. *Journal of Educational Psychology Monograph*, 1969, **60**(6, Part 2).

Frase, L. T. Influence of sentence order and amount of higher level of text processing upon reproductive and productive memory. *American Educational Research Journal*, 1970, **7**, 307–319.

Frase, L. T. Prose processing. In G. H. Bower (Ed.), *The psychology of learning and motivation* (Vol. 9). New York: Academic Press, 1975.

Glass, A. L., & Holyoak, K. J. Alternative conceptions of semantic theory. *Cognition*, 1975, **3**, 313–339.

Griggs, R. A. Logical processing of set inclusion relations in meaningful text. *Memory & Cognition*, 1976, **4**, 730–740. (a)

Griggs, R. A. Recognition memory for deducible information. *Memory & Cognition*, 1976, **4**, 643–647. (b)

Griggs, R. A. Reproductive and productive recall of set inclusion information. *Bulletin of the Psychomic Society*, 1977, **9**, 148–150.

Griggs, R. A., & Keen, D. M. *The role of test procedure in linguistic integration studies.* In preparation.

Griggs, R. A., & Osterman, L. J. *Processing artificial set inclusion information.* In preparation.

Johnson, D. M. *Systematic introduction to the psychology of thinking.* New York: Harper & Row, 1972.

Lawson, R. L. Representation of individual sentences and holistic ideas. *Journal of Experimental Psychology: Human Learning and Memory*, 1977, **3**, 1–9.

McCloskey, M., & Glucksberg, S. *Semantic memory: Test of a feature comparison model.* Paper presented at the meeting of the American Psychological Association, Washington, D.C., September 1976.

Potts, G. R. Information processing strategies used in the encoding of linear orderings. *Journal of Verbal Learning and Verbal Behavior*, 1972, **11**, 727–740.

Potts, G. R. Memory for redundant information. *Memory & Cognition*, 1973, **1**, 467–470.

Potts, G. R. Storing and retrieving information about ordered relationships. *Journal of Experimental Psychology*, 1974, **103**, 431–439.

Potts, G. R. Bringing order to cognitive structures. In F. Restle, R. M. Shiffrin, N. J. Castellan, H. R. Lindman, & D. B. Pisoni (Eds.), *Cognitive theory* (Vol. 1). Hillsdale, N.J.: Erlbaum, 1975.

Potts, G. R. Artificial logical relations and their relevance to semantic memory. *Journal of Experimental Psychology: Human Learning and Memory*, 1976, **2**, 746–758.

Reitman, J. S., & Bower, G. H. Storage and later recognition of exemplars of concepts. *Cognitive Psychology*, 1973, **4**, 194–206.

Revlis, R. Syllogistic reasoning: Logical decisions from a complex data base. In R. J. Falmagne (Ed.), *Reasoning: Representation and process.* Hillsdale, N.J.: Erlbaum, 1975.

Scholz, K. W., & Potts, G. R. Cognitive processing of linear orderings. *Journal of Experimental Psychology*, 1974, **102**, 323–326.

Smith, E. E., Shoben, E. J., & Rips, L. J. Structure and process in semantic memory: A featural model for semantic decisions. *Psychological Review*, 1974, **81**, 214–241.

Tzeng, O. J. L. Sentence memory: Recognition and inferences. *Journal of Experimental Psychology: Human Learning and Memory*, 1975, **1**, 720–726.

Woodworth, R. S., & Sells, S. B. An atmosphere effect in formal syllogistic reasoning. *Journal of Experimental Psychology*, 1935, **18**, 451–460.

INFERENCE AND READING

Lawrence T. Frase
National Institute of Education

To correctly evaluate a standard syllogistic argument like "All S are M; All M are P; therefore, All S are P" requires a rather sophisticated cognitive apparatus. But suppose that this argument occurs not in the bald-faced form in which it is presented here but as an argument embedded in ordinary discourse.

Consider the complications. Within each sentence, words may be substituted for the letters S, M, and P. Furthermore, in one sentence the subject might be the word *singer*, in another sentence a synonym like *vocalist* might be used. The order of the sentences might be changed. For instance, the conclusion might be given first. In addition, numerous supporting or irrelevant sentences might be added to the text. The distance of the premises from each other might vary from one text to another. Finally, the reader's evaluation of the argument might be required some time after the test has been read,

Any views expressed here are the author's own and do not represent the views of the National Institute of Education. No official support or endorsement by the National Institute of Education is intended or should be inferred.

185

making memory, as well as the comparison of propositions, a significant factor in performance.

With these few examples, we can begin to see how the demands of reading go beyond the demands of the skeletal syllogistic form. Yet at the heart of the matter lies the basic problem of how people store and combine information from two different propositions. Perhaps Aristotle was right; the syllogism has implicit within it all the problems of human thought.

It's my feeling that the study of syllogistic and other reasoning tasks can contribute to the understanding of reading processes. Having given a brief perspective on some of the complications of reasoning from reading, I now describe some things that reasoning studies say about reading, and some things that reading says about reasoning tasks.

My own work began with studies of formal syllogistic reasoning (Frase, 1966a, 1966b). These studies and others (Frase, 1968a, 1968b; Pezzoli & Frase, 1968) were conducted within the framework of associative learning theory. Later, the syllogistic paradigm was extended to the study of learning in a prose context (Frase, 1969, 1972). The rationale for this extension was that *sorites*, or extended syllogistic arguments, provide an experimental task with clearly definable contents and learning outcomes. Being able to define objectively text contents and learning outcomes is a rather substantial methodological problem in reading research. Furthermore, reasoning problems, in a prose context, appears to have some practical relevance. As a consequence of our work on prose, we abandoned a simple associative framework.

THE DATA BASE AND MANIPULATION PROBLEMS

What do reasoning studies have to say about reading? To simplify, there are two general problems in reasoning from written materials. The first general problem for the reader is to develop an appropriate data base. That is, to derive from a text a set of propositions (or perhaps images) from which reasoning can proceed. The data base problem includes two subproblems: (a) the *representation* problem, i.e., to arrive at appropriate internal representations of propositions from reading, and (b) the *storage* problem, i.e., to make those representations stable memory contents.

The second general problem in reading is the manipulation of the data base, i.e., using appropriate strategies and tactics to retrieve and compare propositions, to produce conclusions, etc. So we have two general problems: the data base problem and the manipulation problem. The data base problem seems in two ways more important than the manipulation problem. First, there is the a priori argument that a data base is a necessary condition for manipulation. Put simply, one cannot reason with contents that do not exist in the mind. Second, there is the empirical evidence that what people remember from reading is often only a faint shadow of what they have read. Reasoning aside, just getting the basic information into the mind is not a trivial problem.

Is this simple model of reading defensible? My perception of the data base and manipulation problems is presented below. In particular, I will explain why the simple notion of the text as a data base for meaningful reading has got to be wrong, and what this implies for models of reading.

THE DATA BASE PROBLEM

Representation

Achieving adequate representation of the propositions presented in sentences is closely tied to the general topic of reading comprehension in general. There are two subproblems concerning representation, problems of *partial representation* and *optional representation*. Partial representation is concerned with whether all relevant features of a sentence are or need to be encoded. Optional representation is concerned with the form of representation, given that a sentence is completely represented.

Partial representation. Consider first, whether a reader responds to entire propositions or just to parts of them. Revlis' (1975) feature selection model is relevant here. The model deals with the representation of syllogistic premises as an outgrowth of the selection of features (quantity and polarity) which can be used to produce composite representations of premises. The model does not talk about complex internal representations of class inclusion statements. This alogical selective mechanism may neglect a significant portion of the "meaning" of a proposition, but it makes fairly accutate predictions about syllogistic errors. Revlis' (1975) data suggest that errors on syllogisms are due in part to an incomplete data base.

But I am not sure whether we should call a feature selection model unreasonable, even though it appears to be alogical. One can reject many syllogisms as invalid without dealing with a complete representation of the set inclusions implied by matching the quantifier in the conclusion with the quantifiers in the premises. This could be done on the basis of knowing the logical rule, "If one premise is particular, the conclusion is particular; if both premises are particular, there is no conclusion." It might also be done on the basis of an intuitive feeling that if there is some uncertainty in the premises (one or both are particular) then the conclusion shouldn't be too certain (universal). With the latter strategy, a person can correctly evaluate the validity of 96 different syllogisms.

Suppose we assume that reasoners fully represent premises of a syllogism, and that errors in reasoning arise from the fact that some propositions have multiple interpretations. As the number of potential interpretations of the two premises increases, then errors in reasoning should increase. If the joint product of the two premises generally determines the difficulty of evaluating a conclusion, then the forms of the two premises should interact to produce more or fewer errors in reasoning. Error data on all 256 standard syllogisms have been collected. Analysis of these data shows that, over all 256 syllogisms, the forms of the two premises do not interact, although the form of each premise interacts strongly with the form of the conclusion. These findings suggest that, considering the full range of syllogistic arguments, many can be solved with a strategy that entails the selection of a few critical features. To understand these findings fully, we would have to look closely into the conditions of the experimental task as well as the form of the arguments that were evaluated. Regardless, I think that my general point is a valid one. Correct performance can often proceed on the basis of information which is something less than the nominal information presented to the subject.

What I have represented is not particularly new. For instance, in 1962 Henle forcefully argued that the task presented to a reasoner may only weakly reflect the task undertaken. Henle found, among other strategies, two common strategies of reasoning. These reflect what might be called errors of representation. One such error was the omission of a premise failure to accept the logical task, e.g., to disregard the premises entirely and to evaluate the content of the conclusion alone. Errors like this, if we want to call them errors, reflect ways in which a subject tries to simplify the task presented. Here, I believe, reasoning studies have a great deal to say about reading, because reading involves a complex stimulus for which simplifying strategies are important.

Yet we know very little about these simplifying strategies in reading, although I can think of some rather obvious examples. For instance, in the area of programmed instruction, Anderson (1970) reported studies showing that readers do not respond to entire frames of a text. Instead, they may copy words which are overprompted (by underlining) in order to fill in blanks. Readers even look ahead and copy correct answers in programmed materials without reading the instructional portion of a text at all. Anderson's (1970) data show that overprompting in a text and subjects' copying activities are strongly related to posttest performance.

The prereading information that is given to a reader strongly constrains what is learned. A large number of studies have been conducted on the learning consequences of asking people questions about a passage before they read it (Anderson & Biddle, 1975). In over 70% of these studies, subjects who are asked questions learn less of the question-incidental information than subjects who read without questions. Of course, the questioned subjects learn a great deal more of the question-relevant information than subjects who do not receive questions before reading. A recent study by Kaplan (1976) found a strong relationship between the correct identification of relevant material in a text and subjects' posttest performances. Studies that we conducted (Frase, 1972) suggest that the reasoning performance of fourth grade children can be improved by cueing them to the few critical features of relationships that are embedded in a text. For instance, the children read texts in which were embedded sentences of the form "The small thing was red. The red thing was a bag. The bag was full of money." The children read the text and verified sentences like "The small thing was a bag," which entails using two sentences mediated by the word *red*. Performance on these problems averaged 64% for uncued subjects. Cueing the subjects before they read to pay special attention to critical terms like *the red thing* raised performance to 94%. I am suggesting here that specific guidance to a reader, in the form of questions, learning objectives, or other cues, can provide the reader with a simplifying strategy that greatly reduces the demands of ordinary reading.

I believe that these strategies are important for reading. If they show up in reasoning with the sparse contents of a syllogism, they seem all the more important for ordinary discourse. Yet we know very little about these simplifying strategies, much less about whether they can be taught. Why? Part of the problem is that we have not developed many usable task models—models of potential text structures and how the reader's activities might ignore or concentrate upon various aspects of those structures. Research by Fredericksen (1975) and others move in this direction, but a lot remains to be done before we can develop instructional rules and algorithms for decomposing the complexities of text.

Optional representation. A variety of reasoning studies suggest that the premises of a syllogism may be completely represented, but in a form which departs from the correct or intended meaning. Ceraso and Provitera (1971) have described the possibilities of interpreting assertions such as "All A's are B's." This might be interpreted to mean that A is a subset of B, or that A is coextensive with B. Chapman and Chapman (1959) found that subjects frequently interpret "All A are B" to mean that "All B are A." We conducted several studies (Frase, 1969) in which sorites were embedded in brief text. If subjects had read that "All Fundalas are hill people. All hill people are farmers," they are likely to recall that "All hill people were Fundalas." They were also likely to infer, although weakly, that "All farmers were Fundalas." So these conversion errors apparently occur within discourse more extended than the simple syllogism.

Dawes (1966) also conducted studies in which such set relations were embedded in prose. He found that distortions tended strongly toward overgeneralizations, i.e., recalling a disjunctive relation as nested. Dawes considered these distortions to be simplifications of the material read, because a disjunctive relation (as he used the term) is complex in the sense that two sets in a disjunctive relation have elements in common, but neither set is included in the other. In short, distortions of a text apparently move in the direction of less qualified propositions, i.e., more simple structures.

Distortions of representation have some bearing on studies of reading. Many reading studies are concerned with what subjects remember from reading, yet it is not possible to distinguish memory from representational activities on the basis of the experimental procedures used. It is possible that apparent distortions of recall are due to reasonable conjectures of a subject based upon a data base somewhat different from the nominal text. There is a strong need for normative data on simple interpretive (or comprehension) activities of subjects before recall can unambiguously be studied. Studies of reading might take a cue from reasoning experiments in distinguishing between earlier representational activities and later manipulations performed upon those representations.

Studies of reasoning also may have some implications for writing. For instance, Ceraso and Provitera (1971) found that simplified versions of premises, which constrained the representation of premises, improved reasoning performance considerably. Griggs (see Chapter 7) found that careful instructions about how to interpret sentences improved reasoning. The thrust of these studies is to suggest the need for greater precision of expression in discourse. Our own work on technical documents in the Bell System confirms that a variety of ambiguities of reference may occur in documents that are otherwise well written (Frase & Fischer, 1976).

Storage

Once a proposition is correctly represented in working memory, it begins to decay unless special steps are taken to insure its stability. Earlier in this chapter, I made a simple assertion—namely, that even when a proposition is correctly represented, if it is not available in memory, correct reasoning cannot proceed. We looked at the conditional probabilities from a study (Frase, 1973) concerning the integration of text information. In this study, subjects read a series of sentences which listed the attributes of various sailboats in separate sentences. For instance, two sentences might be "The Winston Churchill had a green hull. The Winston Churchill's speed was 12 knots." After reading, the subjects were asked questions that required recall of the text sentences. They were also asked questions that required the integration of information from different text sentences. An integration question might be "What was the speed of the ship with the green hull?" We found that, if responses to neither of the required text sentences were correct, the proportion of a correct integration response was .52. If one text response was correct, the proportion of a correct integration was .55. If responses to both required text sentences were correct, the proportion of a correct integration was .89. A related study by Stetson (1974) explored childrens' ability to draw inferences from reversible and nonreversible relations expressed in a text. Chance scores in Stetson's recognition task were .50. The proportion of a correct inference, given that the necessary premises were not in memory, was .65. The proportion of a correct inference, given that the premises were in memory, was .91.

There is something interesting about the data reviewed above. Although it is clear that knowing the text helps integration performance, knowledge of the basic text, from which higher level outcomes should be drawn, is neither a completely necessary nor sufficient condition for correct performance. For instance, Stetson's subjects performed above chance without correctly responding to questions about the premises. In none of the studies was performance perfect, given that the necessary text was in memory. Recent studies by Moeser (1976) confirm that children may be unable to draw inferences even though they recall the necessary facts. In other words, the notion of the text data base as a necessary or sufficient condition for manipulation must be approached cautiously. Later in this chapter, some factors that might contribute to correct reasoning when the data base is deficient will be considered. Sequence is one of these factors, but many reasoning studies (e.g., Frase, 1966b) show that subjects' prior knowledge about the veracity of propositions is a potent factor in performance.

A variety of studies show that the recall of propositions is determined by the context in which the propositions are embedded. Rothkopf (1972) cites data showing that recall for text information is inversely related to the number of irrelevant facts in a text. But suppose that the additional information in the text consists of the inferences which can be drawn from the premises stated in the text. We can think of this as structurally related information. Stetson (1974) had children learn texts which varied in the number of inferences that were explicitly stated in the text along with the premises. In an extreme condition, 50% of the text consisted of inferences. Stetson's data show that under these conditions, subjects not only learned the inferences, but their retention of the premises was as high as a group that had read only the premises. In short, it was possible to teach structurally related information without depressing the retention of the base text information.

MANIPULATION

Propositions are correctly represented in memory, and they are well stored. What might determine whether subjects can integrate the information?

One important variable appears to be the sequence of information presented to the reader. In one experiment (Frase, 1970), subjects read sorites embedded in text in a forward order; e.g., "All the hill people are wealthy. All the wealthy people are aggressive." The linkage between sentences occurs consecutively in the text in this forward order. In another condition, the order of sentences was reversed. For subjects who had read these two different orders, there were no differences in recognition of the text sentences. However, the forward order resulted in a 48% advantage on the correct recognition of inferences. Furthermore, the forward order of premises resulted in highly structured free recall protocols, i.e., subjects' protocols matched the order of premises given in the text. In a recent study, Moeser (1976) also found evidence for strong effects of the sequence of presentation on inference operations for children.

A question arises whether sequence affects the manipulation of stored propositions, or whether it affects the production of weakly learned associations. Data suggest that sequence may provide an additional cue to the correct combination of weakly learned associations, i.e., a structural schema or rule about how to combine items. In one study (Frase, 1973), we had subjects learn a text describing the colors of the masts of various sailboats. They learned the text to a criterion of one perfect free recall. The text consisted of sentences of the form "The foremast of the Squid was blue. The mainmast of the Squid was red." A prompted recall test contained items testing for text recall, like "What was the color of the foremast of the Squid?" Integration items were also given, such as "What was the color of the foremast of the ship with the red mainmast?" The sentences in the original text were presented in two different sequences. In one sequence, the structure was constant across paragraphs. For instance, the color of the foremast was first, the color of the mainmast was second, etc., in all paragraphs. In the other sequence, the order of information was varied from paragraph to paragraph. When we analyzed the probability of a correct integration, given that both subordinate text items had been recalled, we found no difference between the two sequences. On the other hand, the sequence had large effects on integration performance, given that both subordinate text sentences were not recalled. The proportion of a correct integration item for the constant sequence was .60; for the variable sequence it was .45. These data are consistent with the assumption that sequence tends to facilitate the production of weakly learned associations. The point here is that the adequacy of storage depends upon the performances that will *later* be required. Characteristics of storage may contain cues to higher order structural properties of a text.

CONCLUSIONS

I started off with a simple model of reading that assumes that readers represent a text as given, store propositions, and then manipulate those propositions to produce various learning outcomes. Evidence suggests that this simple model of reading is incomplete in important ways. Partial and optional representation of a text appear to be common outcomes of reading in reasoning and instructional contexts. The nominal text as a necessary or sufficient data base for higher level outcomes is just too simple a notion. The effective data base and manipulations of that base appear to be outgrowths of each other.

What do these ruminations suggest about models of reading? The data say that reading is far from a passive activity. In particular, passivity is notably absent in an early stage of learning or reasoning from text, specifically, during the selection and representation of information displayed to the reader. Important kinds of comprehension activities appear to be driven by remotely learned procedures, or strategies, as opposed to being driven only by the propositions presented in the text. I believe that a greater emphasis on strategies of selection and representation is called for, rather than a strong emphasis on memory. In addition, a realistic perspective is needed on the ecological validity of the kinds of relations that are studied. In this respect, common reading tasks can contribute to studies of reasoning by providing a sample of the kinds of relations with which a reader is often confronted. What I have called "relations" might not look at all like class inclusion statements. We know that there are important differences between relations of class inclusion and temporal order events. But it is possible that the effective stimulus for a reader might consist of extensive segments of information which others have called, e.g., scripts. Regardless, I suspect that we can find important strategies of reading and that these strategies are coupled in important ways to partial and optional representational schemes, i.e., schemes for simplifying and reducing the complexities of prose discourse.

REFERENCES

Anderson, R. C. Control of student mediating processes during verbal learning and instruction. *Review of Educational Research*, 1970, **40**, 349–369.

Anderson, R. C., & Biddle, W. B. On asking people questions about what they are reading. In G. H. Bower (Ed.), *The psychology of learning and motivation* (Vol. 9). New York: Academis Press, 1975.

Ceraso, J., & Provitera, A. Sources of error in syllogistic reasoning. *Cognitive Psychology*, 1971, **2**, 400–410.

Chapman, L. J., & Chapman, J. P. Atmosphere effect re-examined. *Journal of Experimental Psychology*, 1959, **58**, 220–226.

Dawes, R. M. Memory and the distortion of meaningful writtern material. *British Journal of Psychology*, 1966, **57**, 77–86.

Frase, L. T. Belief, incongruity, and syllogistic reasoning. *Psychological Reports*, 1966, **18**, 982. (a)

Frase, L. T. Validity judgments of syllogisms in relation to two sets of terms. *Journal of Educational Psychology*, 1966, **57**, 239–245. (b)

Frase, L. T. Associative factors in syllogistic reasoning. *Journal of Experimental Psychology*, 1968, **76**, 407–412. (a)

Frase, L. T. Effects of semantic incompatibility upon deductive reasoning. *Psychonomic Science*, 1968, **12**, 64. (b)

Frase, L. T. A structural analysis of the knowledge that results from thinking about text. *Journal of Educational Psychology Monograph*, 1969, **60**, (6, Part 2).

Frase, L. T. Influence of sentence order and higher level text processing upon reproductive and productive memory. *American Educational Research Journal*, 1970, **7**, 307–319.

Frase, L. T. Maintenance and control in the acquisition of knowledge from written materials. In J. B. Carroll & R. O. Freedle (Eds.), *Language comprehension and the acquisition of knowledge*. Washington, D.C.: Winston, 1972.

Frase, L. T. Integration of written text. *Journal of Educational Psychology*, 1973, **65**, 252–261.

Frase, L. T., & Fischer, R. Rating technical documents. Murray Hill, N.J.: Bell Laboratories, 1976.

Frederiksen, C. H. Acquisition of semantic information from discourse: Effects of repeated exposure. *Journal of Verbal Learning and Verbal Behavior*, 1975, **14**, 158–169.

Henle, M. On the relation between logic and thinking. *Psychological Review*, 1962, **69**, 366–378.

Kaplan, R. Effects of grouping and response characteristics of instructional objectives when learning from prose. *Journal of Educational Psychology*, 1976, **68**, 424–430.

Moeser, S. D. Inferential reasoning in episodic memory. *Journal of Verbal Learning and Verbal Behavior*, 1976, **15**, 193–212.

Pezzoli, J. A., & Frase, L. T. Mediated facilitation of syllogistic reasoning. *Journal of Experimental Psychology*, 1968, **78**, 228–232.

Revlis, R. Two models of syllogistic reasoning: Feature selection and conversion. *Journal of Verbal Learning and Verbal Behavior*, 1975, **14**, 180–195.

Rothkopf, E. Z. Structural text features and the control of processes in learning from written materials. In J. B. Carroll & R. O. Freedle (Eds.), *Language comprehension and the acquisition of knowledge*. Washington, D.C.: Winston, 1972.

Stetson, P. C. Verbal transitivity in children. (Doctoral dissertation, University of Delaware, 1974). *Dissertation Abstracts International*, 1974, **35**, 2064-A.

MATHEMATICAL REASONING

MAKING INFERENCES ABOUT RELEVANCE IN UNDERSTANDING PROBLEMS

C. Susan Robinson and John R. Hayes
Carnegie-Mellon University

The study reported here was conceived as part of a larger research project on the processes by which humans come to understand a new problem. Making inferences about relevance is viewed as one of those processes.

Hayes and Simon (1974) proposed the UNDERSTAND program, diagrammed in Figure 1, as a model for human processes involved in understanding problem texts. This program has two subprocesses—PARSE and CONSTRUCT. PARSE performs syntactic and semantic analysis of the input text to provide a linguistically analyzed input for CONSTRUCT. CONSTRUCT takes the analyzed text and builds a representation of the problem in a form which a general problem-solving program such as GPS (Newell & Simon, 1972) could accept in order to solve the problem.

Hayes, Waterman, and Robinson (1977) suggest that the process of understanding involves another subprocess—selective attention—which might be added between the PARSE and CONSTRUCT subprocesses. It is that subprocess of selective attention with which this chapter will be concerned.

The following excerpt from the protocol of a subject reading a problem for the first time (Hayes & Simon, 1975) illustrates the operation of a process of

195

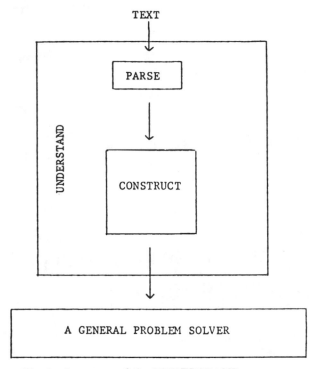

Fig. 1. Structure of the UNDERSTAND program.

selective attention: "Three five-handed extra-terrestrial monsters were holding three crystal globes. OK. Because of the quantum-mechanical peculiarities of their neighborhood—forget that garbage!"

In this protocol the subject has made some decisions about what is and is not relevant to the problem before finishing the second sentence. Clearly, the subject was able to make relevance judgments before he fully understood the problem. (This is the sort of partial representation that Frase discusses in his chapter in this volume.)

In the Hayes, Waterman, and Robinson study, subjects made judgments of importance to problem solution regarding the sentences of a word problem. In this study the authors found that:

1. Subjects' judgments of relevance changed from a first reading to a second reading.

2. Subjects' judgments were affected by the position of the question (at the beginning or end of the problem text).

3. Good prediction could be made of the subjects' changing behavior noted in 1. and 2. above, using a computer program called ATTEND.

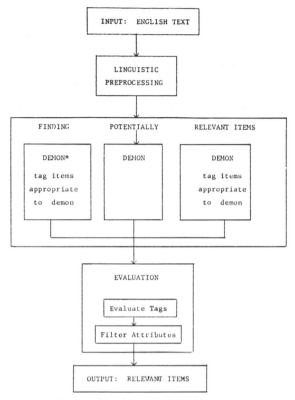

*Any number of appropriate demons can be used.

Fig. 2. Model of ATTEND.

ATTEND, diagrammed in Figure 2, has a PANDEMONIUM-like monitor (Selfridge, 1959) with *demons* for detecting problem features. When a demon detects an example of the feature for which it is attuned, it demands attention from the monitor. The demons which demand the most attention from the monitor receive it. Demons which demand little attention are ignored. The process by which the monitor directs its attention is intended as a model of the process by which humans direct their attention.

In a recent preliminary study subjects were asked to solve the following algebra word problem:

A crop-dusting plane carries 2,000 pounds of Rotenone dusting compound, 250 pounds of high test fuel, a pilot highly skilled in low-altitude flying, and a duster-machinery operator, the pilot's younger brother. The plane must dust a rectangular tobacco field 0.5 miles wide by 0.6 miles long. The dusting compound must be spread with a density of 200 pounds per 0.001 square mile. Further, the compound must be spread between 6 A.M. and 9 A.M., when there is sufficient light and before the morning dew has evaporated, to assure the adherence of the compound to the plants. The plane can dust a 44 foot wide strip at one time. The plane flies the length of the field with a 6 m.p.h. tailwind and back against the same headwind. With the wind, the plane uses fuel at a rate of 60 pounds per hour. Against the wind, it uses fuel at the rate of 80 pounds per hour. The ratio of flying time against the wind to time with the wind if 9:8. The duster operator must try to spread the compound uniformly on the ground despite varying speed.

Some preliminary observations of subjects solving this problem suggested a potential failure of the ATTEND model. On first reading the subjects judged nearly every element of the problem which contained a number—i.e., most of the problem—as relevant. On second reading, however, they judged only a few elements to be relevant—those which concerned flying with and against the wind. Interpreted in terms of the ATTEND model, this behavior would seem to require that a demon which demands relatively little attention (i.e., it tags few items as relevant) should win out against fierce competition. This competition might consist of a few demons who demand lots of attention or of many demons, each demanding a little attention. In neither case does it seem likely that the ATTEND model with its PANDEMONIUM monitor would behave as these subjects did. The present study was conducted to provide further information concerning this issue.

METHOD

Subjects

Subjects were male and female undergraduate or graduate students at Carnegie-Mellon University or the University of Pittsburgh. Each was paid $2.00 for his or her participation in the study.

Due to the algebraic nature of the problem, subjects who had taken no algebra courses in school and those who received poor (lower than B) grades in algebra were eliminated. A total of 50 subjects were tested.

Procedure

Subjects were seated in front of a two-field tachistoscope and the experimenter gave the following instructions:

You are going to see an algebra word problem in this machine. We want you to decide which segments are *relevant* and which are *irrelevant* to the solution of this problem. We define relevant as:

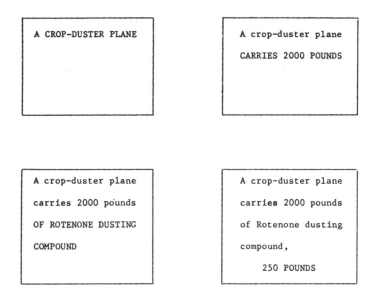

Fig. 3. Sample stimulus cards

"without that particular piece of information, you couldn't solve the problem," and irrelevant as: "you could solve the problem even if you didn't have that piece of information."

The problem will be presented to you segment by segment, rather than all at once, and you will always be able to see the segments which preceded the one you are judging at any given time.

For example, the first card you see will have phrase one on it, the second card will have phrases one and two on it, the third card will have phrases one, two, and three on it, and so on. The phrase which you are to judge will always be in capital letters at the bottom of the card. [See Figure 3 for sample stimulus cards.] Do not attempt to solve the problem.

Phrases were presented cumulatively to minimize the effect of memory load on judgments.

Obviously, you will have very little information with which to make your decisions about the first few segments, but do the best you can. When you reach the end of the problem, we will repeat the task and you will have a chance to re-judge each segment after having seen the entire problem.

The experimenter then gave instructions to the subject for operation of the apparatus. The subject controlled the presentation of each stimulus. The stimulus presentation was terminated when the subject made a response.

Subjects were randomly assigned to one of two conditions (25 per group): question presented before problem text ("Q first") and question presented after problem text ("Q last"). Those subjects in the Q first group also heard the following:

> The first segment which you will see is the question to the problem that would ordinarily appear at the end of the problem. You don't have to make a relevance judgment about the question, since it is clearly necessary to the solution of the problem.

Subjects in the Q last group heard a modified version of the previous paragraph after judging the last segment of the problem:

> The next segment which you will see is the question to the problem. You don't have to make a relevance judgment about the question, since it is clearly necessary to the solution of the problem.

RESULTS

Subjects judged each segment of the problem twice. The first and second judgments will be referred to as Pass 1 and Pass 2, respectively.

The experimenter recorded (a) a judgment of relevance or irrelevance, and (b) a reaction time in milliseconds (from stimulus onset to the time of subject response) for each segment of Pass 1 and Pass 2.

Relevance Judgments

The text segments were grouped into four categories (see Table 1):

1. *Problem-relevant segments*—those segments which are in fact essential for solution of the problem;
2. *Space segments*—segments pertaining to length or area;
3. *Weight segments*—segments pertaining to weight;
4. *Other segments*—all segments not in groups 1, 2, or 3.

Note that none of the segments in categories 2, 3, and 4 is essential for the solution of the problem. Our identification of space and weight categories reflects our hypothesis that subjects use space and weight demons. We will present evidence to support this hypothesis below.

We feel that the subjects may also use a SPEED demon (alas!). However, since the speed segments are confounded with the relevant segments, we won't be able to analyze these categories separately.

Table 1. Grouped Items and Proportion of Relevant Judgments

	Q first		Q last	
	Pass 1	Pass 2	Pass 1	Pass 2

1. Problem-relevant items
  with a 6 m.p.h. tailwind)
  back against the same headwind)
  ratio of speed w/t against wind is 9.8)
	.93	.92	.84	.89

2. Space items
  plane must dust rectangular tobacco)
    field)
  .5 miles wide)
  .6 miles long)
  per .001 sq. mile)
  44 ft. wide strip)
  plane flies length of field)
	.65	.65	.93	.45

3. Weight items
  2000#   60# per hour)
   250#   80# per hour)
  with a density)
   200#)
	.77	.65	.93	.48

Categories 2. and 3. combined	.82 (Pass 1)		.56 (Pass 2)	

4. Irrelevant/other items
  a crop-dusting plane)
  of Rotenone dusting compound)
  of high test fuel)
  a pilot)
  highly skilled in low-altitude flying)
  a duster-machinery operator)
  the pilot's younger brother)
  the compound must be spread)
    between 6 A.M. and 9 A.M.)
    when there is sufficient light and)
    before dew has evaporated to as-)
    sure adherence of compound)
  the compound must be spread uni-)
    formly despite varying speed)
	.20	.14	.35	.11

The results in Table 1 show that both on Pass 1 and Pass 2, a large proportion of subjects judge the items which are actually problem-relevant as relevant, and the other items as irrelevant. Clearly, the subjects do a good job of filtering out some irrelevant material during the first reading. Performance in rejecting irrelevant segments improves from first to second reading. For example, when space and weight items are combined, they are judged relevant in 82% of cases on Pass 1, but this drops to 56% on Pass 2. The drop is most dramatic in the Q last group (from an average of 93% relevant to 47%, on average, on Pass 2).

As was observed in the Hinsley, Hayes, and Simon study (1977), placing the question before the problem text was less helpful than might be expected. Results will be discussed in signal detection terminology: a "hit" represents a correct response of *relevant*; a "false alarm" is a response of *relevant* when the item is in fact *irrelevant*. A good performance rate is one in which subjects make a maximum of hits and a minimum of false alarms.

On Pass 1 of the problem, the Q first group makes fewer false alarms than the Q last group, both in the space and weight categories and the other category. Also, their proportion of hits is greater than that of the Q last group. It appears that reading the question before the problem text has given subjects in the Q first group an advantage over the Q last group. On Pass 2, however, the performance of the Q first group does not improve significantly; the subjects in this group make nearly as many false alarms as they did on Pass 1. By contrast, the Q last subjects not only decrease their false alarm rate, but they surpass the Pass 1 *and* the Pass 2 performances of the Q first group for all irrelevant items. The Q first subjects do not decrease their rate of false alarms significantly. The Q last subjects decrease their false alarm rate significantly for all types of irrelevant items (for space and weight items, $p < .01$; for other items, $p < .01$). Q first subjects retain a slightly (nonsignificant) better performance rate on problem-relevant items both on Pass 1 and Pass 2.

If the subjects do use demons such as the space and weight demons proposed above, we would expect this fact to be reflected in their behavior. If there is a set of segments tagged as relevant by a space demon, we would expect that a subject would tend to judge either all of the segments or none of them as relevant, depending on whether or not he was using the space demon. If some subjects use the demon and others do not, then judgments of the various segments should be positively correlated and not independent.

To test the independence of the subjects' relevance judgments of the space and weight segments, we employed the following procedure. First, for each item, we found the proportion of subjects who judged that segment relevant. Next, using these proportions and assuming that the judgments of individual segments are independent, we computed the numbers of subjects who would be expected to judge two or fewer segments relevant, three or four segments relevant, and five or more segments relevant. (There are six space and six weight segments.) Finally, these expected numbers were compared to the observed numbers by chi-squared tests. The results are given below.

Space segments. On Pass 1 for the Q first subjects, observed values are significantly different from the expected values (χ^2 = 9.83, $p < .01$), with more cells than expected in the two extreme groups. For the Q last subjects on Pass 1, both expected probabilities and observed values are so close to 100% that no significant difference could be obtained. This result would be expected if nearly all of the Q last subjects used a space demon.

On Pass 2, both the Q first and Q last groups differ significantly from the expected probabilities, with more subjects in the direction of the extreme (χ^2 = 6.73, $p < .05$ for Q first; χ^2 = 6.00, $p < .05$ for Q last).

Weight segments. On Pass 1, both the Q first and Q last groups differ significantly from the values expected for their groups, but again, expected values in the low-occurrence cells are zero or near zero, making the results unreliable. As before, the Q last group judges almost all of the segments relevant.

On Pass 2, both groups differ significantly from expected values in the direction our hypothesis suggests (for Q first, χ^2 = 12.56, $p < .01$; for Q last, χ^2 = 6.42, $p < .05$). The results then seem quite consistent with the assumption that our subjects used both a space and a weight demon.

Reaction Times

Z-scores were computed for subjects' reaction times and were used in the data analyses.

Problem-relevant items. On Pass 1 and Pass 2, when Q first subjects judges these segments correctly (made hits), their mean reaction times are significantly faster (z = 2.08, $p < .04$ for Pass 1; z = 2.25, $p < .02$ for Pass 2) than their reaction times for misses (judging a relevant item irrelevant). Differences in the Q last subjects' mean reaction times for hits and misses are in the same direction as for Q first subjects, but the differences are not significant on Pass 1 or Pass 2.

On Pass 1, Q first subjects take significantly longer than Q last subjects to make a miss (z = 2.34, $p < .02$). On Pass 2, Q first subjects are significantly faster than Q last subjects to make hits (z = 3.44, $p < .001$).

Overall, performance of Q first subjects is better than Q last subjects for problem-relevant items.

Irrelevant items. Items irrelevant to the solution of the problems were divided into space and weight segments and other segments in the manner described in the previous section:

Table 2. Reaction Time Means for Item Categories

Pass 1		Pass 2	

Problem-relevant items

QFR	5110	$z = 2.08, p < .04$	QFR	3193	$z = 2.25, p < .02$
QFI	8352		QFI	5386	$z = 3.44, p < .001$
QLR	5560	$z = 2.34, p < .02$	QLR	4160	
QLI	6293		QLI	5465	

Space and weight items

QFR	4507	$z = 3.05, p < .002$	QFR	3048	
QFI	5534		QFI	3535	
QLR	3556	$z = 2.08, p < .004$	QLR	4608	
QLI	4991		QLI	3556	

Irrelevant/other items

QFR	5976	$z = 2.25, p < .02$	QFR	3841	$z = 2.60, p < .009$
QFI	3515		QFI	2471	$z = 2.63, p < .008$
QLR	4608		QLR	5379	$z = 3.40, p < .001$
QLI	3556		QLI	2607	

Note. – Reaction time is in milliseconds.
QFR = Question first group, judging item as relevant[a]
QFI = Question first group, judging item as irrelevant[b]
QLR = Question last group, judging item as relevant[a]
QLI = Question last group, judging item as irrelevant[b]
[a] For problem-relevant items, this is a "hit"; for all other items, this is a "false alarm."
[b] For problem-relevant items, this is a "miss"; for all other items, this is a "correct rejection."

1. When judging space and weight segments on Pass 1, Q last subjects are significantly faster than Q first subjects when making false alarms ($z = 3.05$, $p < .002$) as well as significantly faster than Q first subjects when making correct rejections of these phrases ($z = 2.08$, $p < .004$). These results, taken with the hit proportions given previously, indicate that on Pass 1, Q first subjects have a better speed/accuracy performance. On Pass 2, this is not so. There are no significant reaction time differences between the groups, and,

therefore, since the Q last group has a better hit versus false alarm rate than the Q first group on Pass 2, it appears that the Q last group has attained a superior speed/accuracy performance.

2. When judging other segments on Pass 1, Q first subjects are significantly faster when making correct rejections than when making false alarms (for Pass 1, $z = 2.25, p < .02$). They also make fewer false alarms than the Q last group on Pass 1, giving them an overall better speed/accuracy performance. On Pass 2, however, even though Q first subjects are again significantly faster ($z = 2.60, p < .009$) when making correct rejections than when making false alarms, the Q last group is also significantly faster ($z = 3.40, p < .001$) in this respect. Also, on Pass 2 the Q last group is significantly slower then the Q first group when making false alarms ($z = 2.63, p < .008$).

Combining this information with the data showing that Q last subjects are making fewer false alarms than Q first subjects on Pass 2, it appears that Q last subjects have again attained an overall better speed/accuracy performance than the Q first group.

Comparing reaction time of space and weight segments to those of other segments. A sign test was performed to test for reaction time differences within each group for the two types of space and weight segments and for other segments. On Pass 1, both groups are faster when making false alarms about space and weight segments than when making false alarms about other segments ($p < .05$ for Q first group; $p < .01$ for Q last group). On Pass 2, both groups are slower to make correct rejections of space and weight segments than to make correct rejections of other segments ($p < .01$ for Q first group; $p < .05$ for Q last group).

DISCUSSION

The major result of this study is to confirm the suspicions raised by preliminary observations—i.e., for some problems, the ATTEND program does not provide an adequate description of the processes by which humans make relevance judgments. The problem is this: For the Q last group at least, two reasonably healthy demons, space and weight (each of which identifies six segments as relevant), lose out in competition with a demon (not clearly identified) which tags between three and six segments as relevant. ATTEND has no adequate mechanism for ignoring a demon who continues to shout loudly, but this is just what has happened. Our task now is to explain why the ATTEND program, which succeeded quite well in accounting for human behavior in other problems, failed to do so in this problem.

Hinsley et al. (1977) noted that some problems are recognized as members of a category for which the problem solver has a solution schema. Such schemas contain information about such things as what to attend to in the problem, how to represent it, relevant equations, etc. river current problems are an example of a problem type for which many subjects have a solution schema. The crop-duster problem is a river current type. These investigators also found that some problems were not recognized as members of a category and were solved by a fallback procedure which did not depend on a specialized solution schema. We suggest that the problems in the Hayes, Waterman, and Robinson study were of this sort. We suggest further that the ATTEND model represents the fallback procedure for directing attention in problems which have no specialized solution schema. In the present study subjects may employ the ATTEND procedure for making relevance judgments until they recognize that the problem is of a type for which they have a schema. When the problem type has been recognized, they may then narrow their attention to a few aspects of the problem specified by the schema.

A second result of the study is to confirm the observation of Hayes et al. (1977) that in some cases placing the question first does not help the subject to differentiate relevant from irrelevant problem segments. On Pass 1, the Q first subjects were superior to the Q last subjects, as measured by hit rate, false alarm rate, and response time. On Pass 2, however, the groups were essentially equal in hit rate and response time, but the Q last group showed a lower false alarm rate and hence superior performance overall.

REFERENCES

Hayes, J. R., & Simon, H. A. Understanding written problem instruction. In L. Gregg (Ed.), *Knowledge and cognition.* Hillsdale, N.J.: Erlbaum, 1974.

Hayes, J. R., & Simon, H. A. *Psychological differences among problem isomorphs* (CIP Working Paper #303). Pittsburgh: Carnegie-Mellon University, August 1975.

Hayes, J. R., Waterman, D. A., & Robinson, C. S. Identifying the relevant aspects of a problem text. *Cognitive Science,* 1977, in press.

Hinsley, D., Hayes, J. R., & Simon, H. A. From words to equations. In P. Carpenter & M. Just (Eds.), *Cognitive processes in comprehension.* Hillsdale, N.J.: Erlbaum, 1977.

Newell, A., & Simon, H. A. *Human problem solving.* Englewood Cliffs, N.J.: Prentice-Hall, 1972.

Selfridge, O. G. Pandemonium: A paradigm for learning. In *Symposium on the mechanization of thought processes.* London: H. M. Stationery Office, 1959.

EFFECTS OF MEANINGFULNESS ON THE REPRESENTATION OF KNOWLEDGE AND THE PROCESS OF INFERENCE FOR MATHEMATICAL PROBLEM SOLVING

Richard E. Mayer
University of California, Santa Barbara

INTRODUCTION

Inference

Humans are capable of, among other things, a quite curious and important intellectual feat: the process of *inferential reasoning*. The *process* of drawing inferences involves the combining of existing knowledge to produce new (for the reasoner) knowledge. The main *outcome* of inferential reasoning is that a new (for the reasoner) relationship is discovered based on existing (or presented) knowledge.

The traditional Gestalt approach attempted to describe the reasoning process in terms of *restructuring*: the arranging of existing knowledge in a new or novel way (Duncker, 1945; Kohler, 1927; Maier, 1931; Wertheimer, 1959).

Partial support for this report was provided by a General Research Grant from the Academic Senate of the University of California, Santa Barbara, and Grant SED77-19875 from the National Science Foundation.

The mathematician, Polya (1968), expressed this idea as finding a "connection" between things that had previously been separated. A second contribution of the Gestaltists was the distinction between two types of memory representations for problem solving—namely, *structural understanding versus arbitrary associations* (Katona, 1940; Wertheimer, 1959). Although these ideas have some intuitive appeal, they have, with a few exceptions, lacked the rigor and precision necessary for experimental testing and clarification.

More recently, the information processing approach has been explored as a way of providing precision and analysis for the older Gestalt speculations. *Precision* is afforded by developing models (e.g., flow charts, computer programs, knowledge structures) which allow clear predictions; *analysis* is afforded by investigating the (cognitive) locus of various effects. One important contribution of this approach is a distinction between *memory structures* and *memory processes*. This chapter will explore the idea that certain stimulus variables may affect the nature of the memory representation for new information and/or the solution algorithm which is applied to it in the course of inferential reasoning. In particular, it will attempt to use existing information processing techniques to describe structural differences between *meaningful* and *rote* memory representations, and to describe how these structural differences affect specific stages in the restructuring process.

Meaningfulness and Mathematical Reasoning

The present chapter will focus on the role of meaningfulness in mathematical reasoning. The tasks that will be explored all involve drawing inferences from quantitative information and include the following:

1. *Path finding*—locating how many legs are involved in a path from one term to another via a network of interlocking paired associates, such as Hayes' (1966) spy problems.
2. *Algebra problems*—solving simultaneous algebra equations, such as Mayer and Greeno's (1975) algebra problem.
3. *Linear orderings*—determining the relative position of two variables in a four-term linear ordering when the relations are expressed in terms of numbers, modified from Potts' (1972) linear ordering problems.
4. *Serial counting*—determining the next items in a base 3 counting sequence, modified from Pollio and Reinhart's (1970) counting problem.

Although these tasks, of course, do not represent an exhaustive list of mathematical inference tasks, they will offer some breadth to the discussion.

The definition of meaningfulness is a far more difficult undertaking. For the present tasks, meaningfulness is operationally manipulated by expressing the terms as letter symbols (*low meaningful*) or as words or numerals which are logically related to one another (*high meaninful*); thus, a meaningful context of learning is simply the availability of a symbol-to-symbol conversion list for relating terms in letter form to terms in word form. On a less operational level, a meaningful context of learning involves providing a means for subjects to relate the presented information to experiences and knowledge already in memory. Although this definition is different, and less precise, than traditional verbal learning measures, it does allow testable predictions which will be described in the subsequent sections.

There is some existing evidence that "meaningfulness" of the presented information influences inference. Research, mainly by social psychologists, has revealed a "meaning effect" for syllogistic reasoning in which abstract and meaningful syllogisms of the same form and mood may not elicit the same patterns of performance; e.g., subjects tend to be influenced by the desirability of the conclusions or the consistency of the premises and the conclusion with past experience (see Johnson, 1972; see also Revlin & Leirer, Chap. 3).

In a promising study, Paige and Simon (1966) asked subjects to solve algebra story problems and to draw diagrams to represent the information from the questions; errors in solution could be related to incorrect or nonintegrated representations of the presented information. Such results are interesting because they suggest that information can be encoded in a fragmented way that hinders problem-solving performance.

A related issue is whether different presentation formats might lead to "correct" representations that differ in the way they are structured in memory. Scandura and his associates (Scandura, 1970; Ehrenpreis & Scandura, 1974) have argued that the same mathematical problem-solving behavior can be maintained by a set of discrete, low-level rules (e.g., single associations) or by a more general, higher order rule system that can generate the discrete rules. In one study, Ehrenpreis and Scandura taught a mathematical skill by presenting the discrete, low-level rules or the higher order rules; although both instructional groups performed similarly on a test of the specifically taught skill, the higher order group showed superior transfer to new tasks.

The present chapter summarizes a series of experiments carried out over the past four years concerning the question of whether different memory representations and/or solution algorithms can be acquired for the same problem-solving information. It includes re-analysis of previously reported work (path finding and algebra problems) and highlights of new work (linear orderings and counting).

As a matter of consistency, this chapter will distinguish between *high meaningful* and *low meaningful* presentation formats for each of the four tasks.

In addition, for each task, *rote* and *integrated cognitive structures* for the presented information will be suggested, and solution algorithms to be applied to each structure will be presented. Predictions will be offered to test the idea that high meaningful presentation format leads to integrated cognitive structures, and low meaningful presentation format leads to rote structures. In addition, an attempt will be made to pinpoint which stages in the solution algorithm are influenced by the differences in cognitive structure.

PATH FINDING PROBLEMS

Task

In his study of "spy problems," Hayes (1966) asked subjects to memorize a connection list containing pairs of spies who could communicate a message from the first member of the pair to the second; the list consisted of unrelated words such as ADJECTIVE to SHOWER, BEEF and TAFT, SHOWER to CLERK, ADJECTIVE to PARCHESI, SHOWER to BEEF, etc. Subjects were asked to indicate how to get a message from one spy, via a chain of spies, to a goal spy. The studies discussed in this section used a modified version of this task so that the meaningfulness of the information could be varied, and quantitative questions could be asked.

Subjects were asked to memorize a list of paired associates, as shown in Table 1, and were told that each pair represents a one-way path from the first member of the pair to the second. Table 1 shows two different formats for presenting the paired associates:

> *low meaningful:* the nonsense list on the left side of the table, in which subjects are told that the letter-to-letter pairs are one-way paths between letters.
> *high meaningful:* the airline flights given in the right half of the table, in which subjects are told the city-to-city pairs are one-way flights between U.S. cities and are given a map of the U.S. with the cities indicated.

A third format shown in the middle of Table 1 is the word-to-word format in which subjects are told the words are code names for spies who can pass messages (after Hayes, 1966). The results of several studies indicated that this format produces performance that is indistinguishable from the letter format, so there is some justification for classifying it as low meaningful even though words are involved. For further details, see Mayer (1976).

For the test that followed, subjects were told that single paths could be put together to form longer chains. Several questions could be asked which require quantitative reasoning:

Table 1. Some Formats for Presenting Path Finding Information

Letters (Low meaningful)	Words (Low meaningful)	Story (High meaningful)
1. C to N	1. CLERK to NEIGHBOR	1. CHICAGO to NEW YORK
2. H to L	2. HANDLE to LEAGUE	2. HOUSTON to LOS ANGELES
3. S to C	3. SAND to CLERK	3. SEATTLE to CHICAGO
4. N to M	4. NEIGHBOR to MOUTH	4. NEW YORK to MIAMI
5. H to C	5. HANDLE to CLERK	5. HOUSTON to CHICAGO
6. L to S	6. LEAGUE to SAND	6. LOS ANGELES to SEATTLE
7. M to H	7. MOUTH to HANDLE	7. MIAMI to HOUSTON
8. L to C	8. LEAGUE to CLERK	8. LOS ANGELES to CHICAGO
9. H to N	9. HANDLE to NEIGHBOR	9. HOUSTON to NEW YORK

judgment of journey lenght—e.g., "Are there 5 legs from S to L, taking the shortest route?" (Answer: Yes.)

judgment of journey number—e.g., "Is the sum of the path numbers from S to L equal to 17?" (Answer: Yes, since $3 + 1 + 4 + 7 + 2 = 17$.)

Note that these questions may vary the number of computational inferences required for solution; e.g., questions about C to N require no inference steps, S to N requires 1 inference, C to H requires 3, C to L requires 4, and S to L requires 5.

Structures and Algorithms

The new information (i.e., the nine paths) could be structured in memory in several different ways, and some of the possibilities are shown in Table 2. These structures can be divided into two groups:

rote cognitive structure: the unreferences, tagged list on the left side of the table; each pair has a tag indicating the path number, but there is no reference to other pairs with the same terms.

integrated cognitive structure: the referenced, tagged list (middle of table) or the tagged image (right side of table); each pair has a tag indicating the path number, and there are references to other locations for each term.

The structures differ mainly with respect to *referencing*; the integrated structures indicate where each right-side term serves as a left-side term, while the rote structure does not.

Table 2. Some Knowledge Structures for Path Finding Information

Unreferenced list (Rote)	*Referenced list* (Integrated)	*Referenced image* (Integrated)
1. C → N	1. C → N(4)	
2. H → L	2. H → L(6, 8)	
3. S → C	3. S → C(1)	
4. N → M	4. N → M(7)	
5. H → C	5. H → C(1)	
6. L → S	6. L → S(3)	
7. M → H	7. M → H(2, 5, 9)	
8. L → C	8. L → C(1)	
9. H → N	9. H → N(4)	

The *path selection* algorithm shown in Figure 1 could be applied to either structure. Although it is able to handle only judgments of path length, it could easily be modified (with a different procedure for incrementing the counter) to handle judgments of path number. The procedure for answering questions such as "Are there 5 legs from S to L?" is as follows:

1. Set the counter to 0.
2. Input the starting (S) and ending terms (L) and number of legs (5).
3. Check to make sure the first term and the last term are on the list. If not, stop; otherwise go on to step 4.
4. Select a path that begins with the starting term (e.g., S to C).
5. Check to see whether the right-side terms has been located earlier in a previous loop. If yes, discard that path and recycle to step 4; otherwise, go on to step 6.
6. Increment counter by 1.
7. Check to see whether the second term (C) in the path that was located in step 4, is the ending term (L). If yes, go to step 8, otherwise go on to step 9.
8. Check to see if the number in the counter is the same as the number in the question (5). If yes, answer *yes*; if not, answer *no*.
9. Change the starting term you are searching for to the right-side member of the pair; then go on to step 4.

In the present problem, the system will return to step 4 to search for C to N, then it will return for N to M, then M to H, and finally H to L. After these four loops, the ending term will be found (L), and the counter will have been incremented to 5 so that the answer is *yes*.

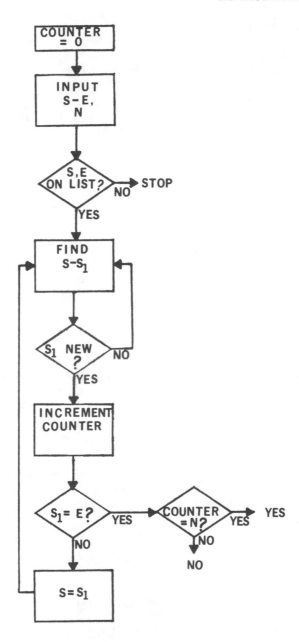

Fig. 1. Path selection algorithm for path finding task.

Note. S is starting term, E is ending term, N is number of paths, S_1 is right hand member of a S-to-S_1 pair.

Predictions and Data

This analysis suggests that subjects with integrated and rote structures would perform differently on the problem-solving test. Subjects with integrated structures would be expected to perform faster than rote subjects on problems requiring putting paths together into long chains, mainly because search time for connecting paths (step 9 to step 4) would be reduced for referenced terms. Referencing reduces the time needed to locate the next path, while subjects with unreferenced lists must search through the list to find the path that begins with the target term. No such advantage would be expected for integrated subjects when the problems involved only *one* path (no inferences) since the path search process (step 4) would be the same for both structures, or perhaps slightly slower for integrated subjects by virtue of having more information (reference information) to deal with.

One prediction that can be addressed is that low meaningful format more likely leads to a rote structure, and high meaningful format leads to an integrated structure. One specific performance prediction that follows is that the letters group should take longer than the story group to perform on inference questions that require several inferences (such as concerning S to L), but the difference would disappear on retention questions which require no inferences (such as concerning S to C). This prediction was upheld in two separate experiments—one using calculated answers and one using yes-no judgments. In both cases there was reliable interaction between the groups by number of inferences in the question; e.g., the time to answer judgment questions with no inferences averaged 4.4 seconds for letters subjects and 4.8 seconds for the story group, but long inferences (4 to 5 steps) took an average of 20.1 seconds for the letters group and 12.0 seconds for the story group (Mayer, 1976, Experiments 1 and 2).

In a more controlled study, subjects memorized the list of nine letter-to-letter connections but were told either before or after learning that the pairs referred to airline flights between cities. Thus, some subjects were given a list consisting of letter-to-city conversions (C = Chicago, H = Houston, N = New York, etc.) for 60 seconds before learning, and some received the same list and instructions after learning. Although all subjects took the test in letters format only, there was the predicted pattern of interaction. Both groups performed about the same on no-inference questions, but the Before group performed better on problems requiring inference (Mayer, 1976, Experiement 3).

Table 3 shows a re-analysis of a typical result by Mayer (1976, Experiment 2). Regression lines fit to the curves revealed that the letters group had a slightly lower intercept than the story group (a = 4.40 vs. 5.35) which is consistent with the idea that referencing added some overall burden; however,

Table 3. Re-analysis of Data from Experiment 2 of Mayer (1976)

	Inference size					Regression line		
	0	1	2	3	4	a	b	r^2
RT obtained for letters group	4.3	9.5	15.4	19.7	24.8	4.40	5.15	99.8
RT predicted for letters group	4.4	9.5	14.7	19.8	25.0			
RT obtained for story group	4.8	6.8	10.3	12.9	13.6	5.35	2.35	95.4
RT predicted for story group	5.4	7.7	10.1	12.4	14.7			

Note. $-$ a = intercept, b = slope, and r^2 = the percentage of explained variance for the regression line.

RT = reaction time in seconds.

the slope of the line for the story group is much less steep than that for the letters group (b = 2.35 vs. 5.15). Since each recycle back through step 4 added only 2.35 seconds for the story group but added 5.15 for the letters group, these results are consistent with the idea that search time for the "next" leg in the journey was more than twice as fast with referenced structures. In the present case "meaningful format" and "integrated structure" is manifested in shorter search time for the "next" link in the inference chain.

ALGEBRAIC PROBLEMS

Task

In a recent series of experiments (Mayer & Greeno, 1975) subjects were asked to learn an interlocking set of equations. The equations could be presented in several different contexts, including:

> *low meaningful:* presenting the equations as relations among nonsense letters, as shown on the left side of Table 4.
> *high meaningful:* presenting the equations as a story with each term given a name that was logically related to the others in the equations, as shown on the right side of Table 4.

Although both formats presented the same relations among the same variables (with only different symbols used for the variables), the high meaningful

Table 4. Some Formats for Presenting Algebraic Information

Letters (Low meaning- ful)	Story (High meaningful)
Four equations	
(1) V = F − L	Driving time = arrival − leaving time
(2) D = V*A	Distance = driving time * average speed
(3) M = D/G	Gas mileage = distance/gas used
(4) T = V + P	Total time = driving time + preparation time
Nine equations	
(A1) V = A x H	Volume = area x height
(A2) H = E − B	Height = stopping point − starting point
(A3) A = L x S	Area = length x width
(B1) W = O x D	Work = weight x distance
(B2) M = O x H	Potential energy = weight x height
(B3) R = W/T	Power = work/time
(C1) N = O/V	Density = weight/volume
(C2) O = Y x C	Weight = mass x acceleration
(C3) F = O/A	Pressure = weight/area

format may have allowed subjects a means of relating the new equations to their past experience.

In some experiments subjects memorized the four equations on the top of Table 4 (either in letter or story format). In other experiments subjects memorized the nine equations given in the lower part of the table (in either letter or story format) by memorizing three sets of three equations. For example, a subject would memorize A1, A2, A3 to criterion, then memorize B1, B2, B3 to criterion, and then learn C1, C2, and C3; other subjects in each treatment group memorized the equations groups as A1, B1, C1/A2, B2, C2/A3, B3, C3.

The test could consist of asking subjects to perform the following:

> *judgments of computability*—e.g., "Given values for F, L, and A, is it possible to determine a value for D?" (Answer: Yes).

Note that computability judgments may vary the length of the required inference chain; e.g., for a set of three equations, questions may deal with only one equation and no substitutions (0-size), two equations and one substitution (1-size), or all three and two substitutions (2-size).

Table 5. Some Knowledge Structures for Algebraic Information

Equations (Rote)	Abbreviated referenced list (Integrated)	Spatial image (Integrated)

$V = F - L$
$D = V*A$
$M = D/G$
$T = V + P$
	1. V(4), F, L
	2. D(3), V(1, 4), A
	3. M, D(2), G
	4. T, V(1, 2), P
		A — D — V
		   | / \
		  G F T
		  | | |
		  M L P

For subjects given all nine equations, questions were based on only three of the equations. For half the letters group and half the story group the test equations had all been memorized in the same set during learning (e.g., A2, B2, C2 for the presentation organization A1, B1, C1/A2, B2, C2/A3, B3, C3; or B1, B2, B3 for the presentation organization A1, A2, A3/B1, B2, B3/C1, C2, C3); for the other subjects in each group the test equations came from each of the three separate sets (e.g., A2, B2, C2 from A1, A2, A3/B1, B2, B3/C1, C2, C3; or B1, B2, B3 from A1, B1, C1/A3, B3, C3). This yields four main groups: letters subjects who were tested on one set (letters-1), letters subjects who were tested on equations from all three sets (letters-3), story subjects who were tested on one set (story-1), and story subjects who were tested on equations from all three sets (story-3).

Structures and Algorithms

There are several ways in which the new knowledge (i.e., the equations) could be structured in a subject's long-term memory. Three possible cognitive structures for a set of four equations are given in Table 5. These structures may be divided into two general types:

> *rote cognitive structure:* an exact duplication of the four equations, as shown on the left side of the table.
> *integrated cognitive structure:* the abbreviated referenced list or the spatial image given on the right side of the table.

The referenced list and the spatial image differ from the rote structure in two important ways: Details have been eliminated (i.e., signs and numbers), and pointers have been provided for each term that appears in more than one equation. For example, the referenced list shows that the D in equation 2 is referenced to equation 3 (by parentheses) to indicate that D also appears there.

There are several algorithms that could be applied to either of these structures. Malin (1973) has suggested two solution algorithms that would be

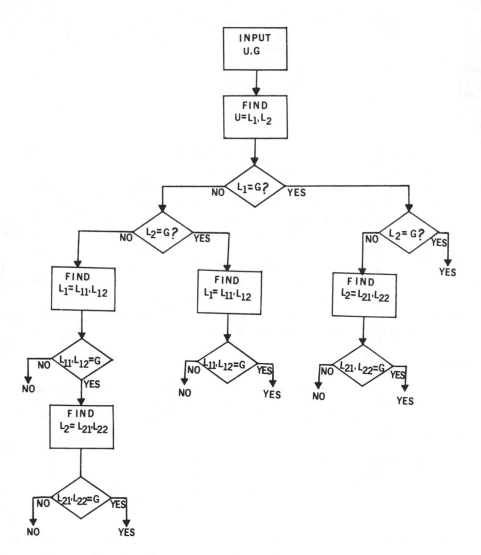

Fig. 2. Backward algorithm for algebra task.

Note. U is the unknown variable, G is the given variables, L_1 and L_2 are other variables in the equation with U, L_{11} and L_{12} are other variables in the equation with L_1, and L_{21} and L_{22} are other variables in the equation with L_2.

applicable to either structure: a *forward algorithm* in which the subject "works forward" (Polya, 1968) from the givens to the unknown, and a *backward algorithm* in which the subject "works backward" (Polya, 1968) from the unknown to the goal. Since both models generate similar general predictions[1] with respect to the inference size, only the backward algorithm will be described in this section. The backward algorithm for computability judgments is given in Figure 2 and is summarized below for the problem "Given T, R, M, H, could you find D?"

1. Input the unknown (D) and the givens (T, R, M, H,).
2. Find the equation with the unknown in it and store the two letters that are in the same equation (D is in the same equation as W and O).
3. Check to see if the first needed letter (W) is in the given set. If yes, go on to step 11; otherwise, go on to step 4.
4. Check to see if the second needed letter (O) is in the given set. If yes, go on to step 9; otherwise, go to step 5.
5. Find the equation with the first needed letter in it and store the two letters that are in the same equation (W is in an equation with T and R).
6. Check to see if the two letters (T and R) needed to find the first needed letter (W) are in the given set. (T and R are in the given set). If no, answer *no*; otherwise, go on to step 7.
7. Find the equation with the second needed letter in it and store the two letters that are in the same equation (O is in the equation with M and H).
8. Check to see if the two letters (M and H) needed to find the second needed letter (O) are in the given set. (M and H are in the given set.) If no, answer *no*; otherwise, answer *yes*.
9. Find the equation with the first needed letter in it and store the two letters that are in the same equation.
10. Check to see if the two letters are in the given set. If no, answer *no*; if yes, answer *yes*.
11. Check to see if the second needed letter is in the given set. If yes, answer *yes*; if no, go on to step 12.
12. Find the equation with the second needed letter in it and store the two letters that are in the same equation.
13. Check to see if the two letters are in the given set. If no, answer *no*; if yes, answer *yes*.

There are several additional features of this model that require clarification. For example, in steps 5, 7, 9, and 12, if more than one equation may be

---

[1] The models often predict different performance for specific problems, but these differences are not directly relevant for this chapter.

found, then the system must try each before answering *no*. This problem adds some ambiguity to predictions but, in general, 2-size problems require more processing (i.e., more recycles to steps 5, 7, 9, or 12) than 1-size problems, and 1-size problems require more processing than 0-size.

Predictions and Data

Several performance predictions may be generated to test the idea that low meaningful format leads to rote cognitive structure while high meaningful format more likely leads to the development of an integrated structure. One performance prediction is that high meaningful format subjects should perform better (e.g., faster) on problems requiring long chains of inference than low meaningful subjects, but there should be no difference for retention (0-size) questions. This prediction is based on the idea that locating the "next" equation for a target variable (as in steps, 5, 7, 9, and 12) should be faster for subjects with referenced structures; however, problems requiring only steps 1 through 4 do not rely on referencing, and, therefore, the meaningful structure would not show an advantage. This prediction was upheld in two experiments, one in which subjects actually calculated answers (Distance = 90 miles, gas used = 5 gal., Find gas mileage), and one in which subjects made judgments of computability (Mayer & Greeno, 1975, Experiments 1 and 2).

A stronger test of the distinction between two types of cognitive structure for the two format groups concerns the experiment with nine equations. If low meaningful subjects retain the equations in their original form but high meaningful format encourages an integrated structuring, then one prediction is that letters subjects should perform much better if the test concerns three equations which all come from the same set (due to reduced search time) but that input organization should have no effect for high meaningful subjects who have referenced the entire list. For example, letters subjects may develop some local referencing for each set while story subjects develop complete referencing for all nine equations. This result was obtained (using computability judgments) and is summarized in Table 6 (Mayer & Greeno, 1975, Experiment 4).

Regression lines were fit to the RT data (for true-correct) for all four groups. The story-1 and story-3 groups displayed similar intercepts (a = 4.75 seconds and a 3.70 seconds, respectively) and almost identical slopes (b = 2.25 and b = 2.50, respectively). Apparently, each additional required equation added about 2.25 to 2.50 seconds in processing time, but both groups were able to perform the search equally rapidly due to similar referencing for both groups. However, the letter-1 and letter-3 groups differed greatly with respect to slope (b = 1.80 seconds and b = 5.50 seconds, respectively). Apparently,

Table 6. Re-analysis of Data from Experiment 4 of Mayer and Greeno (1975)

Group	Inference size			Regression line		
	0	1	2	a	b	r^2
RT obtained for letter-1 group	3.0	5.6	6.5			
RT predicted for letter-1 group	3.2	5.0	6.8	3.25	1.80	94.5
RT obtained for letter-3 group	3.2	6.9	14.2			
RT predicted for letter-3 group	2.6	8.1	13.6	2.60	5.50	96.4
RT obtained for story-1 group	4.5	7.4	9.0			
RT predicted for story-1 group	4.7	7.0	9.2	4.75	2.25	97.5
RT obtained for story-3 group	3.5	6.7	8.5			
RT predicted for story-3 group	3.7	6.2	8.7	3.70	2.50	97.4

Note. $-$ a = intercept, b $-$ slope, and r^2 = the percentage of explained variance for the regression line.

RT = reaction time in seconds.

the searches required in steps 5, 7, 9, or 12 added three times as much time for the letter-3 group as compared with letter-1; one implication is that the letter-3 group had to seach through more equations until finding the target. In addition, both groups had lower intercepts than the story groups (a = 2.58 seconds for letter-3 and 3.25 for letter-1), thus suggesting that the referencing of the story group may have added a slight amount of time overall. The same pattern of intercepts and slopes was obtained in comparing the response time data for 0-, 1-, and 2-size problems, combining "true" and "false" questions. Apparently, story subjects acquire more complete referencing that allows faster search time for the "next" equation in the algebraic chain.

QUANTITATIVE LINEAR ORDERING PROBLEMS

Task

Potts (1972, 1974, chapter 6 in this volume) has investigated the structures and algorithms subjects use to answer questions about linear orderings that are

Table 7. Some Formats for Presenting Linear Ordering Information

Letters (Low meaningful)	*Story* (High meaningful)
F = 10*R H = 20*B F = 40*B	In a certain forest the animals are voting for their leader. The frog gets 10 times as many votes as the rabbit. The hawk gets 20 times as many votes as the bear. The frog gets 40 times as many votes as the bear.

presented as part of a meaningful passage. A major finding has been a "distance effect" in which subjects who are presented with information about adjacent pairs (e.g., A > B, B > C, C > D) perform faster or more accurately on questions about remote pairs (A-C, B-D or A-D) than on questions about adjacent pairs (A-B, B-C or C-D). Potts (1972) has offered a process model to account for the data based on the idea that subjects form a visual image or a referenced list; others (Humphreys, 1975) have argued that the data can be accounted for by assuming subjects remember a set of features for each term, such as how many times it appeared on the right or left of a "greater than" relationship. The present study attempted to investigate how linear ordering information is stored and processed for use in quantitative problems and also varied the meaningfulness of the presentation format.

Subjects were asked to read passages, as illustrated in Table 7, for as long as they needed. The passages concerned a four-item linear ordering and presented the quantitative relations among the three remote pairs. The information could be presented in two different formats:

> *low meaningful:* quantitative relational propositions are expressed as a set of nonsense equations with variables presented as meaningless letters (see left side of Table 7).
>
> *high meaningful:* stories are used with variables expressed as names and relations given in the context of meaningful sentences (see right side of Table 7).

Both formats present the same numerical relations among the same terms, and from both the same ordering may be constructed: F = 2*H, H = 5*R, R = 4*B (or F > H, H > R, R > B) where the asteric (*) means "multiplied by."

There are several types of questions that can be asked of subjects including the following:

> *judgment of numeric relations*—e.g., "F = 2*H?" (Answer: Yes)
>
> *judgment of comparative relations*—e.g., "F > H?" (Answer: Yes)

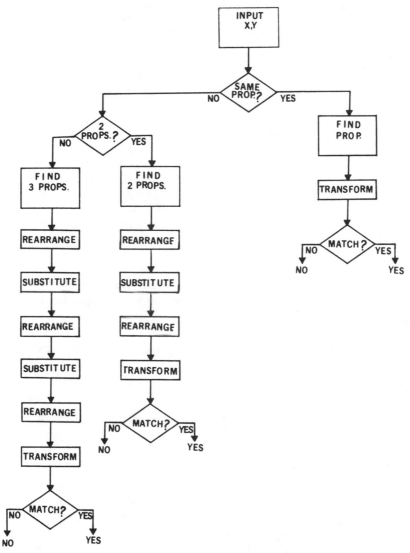

Fig. 3. Quantitative inference algorithm for linear ordering task. *Note.* X and Y are terms in the problem.

Table 8. Some Knowledge Structures for Linear Ordering Information

Feature list (Rote)	Referenced, tagged list (Integrated)
Term-Feature Pairs = {(F, greater greater) (R, less) (H, greater) (B, less less)}	1. F(3) – R →*10 2. H – B(3) →*20 3. F(1) – B(2) →*40
Quantities = {*10, *20, *40}	
where "greater" indicates that term occurred on left on a "greater than" relation and "less" indicates it occurred on the right.	where numbers in parentheses are references to other locations, and numbers to the right of arrows indicate tags such as *10 means the term on the left is 10 times greater than the term on the right.

Since only remote pairs are given, answering even "judgment of comparative relations" requires numerical calculations. In the present situation questions concerning the remote pairs (A-C, B-D, A-D) require no inferences, questions concerning A-B and C-D require substituting one proposition for another (inference size 1), and questions concerning B-C require two substitutions (inference size 2).

In the present study subjects read four passages (in either equation or story format) and answered only one type of questions after each (numeric judgments or comparative judgments); then, on the fifth passage all subjects were given both types of questions.

Structures and Algorithms

How does the subject represent the presented information, and what processes are used to answer judgment questions? Two quite different methods for storing and using information are given in Table 8 and Figures 3 and 4. These structures may be called:

> *rote cognitive structure:* unordered, untagged feature list such as that shown on the left side of the table; each term is associated with its features (in this case, how many times it occurred on the left or right of "greater than" relation), and the specific quantities are stored in a separate unattached list.

integrated cognitive structure: a referenced, tagged list of pairs such as that shown on the right side of the table; each term is referenced for where it appears in another location, and each pair is tagged for the numerical quantity involved.

An equivalent representation for the referenced, tagged list would be a tagged image such as:

A –(10)–C
   B – (20) – D
A — (40) — D

where numbers in parentheses are tags, and vertical columns serve as references. In this case the actual relation between B and C is ambiguous unless attention is paid to the quantities. The high meaningful representation would be most compatible with Potts' model whereas the feature list would be more closely related to Humphrey's model.

Both types of memory representations require different algorithms to generate answers. For example, the algorithms for answering comparative judgment problems are given in Figure 3. The *quantitative inference* algorithm could be used with integrated cognitive structures and would answer 0-, 1-, and 2-step questions as follows.

To answer a 0-size question such as "A $>$ C?" the procedure is:

1. Retrieve A-C propostion (1. A = $10*$C).
2. Transform the proposition into an inequality (A $>$ C).
3. Check to see if the produced inequality matches the question.
If yes, answer *yes*; if no, answer *no*. (Answer is Yes.)

To answer a 1-size question such as "A $>$ B?" the procedure is:

1. Retrieve proposition A-D (3. A = 40*D).
2. Retrieve proposition B-D (2. B = 20*D).
3. Rearrange for common term. (D = A/40, or D = B/20).
4. Substitute propositions into one another (A/40 = B/20).
5. Rearrange new proposition into A-B form (A = 2*B).
6. Transform new proposition into an inequality (A $>$ B).
7. Check to see if the produced inequality matches the question.
If yes, answer *yes*; otherwise, answer *no*.

To answer a 2-size question such as "B $>$ C?" the procedure is:

1. Retrieve A-C proposition (1. A = 10*C).
2. Retrieve B-D proposition (2. B = 20*D).

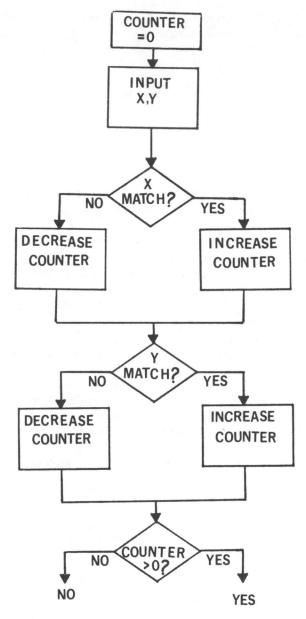

Fig. 4. Feature matching algorithm for linear ordering task.

Note. X and Y are terms in the problem.

3. Retrieve A-D proposition (3. A = 40*D).

4. Rearrange propositions for common term (D = B/20 or D = A/40).

5. Substitute two propositions to eliminate common term (A/40 = B/20).

6. Rearrange new proposition in standard form (A = 2*B).

7. Substitute new and remaining proposition into each other to eliminate common term (2*B = 10*C).

8. Rearrange propositions (B = 5*C).

9. Transform proposition into inequality (B > C).

10. Check to see if the produced inequality matches the question. If yes, answer *yes*; if no, answer *no*.

In all three examples, the answer is *yes* since there is a match. To determine whether a problem is 0-, 1-, or 2-size, the system uses the procedure:

1. Do the two terms in the question appear in the same proposition? If yes, use 0-size procedure; otherwise, go on to step 2.

2. Do the two terms in the question appear in two propositions which have a common term? If yes, use 1-size procedure; otherwise use 2-size procedure.

Note that 1-size problems have all the same processes as 0-size plus some extras; similarly, 2-size problems have all the processes of a 1-size problem plus some extras. This model predicts that 0-size problems should be easiest, 1-size next easiest, and 2-size most difficult.

Figure 4 shows a *feature match* algorithm that could be used with the unordered feature list; according to this model, 0-size problems such as "A > C?" would be answered as follows:

1. Does the position of the first term in the question (A is on the "greater than" side of the inequality) match the position of that term in the memorized feature list (A was "greater than" 2 times)? Answer: Yes, Yes.

2. Does the position of the second term in the question (C is on the "less than" side) match the position of that term in the feature list (C was "less than" 1 time)? Answer: Yes.

3. Add up matches and mismatches. If matches outnumber mismatches, answer *yes*; if mismatches outnumber matches, answer *no*.

For 0-size problems, there are either all matches or all mismatches. The same situation holds for 2-size problems because B is a "greater than" and C is a

Table 9. Obtained and Predicted Proportion Correct Response for Story and Letter Groups by Inference Size

Group	Obtained data Inference size 0	1	2	Model	Predicted data Inference size 0	1	2	r^2
Letter (Passages 1–4)	.70	.62	.71	Feature	.70	.62	.70	.99
Story (Passages 1–4)	.92	.86	.64	Inference	.95	.81	.67	.90
Letter/Comparative (Passage 5)	.85	.69	.83	Feature	.84	.69	.84	.99
Story/Comparative (Passage 5)	1.00	.90	.58	Inference	1.04	.83	.62	.92
Letter/Numeric (Passage 5)	.66	.60	.65	Feature	.66	.60	.66	.98
Story/Numeric (Passage 5)	.98	.84	.58	Inference	1.00	.80	.60	.97

Note. $-r^2$ is a measure of the percentage of explained variance.

"less than." However, 1-size problems always involve a match and a mismatch; e.g., "A > B?" results in a double match for A but a single mismatch for B. This model predicts that 0- and 2-size problems should be equal because they produce consistent match results while 1-size problems should be most difficult.

Predictions and Data

Although the two models (quantitative inference and feature match) give similar performance predictions for situations in which adjacent pairs are given, the present situation with remote, quantitative pairs allows a more powerful test of the two models. If equation format results in the acquisition of a rote/feature representation and story format tends to produce integrated/inference representation, then different patterns of performance are predicted by inference size for the two groups. Table 9 gives the performance of equation and story subjects on making comparative judgments on the first four passages (two separate groups) and on the fifth passage (consisting of subjects who had answered only comparative and only numeric questions on the first four passages). In all cases there is a clear pattern of interaction in the predicted direction: Equation subjects perform just as well on size 0 and size 2 but worse on size 1 problems, while the story subjects show a "negative" distance effect, as predicted by the inference model.

Linear regression lines can be generated as simple versions of the inference and feature models. The simple inference model predicts that each increase in inference size from 0 to 1 to 2 should add a constant amount of error (i.e., constant decrease in proportion correct). The predicted values for inference sizes 0, 1, and 2 are, respectively, $\overline{X} + S$, $\overline{X} - S$, where $\overline{X}$ is the mean of the obtained values and S is the slope of the regression line. The feature model predicts inference sizes 0 and 2 should be equal because both generate two consistent tests while inference size 1 should show a decrement (in proportion correct) since it always produces one match and one mismatch. The predicted values for inference sizes 0, 1, and 2 are, respectively, $\overline{X}$ $\overline{X} - S$, and $\overline{X}$, where $\overline{X}$ is the mean of the obtained values for sizes 0 and 2 and $\overline{X} - S$ is equal to the obtained value of size 1 (or $\overline{X}$, whichever is smaller).

To obtained and predicted data, summarized in Table 9, show that the performance of the story group was best fit by the inference model, and the performance of the letter group was best fit by a feature model, in all cases. Apparently, when the situation is complex and numerical computations are ostensively required, subjects can alter their processing strategies; one factor that influences the structures and algorithms which are used by subjects may be the meaningfulness of the presented premises.

SERIAL COUNTING PROBLEMS

Task

Pollio and Reinhart (1970) taught subjects to count in base 2, 3, or 4 by starting with 1, asking the subject to anticipate the next number, giving the correct answer, and then continuing the series until the subject could anticipate without error. One interesting finding was that subjects learned not only to count, but also to perform some arithmetic such as adding in the bases. The studies discussed in this section used a modified version of this task so that meaningfulness of the counting chain could be varied.

Subjects were asked to learn a list of 18 consecutive counting symbols, based on base 3, using an anticipation method similar to that used by Pollio and Reinhart. However, the list was repeated until the subject could correctly anticipate each of the 18 items for two trials in a row. The series of symbols could be presented in several formats, and the two that were used in the present studies are shown in Table 10. They are:

  low meaningful: a series of letters where each is generated by taking
      the first 18 items in base 3 and then substituting w for 0, d for
      1, and r for 2.
  high meaningful: a series of numbers based on the first 18 items in
      base 3.

Table 10. Some Formats for Presenting Counting Information

Letters (Low meaningful)	*Numerals* (High meaningful)
w	0
d	1
r	2
dw	10
dd	11
dr	12
rw	20
rd	21
rr	22
dww	100
dwd	101
dwr	102
ddw	110
ddd	111
ddr	112
drw	120
drd	121
drr	122
rww	200

Both formats present the same information but use different symbols; since subjects are accustomed to using numbers in base 10, the high meaningful format may serve to encourage subjects to encode the material in a more integrated way.

For the test that followed learning, subjects were asked to perform three tasks:

1. *recall*—write out the 18 items as presented during learning.

2. *addition*—solve several addition problems in base 3 using the same type of symbols as during learning (e.g., dr + dd = ———, or 12 to 11 = ———).

3. *counting*—provide the next 10 items after rww (or 200). Note that the addition and counting tasks require transfer beyond what was given during learning.

Structures and Algorithms

The new counting behavior can be supported by entirely different types of memory structures. For example, Scandura and his associates (1970;

Table 11. Some Knowledge Structures for Counting Information

Discrete low-level associations (Rote)	*Base 3 number system* (Integrated)
w → d	
d → r	S = {w, d, r}
r → dw	
dw → dd	concept of "place value"
dd → dr	
dr → rw	
rw → rd	where S is the ordered set of allowable elements.
rd → rr	
rr → dww	
dww → dwd	
dwd → dwr	
dwr → ddw	
ddw → ddd	
ddd → ddr	
ddr → drw	
drw → drd	
drd → drr	
drr → rww	

Ehrenpreis & Scandura, 1974) provide evidence that mathematical rules may be learned as many discrete, lower level rules or as a higher order, more general rule. These two types of structures for the counting task and the algorithms to support each are shown in Table 11 and Figures 5 and 6. These two structues can be called:

rote cognitive structure: the set of 18 discrete, lower level rules on the left side of the table.
integrated cognitive structure: the ordered set of elements and the concept of place value for use with the higher order algorithm shown on the right side.

The structures contain qualitative differences that cannot be explained in terms of referencing, and each requires a different algorithm.

The *rule selection algorithm* for the low-level rule is quite straightforward; e.g., to count from "dw to rw" the procedure would be as follows:

1. Input the starting term (dw) and the ending term (rw).

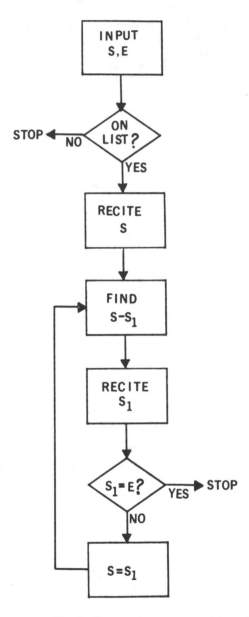

Fig. 5. Rule selection algorithm for counting task.

Note. S is the starting term, E is the ending term, S_1 is the term that follows S in the counting sequence.

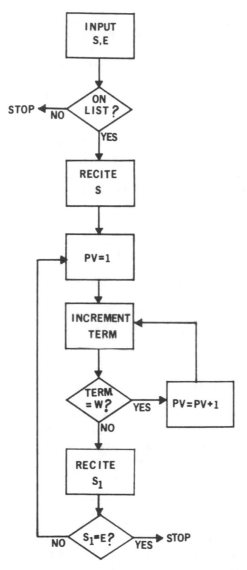

Fig. 6. Place value algorithm for counting behavior.

Note. S is the starting term, E is the ending term, S_1 is the term that follows S in the counting sequence, PV refers to place value.

2. Check to make sure both are on the list. If not, stop; otherwise go on to step 3.

3. Recite the starting term (dw).

4. Find the rule beginning with the starting term (dw → dd).

5. Recite the right-side member of the pair (dd).

6. Check to see if the right side member of the pair is the ending term (rw). If it is, stop; otherwise go on to step 7.

7. Let the right side term (dd) now be the starting term, and recycle to step 4.

In this case, the subject would recycle to find dd → dr and then recycle one more time to find dr → rw. Since rw is the ending term, the subject would then stop.

The *place value algorithm* for the higher order memory representation is based on the subjects' past experience with counting in base 10. To count from "dw to rw" the procedure would be:

1. Input the starting term (dw) and ending term (rw).

2. Check to make sure each place value for each term contains one of the symbols on the list (w, d, or r). If not, stop; otherwise, go on to step 3.

3. Recite the starting term (dw).

4. Concentrate on place value 1 (the symbol most on the right).

5. Increment the number in the place value (w to d) based on the ordered set (w, d, r).

6. Check to see if the new symbol (d) in the place value is a w. If not, recycle to step 8; otherwise, go on to step 7.

7. Concentrate on next place value (i.e., the one just to the left of the current place value), then go back to step 5.

8. Recite the produced term (dd).

9. Check to see if the produced term is the ending term (rw). If no stop, otherwise go on to step 10.

10. Let the produced term (dd) now be the starting term and go on to step 4.

In this case the subject will now go back to step 4, with dd as the starting term and then will produce dr; the production of rw will require a loop from step 6 to 7 to 5. This algorithm is capable of generating sequences not presented in original learning.

Predictions and Data

This analysis suggests that subjects with integrated/higher order representations and rote/discrete representations would perform differently on the problem-solving test. All subjects should perform well on tests of recall since both groups have acquired structures which support counting to 18 in base 3. However, the subjects with an integrated structure should perform better on transfer tests such as addition and extended counting since they have acquired more general rules, while the subjects with discrete structures would not be expected to transfer at all.

If the high meaningful format leads to integrated structures and the low meaningful format leads to rote structures, then the predictions will have been confirmed. In a typical experiment, the letters group achieved only 18% correct in counting and 1% in adding, while the number group achieved 72% and 56% correct, respectively. However, since the test in number format may be easier than the test in letter format, an additional study was conducted in which all subjects learned the sequence of letters and took the test expressed in letters format. Some of the subjects were told *before* learning that "w = 0, d = 1, r = 2", while other subjects were given the same information after learning. As predicted, the two groups both performed at the 100% level on recall, but the Before group scored 50% on the addition test and 61% on the counting test compared with 17% and 21%, respectively, for the After group. Apparently, the short introduction allowed Before subjects to integrate the new series within the context of past experience with base 10, while the After group was forced to encode in a more rigid fashion.

CONCLUSION

Meaningfulness as Context

This chapter summarized experiments on four different tasks involving the role of meaningfulness on mathematical inference. In these studies the concept of meaningfulness was based on the proposition that a *high meaningful presentation format* helps the subject to relate the presented information to his existing knowledge, while a *low meaningful presentation format* gives the identical information without cues for relating the information to past experience. In each task, meaningfulness of presented stimuli was operationally varied by manipulating whether nonsense symbols (i.e., letters) were used to represent each term or whether terms were represented by logically related words (or numerals in the counting task). For cases involving sequencing of a meaningful context (paths task and counting task) meaningfulness was operationally manipulated by presenting a symbol-to-symbol conversion list (letter-to-numeral for the counting task, and letter-to-city for the paths task) either before or after learning. This definition of meaningfulness is considerably different from those developed in traditional verbal learning research (Noble, 1952; Underwood & Schultz, 1960). Although the concept of *meaningfulness as a context* as discussed in this chapter is not as precise or as quantifiable as verbal learning measures for words, the concept does lead to clear predictions that can be tested.

Assimilation

This chapter suggests that the presented information may be *encoded* in different ways depending on the meaningfulness of the presentation format. Apparently, how new information is encoded is a critical variable for complex mathematical reasoning tasks. Previous studies (Mayer, 1975) have distinguished between an acquisition process based on *assimilating* new information to existing knowledge versus *adding* new information as presented to memory. Similarly, Ausubel (1968) has distinguished between *meaningful learning set* in which a subject subsumes new information under higher order concepts already existing in memory and *rote learning set* in which a subject acquires information without assimilating higher order concepts. The *assimilation-to-schema* idea (discussed more fully in Mayer, 1977) predicts that a meaningful context (i.e., the symbol-to-symbol conversion list) presented before learning will result in an assimilation acquisition process whereas the same context presented after learning will result in more rigid, less integrated learning. A more straightforward idea is that since the same information is presented, the same learning process and outcome should result. The results discussed here and elsewhere (Mayer, 1977) favor the assimilation theory.

Integrated Cognitive Structures

"What is learned" due to a meaningful context and assimilative acquisition processes is a central theme of this chapter. Previous studies (Mayer, 1975; Mayer & Greeno, 1972) have described differences in rote versus integrated learning outcomes in terms of internal connections (strong relations among elements that retain the presented relations) and external connections (connections between presented elements and concepts already in memory). Broad or integrated learning outcomes are proposed to have more external connections but weaker internal connections, while rote or narrow structures have strong internal but weak external connections. Norman (1973, p. 158) presents a similar distinction in which new propositions are either interconnected with existing knowledge or added to memory in isolated form. The present chapter provides a modest increment in the level at which differences between rote and integrated structures can be made specific.

For two tasks (paths and algebraic) the structural differences between rote and integrated cognitive structures could be successfully described in terms of *referencing*; i.e., integrated structures contained pointers indicating the location of each term in other propositions, and rote structures lacked such pointers. For each task different knowledge structures could be operated on by the same solution algorithm (path selection algorithm for path task and backward algorithm for algebra task); the effect of referencing could be pinpointed to a savings in search time for finding the "next" proposition in an inference chain. In both tasks a re-analysis of previously reported data revealed that each additional inference step added a constant amount to overall reaction time, but that amount (i.e., the slope of a regression line) was much higher for subjects presumed to have rote structures. Apparently, these subjects had to search through more propositions before finding the "next" one than subjects with referenced (integrated) structures. There was also some evidence that referencing added a slight amount of time overall (intercept of regression line) compared to rote structures, presumably due to the additional referencing information that had to be retained during problem solving.

For two other tasks (linear orderings and counting) the structural difference between rote and integrated cognitive structures was more basic than simply a difference in amount of referencing; in these cases entirely different structures and solution algorithms were presumably acquired. The results of the linear ordering task indicated that high meaningful format subjects acquired a referenced, tagged list and used an inference algorithm to solve problems, while low meaningful format subjects tended to acquire a feature list and use a feature matching algorithm for solution. The structure acquired by the high meaningful subjects is more closely related to that described by Potts (1972, 1974, chapter 6 in this volume); the structure acquired by low meaningful subjects is closer to that described by Humphreys (1975) based on verbal discrimination learning. Similarly, subjects in the counting experiment seemed to have acquired qualitatively different structures. High meaningful subjects tended to acquire an ordered set of symbols, the concept of place value, and a counting algorithm borrowed from base 10 whereas low meaningful subjects learned a set of discrete, lower level rules. These results provide some additional support to Scandura's (1970; Ehrenpreis & Scandura, 1974) claim that the same mathematical behaviors can be maintained by rules which differ greatly in their generality. Apparently, for complex mathematical tasks the same information can be encoded in qualitatively different ways; this chapter provides some examples of what these qualitative differences may be like for specific tasks.

Models

The strategy used in this chapter was to develop simple, specific models of the memory structures and solution algorithms for four different inference tasks and then to examine the obtained performance of subjects against the predictions of the models. This analysis certainly was not intended to deny that there may be alternative models to those tested or alternative descriptions of the findings. For instance, although this chapter emphasizes differences in memory structures for the first two tasks, it may be possible to describe the differences in terms of processing by providing a more detailed description of the processing stages. As an example, instead of relying on the concept of referencing to explain the data for the first two tasks, a process model might detail how the search process could be longer for subjects given low meaningful premises than for subjects given high meaningful information.

Because the group x inference size interaction was not disordinal in the first two tasks, there may be some reason to believe that the performance on recall (non-inference) problems in the first two tasks reflected a floor or ceiling effect; if this is the case, one might argue that there is only an overall difference in "how much is learned" between subjects given high versus low meaningful information. However, the fact that (a) each additional inference step apparently added a constant amount of processing time, and (b) this constant was higher for low meaningful presentation conditions is most consistent with the idea that there were qualitative differences in performance. Certainly, a more convincing argument for qualitative differences is established when a disordinal interaction is obtained such as with linear orderings where one group excels on one type of task and the other group excels on another. Thus, for both linear orderings and counting tasks, the differences between low and high meaningful conditions could be described in terms of both different memory processes and different memory structures.

Although the models suggested herein are preliminary, they do suggest that there may be some consistency in the types of associations used to describe cognitive structures and the types of stages used to describe processing in the four different tasks. As such, they provide a modest step in the larger goal of determining a finite set of "universal" structural and processing components involved in human reasoning.

Implications

The theme of this chapter is that different presentation formats can result in different encodings of the same information. This finding has erious implications both for the conduct of research and theories in cognitive psychology. The study of inference, and the construction of models of the inference process for various tasks, must be conducted with some reference to the way in which presented information is encoded. An important implication of this work is that subtle (and not so subtle) factors may influence how subjects encode presented information for a given task. Models of inference must be broadened to account for an array of inference tasks, and especially for differences in the meaningfulness of the presented material. Potts (1976), e.g., has obtained a distance effect for a linear ordering using "concrete" words as terms; however, there was neither a direct comparison with an "equation" group nor were more complex orderings used. The goal of future research on inference should include an attempt to specify better the structural differences in "what is learned" as a function of different experimental variables and to build broader models based on a larger set of "real world" inference tasks.

There are also several important pedagogic implications of this work. Greeno (1976) has distinguished between *behavioral objectives* and *cognitive objectives* of instruction. This chapter shows that the same problem-solving behavior—mathematical inference—can be maintained by entirely different underlying structures and processes. Instructors must consider not only what terminal behavior is desired, but also what cognitive structures and processes will support that behavior. An analysis of the cognitive objectives of instruction seems particularly important for those skills which will be used as building blocks for more complex skills. There are currently several important models of arithmetic behavior (Groen & Parkman, 1972; Resnick, 1976; Suppes & Groen, 1967; Woods, Resnick & Groen, 1975) which may form the basis for cognitive objectives of arithmetic instruction. However, more work is needed to provide cognitive analyses of more complex tasks.

REFERENCES

Ausubel, D. P. *Educational psychology: A cognitive view*. New York: Holt, Rinehart & Winston, 1968.

Duncker, K. On problem-solving. *Psychological Monographs*, 1945, **58**, (Whole No. 270).

Ehrenpreis, W., & Scandura, J. M. The algorithmic approach to curriculum construction: A field test in mathematics. *Journal of Educational Psychology*, 1974, **66**, 491–496.

Greeno, J. G. Cognitive objectives of instruction: Theory of knowledge for solving problems and answering questions. In D. Khalr (Ed.), *Cognitive and instruction*. Hillsdale, N.J.: Erlbaum, 1976.

Groen, G. J., & Parkman, J. M. A chronometric analysis of simple addition. *Psychological Review*, 1972, **79**, 329–343.

Hayes, J. R. Memory, goals and problem solving. In B. Kleinmuntz (Ed.), *Problem solving research, method, and theory*. New York: Wiley, 1966.

Humphreys, M. S. The derivation of endpoint and distance effects in linear orderings from frequency information. *Journal of Verabal Learning and Verbal Behavior*, 1975, **14**, 496–505.

Johnson, D. M. *A systematic introduction to the psychology of thinking*. New York: Harper & Row, 1972.

Katona, G. *Organizing and memorizing*. New York: Columbia University Press, 1940.

Kohler, W. *The mentality of apes*. New York: Harcourt Brace, 1927.

Maier, N. R. F. Reasoning in humans: II. The solution of a problem and its appearance in consciousness. *Journal of Comparative Psychology*, 1931, **12**, 181-194.

Malin, J. E. T. *An analysis of strategies for solving certain substitution problems.* Ann Arbor, Michigan: Human Performance Center, Technical Report No. 40, 1973.

Mayer, R. E. Information processing variables in learning to solve problems. *Review of Educational Research*, 1975, **45**, 525-541.

Mayer, R. E. Integration of information during problem solving due to a meaningful context of learning. *Memory & Cognition*, 1976, 4, 603-608.

Mayer, R. E. The sequencing of instruction and the concept of assimilation-to-schema. *Instructional Science*, 1977, in press.

Mayer, R. E., & Greeno, J. G. Structural differences between learning outcomes produced by different instructional methods. *Journal of Educational Psychology*, 1972, **63**, 165-173.

Mayer, R. E., & Greeno, J. G. Effects of meaningfulness and organization on problem solving and computability judgments. *Memory & Cognition*, 3, 1975, 356-362.

Noble, C. E. An analysis of meaning. *Psychological Review*, 1952, **59**, 421-430.

Norman, D. A. Memory, knowledge and the answering of questions. In R. L. Solso (Ed.), *Contemporary issues in cognitive psychology.* Washington, D.C.: Winston, 1973.

Paige, J. M., & Simon, H. A. Cognitive processes in solving algebra word problems. In B. Kleinmuntz (Ed.), *Problem solving: Research, method and theory.* New York: Wiley, 1966.

Pollio, H. R., & Reinhart, D. Rules and counting behavior. *Cognitive Psychology*, 1970, **1**, 388-402.

Polya, G. *Mathematical discovery.* New York: Wiley, 1968.

Potts, G. R. Information processing strategies used in the encoding of linear orderings. *Journal of Verbal Learning and Verbal Behavior*, 1972, **11**, 727-740.

Potts, G. R. Storing and retrieving information about ordered relationships. *Journal of Experimental Psychology*, 1974, **103**, 431-439.

Potts, G. R. Artificial logical relations and their relevance to semantic memory. *Journal of Experimental Psychology: Human Learning and Memory*, 1976, 746-758.

Resnick, L. B. Task analysis in instructional design: Some cases from mathematics. In D. Klahr (Ed.), *Cognition and Instruction.* Hillsdale, N.J.: Erlbaum, 1976.

Scandura, J. M. Role of rules in behavior: Toward an operational definition of what (rule) is learned. *Psychological Review*, 1970, **77**, 516-533.

Suppes, P., & Groen, G. Some counting models for first grade performance on simple addition facts. In J. M. Scandura (Ed.), *Research in mathematics education.* Washington, D.C.: Council of Teachers of Mathematics, 1967.

Underwood, B. J., & Schultz, R. W. *Meaningfulness and verbal learning.* Chicago: Lippincott, 1960.

Wertheimer, M. *Productive thinking.* New York: Harper & Row, 1959.

Woods, S. S., Resnick, L. B., & Groen, G. J. An experimental test of five process models for subtraction. *Journal of Educational Psychology,* 1975, **67**, 17–21.

AUTHOR INDEX

SUBJECT INDEX

Numbers in bold face type represent entire chapters. Subject terms that occur at frequent points throughout an entire chapter are referenced to that entire chapter. Subject terms that occur at frequent points throughout the entire volume are: reasoning, syllogism, inference, interpretation, encoding, representation.